AS CITIZENSHIP

AS

CITIZENSHIP

Tim Holden-Rowley and John Blewitt
Edited by Mike Mitchell

Hodder & Stoughton

A MEMBER OF THE HODDER HEADLINE GROUP

Tim Holden-Rowley is head of Sociology and Citizenship at Hyde Clarendon Sixth Form College, part of Tameside College, in Greater Manchester. He would like to thank his colleagues for their support and his students for their insightful observations. Most of all he would like to thank his partner Rachel and daughter Holly for their patience and support in tolerating what has proved to be a lengthy and difficult project.

John Blewitt is Deputy Director of the Department of Lifelong Learning at the University of Exeter. He would like to thank Lorna for her patience.

The publishers would like to thank the following individuals, institutions and companies for permission to reproduce copyright illustrations in this book:

PA Photos: p11 (John Giles), p29 & p75 l (Fiona Hanson), p75 r (Michael Walter), p77 l, p77 r (Martin Keene), p78 l (Malcolm Croft), p78 r (Haydn West), p81 (Yui Mok), p105 (Peter Jordan), p106 (John Stillwell), p107 (David Jones), p109 (Owen Humphries), p112 (Phil Noble), p150, p162 and p166 t (EPA); p90 © Adam Woolfitt/CORBIS, p140 t © David Butow/CORBIS SABA, p140 b © Pizzoli Alberto/Corbis Sygma, p145 Laura Dwight/Corbis; p91 © 2003 Topfoto.co.uk UPPA; p123 Ron Sachs/REX FEATURES, p137 © Ray Tang/REX FEATURES, p138 Nigel R. Barklie/REX FEATURES, p151 © Mike Alsford/REX FEATURES, p160 © Richard Young/REX FEATURES, p164 © Sipa Press/REX FEATURES, p165 © Matt Sadler/REX FEATURES; p152 l & r, 153 © Empics Phil Walter/Mike Egerton/Matthew Ashton; p55 © Steve Bell; p89 courtesy of Leeds City Council; p144 l & r © Carlton Cards; p151 author's own; p149 © Stuart Dunn; p7 *Which?* published by Consumers' Association, 2 Marylebone Road, London NW1 4DF, for further information please phone 0800 252 100.

Every effort has been made to trace and acknowledge ownership of copyright. The publishers will be glad to make suitable arrangements with any copyright holders whom it has not been possible to contact.

Note about the Internet links in the book. The user should be aware that URLs or web addresses change regularly. Every effort has been made to ensure the accuracy of the URLs provided in this book on going to press. It is inevitable, however, that some will change. It is sometimes possible to find a relocated web page, by just typing in the address of the home page for a website in the URL window of your browser.

Orders: please contact Bookpoint Ltd, 130 Milton Park, Abingdon, Oxon OX14 4SB. Telephone: (44) 01235 827720. Fax: (44) 01235 400454. Lines are open from 9.00–6.00, Monday to Saturday, with a 24 hour message answering service. You can also order through our website www.hodderheadline.co.uk.

British Library Cataloguing in Publication Data
A catalogue record for this title is available from the British Library

ISBN 0 340 859 040

First Published 2004
Impression number   10 9 8 7 6 5 4 3 2
Year   2009 2008 2007 2006 2005 2004

Cover photo by Richard Lyon.

Papers used in this book are natural, renewable and recyclable products. They are made from wood grown in sustainable forests. The logging and manufacturing processes conform to the environmental regulations of the country of origin.

Typeset by Phoenix Photosetting, Lordswood, Chatham, Kent.

Printed in Great Britain for Hodder & Stoughton Educational, a division of Hodder Headline, 338 Euston Road, London NW1 3BH by J. W. Arrowsmith, Bristol.

Contents

Foreword

About the book

This book is designed to support the AQA AS Social Science: Citizenship specification.

In Chapters 1–9 the key ideas within the specification are covered. Each chapter is broken into sections to help you plan and structure your learning and contains:

- **Key terms** which define the key ideas and concepts within the chapter
- **Case studies** providing up-to-date, relevant stimulus material to illustrate concepts
- **Activities** based on stimulus material which encourage you to think about the key issues
- **Questions** which allow you to assess what you have learnt
- **Photographs and diagrams** to explain and illustrate the themes
- **Websites** and web-based activities to give you starting points for further research

- **Sample examination questions** to help you reflect on and assess learning but also to give you an idea about what to expect in the examination.

The final chapter contains information about the specification and the three module examinations. The section on the examinations has exam and revision tips but also explains in detail the requirements of the examination papers, the assessment objectives and the skills domains.

At the end of the book there is:

- a list of useful addresses and websites for further help and exploration of the themes in each chapter.
- a glossary – throughout the book glossary terms are in bold the first time they appear in a chapter.

Good luck with your studies, we hope you find your efforts rewarding and purposeful.

	HOW THIS BOOK RELATES TO THE AQA SOCIAL SCIENCE: CITIZENSHIP SPECIFICATION	
Chapter	AQA module	Section
1	1 The Citizen and the State	9.1 Characteristics of Citizenship in the Modern State
2	1 The Citizen and the State	9.2 The Citizen and the Law
3	1 The Citizen and the State	9.3 The Welfare of the Citizen
4	2 The Citizen and the Political Process	10.1 Representative Democracy
5	2 The Citizen and the Political Process	10.2 Political Participation
6	2 The Citizen and the Political Process	10.3 Political Ideology and Political Action
7	3 The Citizen, Society and the Community	11.1 Socialisation
8	3 The Citizen, Society and the Community	11.2 Life-chances and Inequality
9	3 The Citizen, Society and the Community	11.3 The Citizen in the Community

1

Citizenship in the Modern State

In this chapter you will explore characteristics of citizenship in the modern state including:

- contemporary debates about citizenship in the context of the citizen as a consumer, employee, employer, and family member
- rights and duties: the citizen as a member of the state and their legal, political and social rights and responsibilities
- civil and human rights in the UK, Europe and globally (i.e. Human Rights Act, freedom of information).

The chapter is broken into four sections

Key terms

Citizenship – acting on one's rights and duties to become a fully participating member of society

Duty – moral or legal obligation, what one is bound or ought to do

Equality – the idea that every person has an equal right to have his or her material, spiritual and other interests respected by other people

Responsibility – the idea that a person is answerable for his or her actions and so is a proper subject for praise or blame

Rights – a person's entitlements, often referred to as liberties, as a member of society

Values – the worth, significance, or even usefulness, a person or a community places on a **practice**, activity or product

1 Towards a definition of citizenship

This section explores theories and ideas about the nature of citizenship and what it means. It looks at:

- a case study and definition
- the development of the concept of citizenship
- contemporary debates about citizenship
- T H Marshall and the evolution of citizens' rights.

A case study and definition

CASE STUDY: Asylum seekers – a personal story

Bek, 17-year-old asylum seeker from Mitrovica, Kosovo

My name is Bek. I am 17 and I will be 18 next month. I am Kosovan. I come from Mitrovica. It is a big city, the second biggest in Kosovo. I am Albanian and I am a Muslim. Things became really bad when I was 15. Everyone was moving or advising each other to get out and go somewhere safe – the Muslim people, I mean.

I had to escape because my friends and I had been helping the KLA [Kosovo Liberation Army] soldiers – giving them information and clothes and food. At the beginning, they were not really soldiers, but then they became an army. Everybody helped the soldiers – most of my friends were helping them too – you have to, you know, it is for your future. If I had been older then I would have been made to join the army – I would not have had a choice.

One day the Serbian police came round to my house to look for me. I escaped out of the back door. I was really scared. I cannot say what would have happened to me if I had stayed, but it would have been dangerous because I am not a Serb. I escaped with Mila, my friend.

My family wanted me to leave because they knew it was not safe for me. They are in Bosnia now. I really miss my family and, of course, they miss me, but they are happy because I am safe. But it is a long time to be away from my family. I have not had contact with them for five months.

When we left Mitrovica there was another guy with us – an older guy – and he took us to Macedonia in his van. There was carpet in the van and we had to hide underneath it. When we got to Macedonia, Mila and I paid another man 4500 Deutschmarks – half each – to get away in a lorry. I wanted to go to Switzerland because I have some cousins there. I did not know that I was going to England.

We travelled on three different lorries altogether. The driver of the third lorry did not know we were there. It was a big lorry and we hid in the back. We just wanted to escape. We were happy to get away from the war, though we were scared about the next part too. We could tell that we were crossing the sea and that is when we guessed that we were going to England.

The journey to England took three days. We did not have any food; we had nothing. When we got out of the lorry the first thing I wanted to do was get some food.

We were discovered when the lorry stopped at a petrol station and the driver got out to get some stuff. He saw us and told us to get out, but he was not angry. Someone called the police – maybe the driver, I do not know. The police took us to the city centre. There was a translator who helped us to find a solicitor – they said that this was the most important thing. The solicitor gave us a lot of forms to fill in.

I spoke a little bit of English then, which helped. We stayed at the interpreter's house for two or three weeks, and then Mila and I were given a room to stay in by social services. Since then, I have moved about four or five times. Social services give us £35 a week. It is enough to buy food, but not clothes. Things are very expensive.

People are not friendly to me here. The most difficult thing is learning the language and communicating with people. It is very hard. And there are so many forms to fill out. But I have been treated well by social services. I do not know if it is like that for everybody. It is different for different people.

When I see the stories in the newspapers about asylum seekers I feel bad. Some people here have seen the war in Kosovo on the television and then they see Kosovan people here and they can say, 'Yes, it is a good thing and we are going to help them.'

But not everyone is like that. Some of them say, 'What are they doing here, why have they come here?' I have met people like this myself and I can tell you a story about that.

I used to live in a place with three other asylum seekers and something happened there. It was like a racist attack. A lot of people came to the house and smashed up the windows and doors with sticks and baseball bats. One of my friends got hurt and had to go to hospital. I was out at the time. If I had been there with my friends, I would have been very, very frightened. It was really horrible.

We had to move house after that happened – it was too dangerous for us to stay there. The police stayed with us until we moved. Our social worker found me a place to stay.

When I first got here, I did an English course. My English is getting much better but I still find the work very difficult though. I am not sure what I want to do when I finish school – I just have to concentrate so hard on studying English, and if I want to study anything else, I find it hard. I am taking it step by step. When I was growing up I wanted to be an astronaut but I think I am a long way off that. It was just something I wanted to do when I was a kid.

I want to go back to Kosovo. I hope that I can go back next year. I might go to university but I might not. I do not know if it will be safe to go back next year – maybe war will start again. I am still waiting to see if I can stay in Britain. I am waiting to hear from the Home Office whether I have to go back or whether I can have refugee status. I do not know when I will find out.

Reproduced by permission of Oxfam GB, www.oxfam.org.uk

ACTIVITY

1) Why is Bek in the UK?
2) What rights do you think Bek should have?
3) What attitudes should people take towards Bek and people like him who have had similar experiences?
4) In what ways is Bek a non-citizen?

Towards a definition

The sociologist Bryan S Turner recently defined citizenship 'as that set of practices (legal, political, economic and cultural) that define a person as a competent member of society and which, as a consequence, shape the flow of resources to persons and social groups'. The word 'practice' is important because it is a term encompassing the experience of everyday life, social structure and inequality, action and agency, power and relationships, and the distribution of resources within societies and between them. Modifying Turner's argument slightly, citizenship may be said to address the following issues:

- the nature of rights, responsibilities and obligations
- the form or type of such rights, responsibilities and obligations
- the social and political forces that produce practices of various sorts

- the arrangements whereby benefits (or otherwise) are distributed among people or between peoples, or between peoples and the non-human world.

The development of the concept of citizenship

Debates about the nature of citizenship date back thousands of years to the world of Ancient Greece and the Roman Republic, which thrived in the four or five centuries before Christ. Since then, rarely has there been a time when the meaning of citizenship has not been discussed. For the Ancient Greeks being a citizen meant being a member of a political community – in those days a city or *polis*. It also meant:

- being able to participate in the affairs of the city, making decisions about how the city is governed and organised
- going to meetings or assemblies (*fora*) to debate issues like crime, trade, tax, war, etc.
- voting on decisions or taking public office
- *belonging* to the community, exercising rights and fulfilling duties or responsibilities
- being a *man* who owned property. Women, children, foreigners and slaves were not citizens. In fact, this 'cradle of western **democracy**', although exhibiting many worthy characteristics, would by today's standards be considered deeply unfair, unequal and exclusionary.

Ancient Rome also had a similar idea of citizenship in which a degree of exclusivity and participation existed side by side. The aristocracy had full or **substantive citizenship rights** and status, and the plebeians (workers, tradesmen) just had status and no rights. The wealth and power of Ancient Rome were based on slavery and military conquest and as the Republic gave way to the Empire, citizenship was extended to people in conquered lands in order to help with the collection of taxes. In return for the taxes, the conquered peoples would be protected by the Roman army from the barbarian hoards. They were also given a number of legal rights enjoyed by full Roman citizens including freedom to move and trade throughout the Empire. Trial by jury also dates from this time.

In the medieval period, dating from around the fifth century AD to the birth of the Renaissance in the fifteenth century, citizenship as the right to participate in public affairs virtually disappeared except for in a few cities such as Venice and Florence. It was not until the Civil War in England in the 1640s and, more significantly, with the American and French Revolutions in the late eighteenth century, that citizenship became very important to increasing numbers of individuals, groups and nations. Significant changes have occurred and although many of them are considered extremely positive, such as the development of civil, political and social rights, other developments are less encouraging.

Although we are all citizens today, most of us are not particularly active, interested or involved in public affairs. Many people would prefer to vote for their 'pop idol' than for their government.

> 1) What type of people were not citizens in Ancient Greece?
> 2) What was a key benefit of being a citizen of Ancient Rome?

Contemporary debates about citizenship

In his examination of contemporary debates about citizenship, the British political scientist David Miller has identified three models of citizenship.

The liberal model

Citizens enjoy equal status in civil, political and social rights. For a democratic society to grow there can be no second-class citizens. Social policy should aim to get rid of inequalities and injustices. Citizens use elections as their main way of defending their rights.

The consumer model

Citizens have a right to expect a certain level of service, but are also empowered through the operation of various citizen charters or public service agreements to seek some redress if the service is not satisfactory. This is a somewhat selfish understanding of citizenship as it is based on self-interest rather than a sense of collective solidarity.

Citizens as active community members

The citizen is someone who is actively involved in shaping the way his or her community functions. Active citizenship goes beyond individual interests to include a sense of public responsibility and awareness of and participation in civic affairs.

T H Marshall and the evolution of citizen rights

A useful starting point for any discussion of citizenship in the contemporary world is the hugely influential work of sociologist T H Marshall, who wrote in the years immediately following the end of World War II and coinciding with the development of the **welfare state**. Marshall sees the history of the West as being characterised by the successive achievement of a series of key citizen rights.

Civil rights

The achievement of civil rights involved the protection of individual freedoms such as that of the person ('no imprisonment without trial'), 'freedom of speech, thought and faith, the right to own property and to conclude valid contracts, and the right to justice.' The eighteenth century saw many battles over the freedom of the press and the reduction in the random powers of the state. Previously, people might be arrested simply because the rulers did not like or trust them.

Political rights

The achievement of political rights included the right to 'participate in the exercise of political power as a member of a body invested with political authority or as an elector of the members of such a body'. For Marshall, this meant the right to stand for elected office or to vote in local and national elections. It was not until 1928 that all women over the age of 21 got the vote. 40 years later, all 18 year olds got the vote. From this time, political rights were no

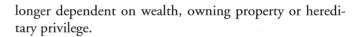

longer dependent on wealth, owning property or hereditary privilege.

Social rights

The twentieth century saw the introduction of a national system of compulsory education up to the age of 16 years, a system of social security and unemployment benefits, and a system of universal healthcare paid out of taxation but free at the point of delivery (the National Health Service). Marshall believed these social rights to education, income support, disability benefits, old age pensions, medical treatment, and decent public housing, etc., would reduce social and economic inequality based on class.

Marshall was a product of his time. He has nothing to say about gender issues (the right of women to be treated equally with men), ethnicity or racial discrimination (the right of different cultural or racial groups, such as Asian or Afro-Caribbean people, to be treated equally), or the right to a clean environment. However, the ideal of equality has been a primary interest for many social movements. These include those seeking to improve the rights of women, black and minority ethnic groups, developing countries, and the local and global environment. It is important to remember that for many feminists equality is about personal and social relationships as well as what happens publicly during elections or in Parliament.

> 1) In what way is society today different from that of 1950 and the one known to the Ancient Greeks and Romans?
> 2) According to Marshall, how have citizenship rights evolved?
> 3) What is missing in Marshall's theory?

2 The citizen and the community

This section explores themes of citizenship in relation to communities and looks at:

- communities and **communitarianism**
- active and responsible citizens; the balance of rights and responsibilities
- consumers' rights.

Communities and communitarianism

Labour and Conservative governments have acknowledged that our democratic processes are in urgent need of reform because of a serious decline of interest and participation in public affairs at virtually every level. People are detached from the political process, from their communities, and from each other. Recent policy and practice has aimed to bring together ideas of community and particularly of responsibility into debates about citizenship.

Citizenship is not merely a matter of personal morality, of learning not to steal or beat people up in the street. Nor is it simply a matter of political effectiveness, of knowing which buttons to press in order to get a government grant or to claim a benefit. If you are going to be an active citizen, involved in doing things on behalf of the community as a whole, then you must have an understanding of what that community stands for. And that in turn means having yourself as a member of a historic community in whose positive achievements you can justifiably take pride, and of whose shortcomings you feel ashamed.

Miller, D (2000) 'Citizenship: What does it mean and why is it important?' in *Tomorrow's Citizens: Critical Debates in Citizenship and Education* **(Pearce and Hallgarten), IPPR, London, p31**

Communitarianism has strongly influenced the social policies of the Labour government since 1997. It is a social philosophy suggesting that communities are best placed to decide and define what they think is right and proper. Many see communitarianism as a way of restoring ideas of shared obligation and social responsibility to citizenship. It should be as much about doing something for others as it is about doing something for yourself.

The family

Amitai Etzioni, a leading communitarian, has argued for many family orientated measures enabling mothers and fathers to devote more time and energy to parenting. This would involve trade unions and employers making it easier for parents to work at home and governments fully endorsing the right of parents to take maternity and even paternity leave. Children have a right to a good family life and to be looked after by their parents. Governments and businesses should make this form of good citizenship easier because children have a right to a good education and this should be provided either by the state or by private bodies. On the other hand, parents have a responsibility to care for their children and children have a responsibility to go to school. To be realistic, a right needs to be exercised and, where necessary, those who fail to fulfil their obligations need to be warned or even punished. Communitarians see the wider community, the government and the law enforcing these rights and responsibilities.

Truancy

In February 2002, the Chief Inspector of Schools in England and Wales published his annual report. This report showed that 10,000 young people aged between 14–16 years were 'missing' from the education system and were not on the records of any school. 5 million school days were lost due to pupil absence. 1 million was a result of truancy, i.e. children staying away from school without the knowledge of their parents, but 4 million days were approved by parents. The government responded by announcing that it would increase the rate at which it issues orders to parents to attend parenting classes. The Secretary of State for Education, Estelle Morris, told *The Independent*: 'Too many [parents] do not understand the damage they do to children's education by taking them out of school.'

Two-day sentences for parents of truants

The home secretary David Blunkett is considering introducing weekend prison sentences for parents who allow their children to persistently truant.

The 'intermittent custody' proposals are due next week in a white paper.

Such a move would mean the offender spending two weekdays or a weekend confined, which would enable them to keep their jobs and deal with family obligations, the Home Office said.

Patricia Amos, the Oxfordshire mother imprisoned by Banbury magistrates in May for allowing her two youngest daughters to miss large amounts of schooling, would have served the weekend sentence under the new law.

It is thought the rates of truancy dropped in the weeks following Ms Amos' sentencing, something referred to as the 'Amos effect'.

But teacher representatives and **charities** said the new proposals did not tackle the root causes of truancy and amounted to nothing more than a 'knee-jerk' reaction.

John Bangs, head of education at the National Union of Teachers, admitted that the threat of prison did seem to be having an effect on truancy rates, but added: 'We need to solve this problem as a societal problem, which schools alone cannot be responsible for.'

A spokesman for the crime reduction charity NACRO, which runs centres for young offenders, said: 'Jailing the parents of truanting children is a simplistic, knee-jerk response to what is often a highly complex problem with no easy answers. While such policies may grab the headlines, they do little to get to grips with the underlying causes of school absenteeism.

'Jailing parents, even if only for weekends, will often make worse the very problems that lead children to truant in the first place.'

The government has been trying to crack down on truancy in recent months, as 50,000 children in England are absent from school with no real excuse on any given day. Town centre sweeps in some of the worst truancy 'hotspots' in the spring netted 12,000 youngsters, many of whom were with their parents.

A spokesman for the Department for Education and Skills said the courts already had the power to jail parents for failing to stop persistent truanting by their children and were expected to use it.

'Truancy blights lives with missed schooling and with some children slipping into a life of crime,' he said. 'Tackling truancy is an important part of the focus on poor behaviour in schools. That involves early intervention through to punishment, if that is necessary, to tackle the problem,' he added.

Polly Curtis, © *The Guardian Unlimited,* **12 July 2002**

ACTIVITY

1) What rights and obligations are involved in the article?
2) Should parents be punished if their children truant from school? Give reasons for your answer.
3) Why did critics use the term 'knee-jerk' when discussing the government's custody proposals?

Active and responsible citizens; the balance of rights and responsibilities

An important aspect of contemporary citizenship is taking an active interest in the public affairs of the community, society and world in which we live. It involves being informed and concerned about our well-being, that of our family, and of other people, too, even if these other people are culturally or geographically remote from us. Many people are not that bothered about things that do not directly affect them. Sometimes this indifference can be attributed to feelings of powerlessness rather than apathy: 'What can I do about it? I am only one person'; '"They" (i.e. organisations, bureaucracies, governments or simply people with the power to make decisions) are not interested in us'; '"They" are only out for themselves'; '"They" are all the same, so why bother?'

However, issues, events or 'their' decisions often do affect us personally. The problem then becomes what to do, how to do it, and whether someone is able to do it. Does someone have the skills, courage or confidence to make themselves heard? Can someone be an active citizen, taking part in civic affairs such as voting or just ensuring that a seller of inferior goods does not get away with it, for example? It may mean being a good parent.

Citizenship involves both rights and responsibilities and duty to carry them out. It is not about being passive. It means doing things even when someone may prefer to do something else. It also means acting as an individual but sometimes acting collectively as a group. An employee has a right to expect to be paid fairly, or at least the statutory minimum wage, and the workplace to conform to legal health and safety standards so that no injuries or illnesses are suffered unnecessarily (the employer's responsibility). The employer has the right to expect the employee to turn up for work on time, do a decent day's work and not pretend to be sick just to stay off work (the employee's responsibility). Employers and employees associations, such as trade unions, exist to monitor and enforce these rights and responsibilities. See Chapters 5 and 6.

Consumers' rights

An individual acting as a consumer, a purchaser of goods and services, or as a supplier, is also involved in a similar network of relationships involving rights and responsibilities. A consumer may investigate the quality of goods before purchase by becoming a member of an organisation like the Consumers' Association. This association publishes product reports and gives advice to members on how to complain or how to take legal action when inferior goods or services are purchased. Sometimes environmental or human rights groups will organise a campaign to persuade people not to buy (boycott) goods that have been made by child labour in the Third World or made by companies whose activities are believed to harm the environment, such as GM foods. These boycotts are a form of collective or joint political/citizen participation and campaigning discussed in Chapters 5 and 6.

CASE STUDY: Victory for consumers on GM labelling

The Consumers' Association has heralded the outcome of today's European Parliament vote on labelling of GM food as a great victory for consumers.

Today's vote by MEPs is another step on the road to a stricter approval process and fuller GM labelling for consumers – with a requirement for GM derived ingredients (such as GM soya oil) to be labelled based on a system of traceability throughout the supply chain.

The Commission's proposal for a 1% threshold for unauthorised GM ingredients has been rejected giving consumers added protection.

The Consumers' Association's own findings have shown that 87% of consumers agree that food containing GM derivatives, which cannot be detected in the final product because they have been processed out, should be labelled as GM.

Sue Davies, Principal Policy Adviser of the Consumers' Association, said:

'This is a fantastic victory for consumer choice. MEPs have shown clear support for European consumers today; however, the battle is not over yet. The proposals have still to be considered by member states in the EU Council.

The UK government has so far taken an anti-consumer stance on this issue, dismissing fuller labelling in favour of a more limited GM-free claim, which would not apply to commodity crops such as GM soya and maize. We hope that they can re-assess their position in light of today's decision and recognise consumer demands for more information and protection.'

Press release, 2 July 2002

http://www.which.net/media/pr/jul02/general/gmvictory.html

1) Explain why the Consumers' Association felt the decision to label GM foods a great victory for consumers.
2) How will consumers benefit?

?

1) **What are the main features of communitarianism?**
2) **In what ways do citizens have both rights and obligations?**
3) **How might a consumer ensure his or her rights are respected?**

3 Human rights and civil rights

This section explores the human and civil rights of citizens and looks at:

- the emergence of human rights
- human rights as universal rights
- human rights and business
- **nationality**, immigration and the 'refugee problem'.

The emergence of human rights

Following the immense hardship and trauma of World War II when millions were murdered in death camps, cities ruined by bombs and countless persons displaced, an international organisation was established to work for peace among all nations. It sought to promote the principle that human beings had universal rights. In December 1948, the United Nations adopted the **Universal Declaration of Human Rights**, providing a standard and a challenge for all nations. It states that the essential dignity and the equal and inalienable rights of 'all members of the human family is the foundation of freedom, justice and peace in the world'.

Human rights are rights that apply to people by virtue of their being human, i.e. having the capacity for moral reasoning, knowing right from wrong. Although not a legally binding instrument, the UN Declaration sets out a series of basic rights including:

- the right to life
- freedom from torture or inhuman or degrading treatment or punishment
- freedom from slavery, servitude, and forced labour
- the right to free movement (mobility)
- the right to food and shelter.

Britain was an active participant in the discussions leading up to the UN Declaration.

At the same time, many European nations wanted to establish a still greater recognition of human rights and freedoms. It created, by international treaty in 1950, a European Convention and a Court of Human Rights. Representing Britain at the first session of the Consultative Assembly of the Council of Europe, the former wartime Prime Minister, Winston Churchill, said:

Once the foundation of human rights is agreed on the lines of the United Nations at Geneva ... we hope that a European court might be set up, before which cases of the violation of these rights in our own body of 12 nations might be brought to the judgement of the civilised world.

Unfortunately, this court did not prove effective for British citizens seeking redress for alleged human rights violations. It was not until 1966 that people could take a case to the European Court. Because questions of parliamentary sovereignty, the power of the legal system, the Cold War, and the fact that Britain still maintained remnants of an undemocratic and racially segregated empire, the Convention did not become part of British law until 1998. With the passing of the Human Rights Act 1998 (put into force from October 2000), Britain finally put on the statute books a 'higher law'. This was a set of principles to which all other laws, policies, practices and procedures must conform.

Human rights as universal rights

Some Asian leaders, such as Suharto and Lee Kuan Yew, who had absolute power, criticised the idea of universal human rights for being Eurocentric, i.e. ignoring the cultural and historical differences of other societies. They said that ideas of individual rights and duties were a product of the western liberal democratic mind and had little to do with the norms and values of countries in East Asia or the Middle East. These traditions interpret the dignity of the individual man or woman differently. Saudia Arabia objected to the 1948 UN Declaration stating that the right to change religion would prevent it from punishing apostasy (the abandoning of a religious faith).

Universalism in human rights is another example of western imperialism. This is where no universal values can be said to exist. Critics of this view state that torture, humiliation, slavery, starvation and hatred are human wrongs and should be seen as international crimes. The international trafficking in women for prostitution is a significant element of globally organised crime. The exploitation of child labour and forced removal of people from their homelands through war or ethnic cleansing are abuses of human rights and criminal activities.

But questions remain: should the values and practices of certain religions and cultures be respected (or tolerated) if they refuse to respect others' beliefs? The Sudanese government has stated that all religions should be respected and that freedom of worship is ensured. In practice, it treats Islam as the state religion denying Christian communities permission to build churches.

Torture

Incidents of torture and ill treatment occurred in 150 countries between 1997–2000. In 80 of those countries, the torture was so severe that the sufferers died. The people who carried out these offences, according to **Amnesty International**, are usually state officials, police officers, intelligence and military personnel. The victims are randomly drawn from social groups already experiencing significant discrimination and disadvantage; e.g. the poor, ethnic minorities, immigrants and refugees, lesbians and gay men. In more than 30 countries, flogging (a form of torture) is sanctioned by law. Since 1997, amputations have been carried out in Afghanistan, Iran, Iraq, Nigeria, Saudi Arabia, Somalia and the Sudan as a form of punishment and intimidation. Over 120 companies have made, sold, marketed and advertised electroshock equipment used by torturers. Human rights organisations regularly campaign against torture and although it remains common, the United Nations Convention Against Torture, itself a product of a previous Amnesty International campaign, provides an important tool for international examination and pressure. By the end of 2000, 119 countries had made the Convention officially valid.

Christopher Avery, the author of Amnesty International's report *Business and Human Rights in a Time of Change*, writes of Asians and Africans as 'being offended by the suggestion that the right to life, freedom from torture, the prohibition of random detention and the right to a fair trial are just western values. Principles of the sacredness of life, of human dignity, and of the importance of justice and fair treatment are reflected in the teaching of all religions and all cultures'. Cultural and ethical **relativism** (saying what is wrong in one society is okay in another) justifies human wrongs. The Runnymede report, *The Future of Multi-Ethnic Britain*, notes that human rights standards provide

a framework for negotiation and minimum guarantees for a shared understanding of certain **substantive moral values:**

Substantive values are those that underpin any defensible conception of the good life. They include people's freedom to plan their own lives, the equal worth of all human beings, and equal opportunities to lead fulfilling lives and to contribute to the collective well-being. Such values are not random and are not those of any one community or society. They are embodied in international human rights standards and form part of the moral dialogue in all parts of the world. On the basis of such values, it is legitimate to ban female circumcision, forced marriages, cruel punishment of children, and repressive and unequal treatment of women, even though these practices may enjoy cultural authority in certain communities.

Parekh B (2000) *The Future of Multi-Ethnic Britain,* **Profile Books, London, pp53–4**

Global citizenship

To say that mass deportations, arrests and imprisonment for no particular reason, and torture are wrong is to be a part of a moral community. To recognise the international and multi-cultural nature of human rights agreements and to speak this language, is to make real an element of **global citizenship**. To act upon this belief is to encourage the correctness of human rights and to do something for others. Individuals do this and so do many organisations. Amnesty International is a worldwide voluntary movement made up of ordinary people who campaign for human rights. It is independent of any government and has no political ideology, economic interest or religion. Its purpose is to encourage people everywhere to promote and protect the human rights set out in the Universal Declaration of Human Rights by raising general awareness and opposing specific abuses of human rights whether committed by government officials or members of armed political groups. The organisation's funding comes purely from donations from its members. It, and individual members of the organisation, can make a difference. Amnesty is part of what is becoming to be known as a **global civil society**.

Human rights and business

Human rights involve individual citizens, businesses and governments. Campaigning may mean citizens attempting to put pressure on governments to combat human rights abuses in other countries. It may mean attempting to use the legal system to bring former dictators like the Chilean president Augusto Pinochet to justice. International action can be very effective. Companies such as Shell and Nike have been severely criticised for human rights abuses, which has led to changes in corporate policy and practice.

In the mid 1990s, Shell had attempted to distance itself from events in Nigeria when Ken Saro-Wiwa (leader of the *Movement for the Survival of the Ogoni* people) and eight others protested against the environmental damage done by oil companies and argued for greater **autonomy** for the Ogoni people. They were arrested, detained illegally in terrible conditions for at least eight months, tried in a special military court that violated international criteria for a fair trial, convicted of murder and then executed. Initially, company spokespeople said this had nothing to do with Shell because the business of Shell was business not politics or human rights. The company was not responsible for the consequences of its economic and financial arrangements with national governments. This attitude was considered by many to be wrong.

Many large companies trading in Third World countries have since tried to redeem the image of big businesses by accepting the idea of 'corporate global citizenship'. In its recent Statement of General Business Principles, Shell now recognises its responsibility

… to conduct business as responsible corporate members of society, to observe the laws of the countries in which they operate, to express support for fundamental human rights in line with the legitimate role of business, and to give proper regard to health, safety and the environment consistent with their commitment to contribute to **sustainable development**.

Avery, CL (2000) *Business and Human Rights in a Time of Change*, **London, Amnesty International UK, p47**

A BBC *Panorama* report (15 October 2000) noted that factories in Cambodia were still manufacturing clothes for both The Gap and Nike with child labour. However, with the rise of the 'ethical consumer' and organised consumer boycotts on an international scale, failure to respect human rights also means a loss of business.

Nationality, immigration and the 'refugee problem'

A basic understanding of citizenship encompasses nationality and the right to live in a particular country with all the civil rights and responsibilities attached. Legally, the British are subjects of Her Majesty and not citizens as they are in France or the USA.

The British Nationality Act 1981

The British Nationality Act 1981 defines several categories of British national who may freely enter the UK unless their passport states otherwise. The application of these rules by immigration officials have sometimes led to accusations of racial or sexual discrimination. These nationality categories include:

- citizens of the British dependent territories
- British overseas citizens
- British protected citizens.

The British Nationality Act 1981 also grants the right of abode to several categories of people if, immediately before 1983 when the Act came into force:

- you were a citizen of the UK and Colonies as a result of being born, naturalised, adopted or registered in the UK
- your parent, either by birth or adoption, was a citizen of the UK
- your grandparents were citizens at the time of your parent's birth or legal adoption
- you had been resident in the UK for five years continuously
- you were then, or had been, the wife of a man with right of abode.

N.B. For the purposes of the Act, a 'parent' includes the mother but not the father of an 'illegitimate' child.

It also includes you if, after 1 January 1983, you were:

- registered or naturalised as a British citizen
- born in the UK when one of your parents was a British citizen or lawfully settled in the UK
- born outside the UK when one of your parents was a British citizen other than by descent.

As a Commonwealth citizen you have the right to live in the UK if, immediately before 1983, your parent at the time of your birth or legal adoption was a UK citizen due to being born in the UK, or you were married to a man with a right of abode.

Refugees

As someone who is escaping war, famine, torture, state or religious persecution, but is not a British citizen, you have no automatic right of abode in the UK and must, as a refugee, apply for asylum. The Immigration and Asylum Act 1999 addresses issues including:

- entry into the UK

- the detention of asylum seekers
- their dispersal around the country and financial support
- the handling of their cases.

The 'refugee problem' has frequently hit the news as people from places such as Albania, Bosnia, Kosovo and Afghanistan have sought asylum in the UK. Many national newspapers, expressing concerns over immigration, have stated this 'problem' should be contained. The number of refugees applying for asylum in Britain reached 70,215 in the 11 months to the end of November 2000: 815 less than in 1999. Of 11,645 decisions taken, only 8% received asylum and 5% given exceptional leave to remain in the UK.

Financial aid

Refugees have a right to minimum social and financial aid in the form of a voucher system. This allows single asylum seekers over 25 to spend up to £36.54 per week (£10 may be cash to meet expenses such as transport costs, telephone calls to lawyers) in a limited number of designated retail outlets. No change can be given for the portion of vouchers that are unused and vouchers will have to be spent within four weeks. The government admitted that administering vouchers is more expensive than giving cash and in 2002 announced a radical reform of the whole asylum system. The campaigning organisation Oxfam has argued that refugees seeking asylum have been stigmatised by both press reports and government policy and would welcome reforms that ease the situation of refugees who experience trauma and face uncertainty and hardship in the UK.

The total income of refugees is around 80% of those people claiming income support. Bureaucratic delays make things worse. The human rights organisation Justice argues that this low level of support, combined with the government's capacity to withdraw all support, raises the issue of whether a refugee could be effectively starved out of the country. Other human and civil rights issues surrounding the situation of refugees include the introduction of ID cards and the concentration of refugees in camps isolated from population centres. There have been examples of racial hostility to refugees in places like Glasgow and wariness from local people when there have been attempts to integrate refugees into some tight-knit former mining or steel communities. However, refugees do have rights if the 1948 UN Declaration and the 1951 Convention on

Anif Maloku (left) and Kadri Gashi, former POWs who escaped the Serbs in Kosovo, at the former RAF base in Finningley near Doncaster where they were staying with a large group of former POWs and other Kosovan refugees, June 1999

Refugees (which Britain has signed in agreement) is applied justly. The problem for them is whether these rights have substance or are purely formal; whether they are granted willingly or grudgingly. Britain, France, Germany and many other countries have provided aid and asylum to some refugees but their long-term future is unclear.

ACTIVITY

Discuss a possible response to each of the following suggested solutions to the 'problem' of growing numbers of asylum seekers. Consider human rights among other aspects in your responses.

- Britain is wealthy and need not restrict entry to any person wishing to enter, refugee or otherwise.
- Quotas should be put in place for each EU country proportionate to their economic status and population size.
- All refugees should be housed in detention centres and given food and clothing but restricted to fenced-off areas within compounds until their claim has been investigated. They should have no working rights at all.
- All asylum seekers should be allowed a temporary stay and to seek employment for one year whilst their claim is processed.
- All refugees and asylum seekers should be sent back to their country of origin and apply from there.

WEB ACTION

Using any search engine, type in 'asylum seekers' and explore the latest news headlines addressing the issues of asylum seekers and refugees.

4 Extending the rights of a citizen

This section explores the role of the state in extending rights to citizens and what citizens can do with these rights. It looks at:

- the European Union
- civil rights and sexual justice: Section 28
- liberty and security
- the Human Rights Act 2000

- freedom of information and the Freedom of Information Act 2000
- citizenship and the environment.

The European Union

In many towns, ordinary people have helped refugees be housed, fed and supported. This extension of civil hospitality is an illustration of a citizenship action that recognises wide social and human responsibilities. However, although these refugees may have had their human rights restored, they are not citizens of the UK. They do not have the right to vote or participate in formal political affairs. Some of them may gain this legal right to work, own property, etc., in time, if they stay in the UK. Being a national citizen grants rights whilst, at the same time, denying rights to others such as foreigners, aliens, visitors, refugees or guest workers. As a citizen of the UK and the European Union (EU), there are certain social, economic and political rights, which are transferable across national boundaries within the Union. The **Maastrict Treaty** of 1992 lists the following individual rights as constituting EU citizenship.

- Freedom of movement and residence on the territory of member states.
- The right to vote and stand for office in local elections and European Parliament elections in the state of residence.
- The right to diplomatic protection by the diplomats of any EU state in a third country.
- The right to petition the European Parliament and the possibility of appealing to an **ombudsman**.

The Maastrict Treaty

The Maastrict Treaty does not offer full (political) citizenship rights; e.g. a resident of the UK cannot vote in the national elections of France and has no right to settle in a member state if they are financially dependent on social security. Maastrict's Social Chapter, based on the European Social Charter of 1961, also offers advanced social and economic rights to EU citizens. This did not immediately apply to British citizens; when signing up to the Maastrict Treaty, Britain was allowed to opt out of the Social Chapter in case it interfered with the working of the free market economy and national political sovereignty. Britain has still to join the single European currency for very similar reasons. In 1997, the Labour government finally accepted the Social Chapter of the Maastrict Treaty.

Although the Social Charter has no legal force, most of its principles have been put into effect through European Community legislation. By 1993, the European Commission had forwarded 47 detailed proposals, including 29 that required legislative action. Among them were some highly controversial proposals including the Working Time Directive, which Britain accepted reluctantly in 1999. The basic rights covered in the Charter include the following.

- Every EU citizen is free to move within the EU and work in any occupation or profession. Every citizen is to be treated equally with any other EU national with regards to employment, working conditions and social protection.
- The continuing aim of the EU to develop legislation to ensure that each employee receives a fair annual leave entitlement, redundancy provision, etc.
- Every worker has the right to an adequate level of social protection with the appropriate social security benefits.
- Employees are entitled to join trade unions and employers are free to form organisations to protect their respective interests.
- Both men and women should have equal opportunity and treatment regardless of employment, education and training.
- Every worker is entitled to satisfactory health and safety conditions in the workplace.
- The minimum age of employment should not be lower than 15 or the minimum school leaving age. Under 18s should not do any night work.
- Every retired worker should have a decent standard of living.
- The disabled are entitled to be integrated fully into society, experiencing adequate provision of training, transport and housing.

These rights established a minimum moral framework for a continuing legislative and political project.

? 1) What are human and civil rights?
2) What is meant by human rights being universal?
3) How did the European Union extend the concept of human rights?

Civil rights and sexual justice: Section 28

Civil rights, sometimes referred to as civil liberties, are political in nature as they are made and enforced by the state. Such rights normally include the right to participate in free and fair elections and the right to a fair and impartial hearing when accused of a criminal offence. They are, to an extent, dependent on the social or societal context in which they are made widely known.

Human and civil rights are impossible to separate, as even a brief glance at the UN Declaration or European Convention shows. The disagreements surrounding Section 28 of the Local Government Act 1988 (forbidding the promotion of homosexuality as being of equal moral significance as heterosexuality) show how human and civil rights are connected. Campaigners against this clause, such as members of the gay rights **pressure group** Stonewall, argue that it is going against the European Convention on Human Rights in denying the liberty of the person. It is also helping to continue prejudice and discrimination against homosexuals. Given the largely unsympathetic attitudes existing in society to homosexuals generally, or, more specifically, gay men in the military, to same-sex marriages, or a gay couple's right to adopt children, they do make a valid point. Homosexuals have frequently been assaulted and, as with the bombing of the gay London pub, the Admiral Duncan, in 1999, even murdered. Article 8 of the European Convention states:

Right to respect of private and family life

1 Everyone has the right to respect for his private and family life, his home and his correspondence.
2 There shall be no interference by a public authority with the exercise of this right except as such as is in accordance with the law and is necessary in a democratic society in the interests of national security, public safety or the economic well being of the country, for the prevention of disorder and crime, for the protection of health and morals, or for the protection of the rights and freedoms of others.

Are homosexuals really a danger to national security or the health, morals or well-being of society? A legal test case brought to the European Court of Human Rights by the civil liberties organisation, Liberty, led to a ruling in September 1999 that the Ministry of Defence had contravened the European Convention in dismissing four persons from the armed forces as a consequence of their sexuality regardless of their excellent service records. The Court stated that the Ministry of Defence's investigations to determine their sexuality, and the consequent discharges, constituted a violation of the right to respect for their private lives. The Court also ruled that the government had not offered convincing arguments to justify the blanket ban on homosexuals serving in the British armed forces.

The belief that homosexual love or sexual inclination is wrong or evil legitimises prejudice and discrimination, which undoubtedly harms many individuals. It harbours a disregard for differences of opinion and ways of living. Toleration has a respectable political and philosophical heritage dating back to John Milton and John Locke in the seventeenth century. We may disagree with the viewpoint, values or lifestyles of certain groups or individuals, but in a **liberal democracy** they have a moral right to toleration, acceptance and equality before the law. It is possible to go further and say that the celebration of difference adds rather than subtracts from the working of democracy. Unreasoned and prejudiced majority opinion can undermine freedom and liberty by fostering hatred and ignorance.

The nineteenth-century political philosopher John Stuart Mill wrote:

[The individual] needs protection against the tyranny of the prevailing opinion and feeling; against the tendency of society to impose, by other means than civil penalties, its own ideas and practices as rules of conduct on those who dissent from them; to fetter the development and, if possible, prevent the formation, of any individuality not in harmony with its ways, and compels all characters to fashion themselves upon the model of its own. There is a limit to the legitimate interference of collective opinion with individual independence, and to find that limit, and maintain it against encroachment, is as indispensable to a good condition of human affairs, as protection against political despotism.

On Liberty, **1859**

The protection or extension of existing moral or legal rights is necessary to the free working of democracy and citizenship. The challenge for Stonewall is to make real some key human rights for the argument that we should all

be free to respect and develop our own sexuality so long as no other person suffers as a result. The Labour government attempted to repeal Section 28 as part of the Local Government Bill but was defeated in the House of Lords by 270 to 228 votes at the end of July 2000. However, many gay rights campaigners feel that the clause will eventually be repealed. Opponents feel that to extend full rights homosexuals would undermine the country's moral and social fabric based as it is on heterosexual marriage and 'the family'.

Section 28

Section 28 is a throwback to a more intolerant age. It has no place in the New Britain.

The Sunday Times, **February 1988**

The attack on lesbians and gay men leading up to Section 28 began as a Private Members Bill tabled by Lord Halsbury in 1986. At the time, the government did not support the Bill on the grounds that it was 'open to harmful misrepresentation'. In the end, the anti-gay rhetoric triumphed and Section 28 was eventually passed on 20 February 1988 as part of the Local Government Bill.

Although never enforced, threatened with judicial review and suspected of being in contravention of the European Convention on Human Rights, Section 28 remains law.

What Section 28 says

28.2A   (1)   A local authority shall not

(a) intentionally promote homosexuality or publish material with the intention of promoting homosexuality;
(b) promote the teaching in any maintained school of the acceptability of homosexuality as a pretended family relationship.

(2) Nothing in subsection (1) above shall be taken to prohibit the doing of anything for the purpose of treating or preventing the spread of disease.

As legislation, Section 28 is confusing and unclear, but its message that lesbians and gay men are less acceptable in society continues to haunt schools and local authorities. In relation to schools, the introduction of local management has reduced the intended impact of the legislation. The Section applies to local authorities, but not to teachers or governors.

Section 28 remains a controversial piece of legislation. It constrains the ability of education authorities to support and advise young people so that they can make informed decisions about their relationships, as well as enshrining in law the notion that homosexuality is unacceptable and undesirable.

www.stonewall.org.uk

1) **Why might a refugee be concerned about his or her human rights?**
2) **What is the relationship between social justice and sexual justice?**
3) **In what ways are gays and lesbians excluded minorities?**

Liberty and security

Few people enjoy insecurity, danger and disorder, unless it is confined to the funfair or the movie channel, but often our search for security, peace and order takes a form that threatens human and civil rights. Crimes against the person and against property have been major issues for many years. Many of us will at one time or another be a victim of a mugging. To combat this, closed circuit television (CCTV) has been installed in shopping centres, high streets, residential estates, car parks, schools and colleges. The monitoring of our every action in these (semi) public places is continuous and largely accepted. It is felt that the technology helps to reduce crime or catch the offenders of a criminal act. A report by NACRO noted that CCTV certainly reduces fear of crime and has more impact on reducing crimes against property rather than personal crime, although the overall effect in reducing crime is only about 5%. Improving street lighting has a better record. The evidence therefore is not as compelling as popular belief assumes and the same report notes that monitoring may sometimes be discriminatory.

Discriminatory monitoring

Those monitoring CCTV have been found to adopt police categories of suspicion when viewing the screens. The target selection of CCTV operators can be massively discriminatory towards males, particularly black males: 'For literally thousands of black and working class youths, however law abiding, it transmits a wholly negative message about their position in society.' When certain sections of the community are randomly monitored, this acts to portray an impression of criminality amongst these groups (certain acts are noticed whilst other groups may be carrying out the same acts unmonitored and unnoticed). It also conveys a message to these individuals that they are not trusted. The Stephen Lawrence Inquiry report places a par-

ticular emphasis upon the use of training to deliver 'racism awareness' and 'valuing cultural diversity'. Improved training for those responsible for monitoring CCTV systems may go some way towards addressing such imbalances.

NACRO Community Safety Briefing: 'To CCTV or Not CCTV', May 2002
www.nacro.org.uk

CCTV

The use of CCTV has grown rapidly, without any proper legal controls. There are now five times as many CCTV cameras as there were five years ago. This lack of statutory regulation has led to widespread invasion of individual privacy. Although CCTV can be useful in the prevention and detection of crime, more recent studies have shown that all too often it does not live up to its promises, and merely displaces crime – often to poorer areas. Liberty believes that tough laws are needed to control the use of CCTV, covering the location and use of cameras, the recruitment and training of CCTV operators, and arrangements for storage of and access to CCTV footage.

www.liberty.org.uk

ACTIVITY

1) Why does CCTV footage suggest that some social or ethnic groups are not to be trusted?
2) Does it matter?

Surveillance

Surveillance is beginning to invade most of our social relationships and political arrangements and although Big Brother may not exactly be watching you, private security firms or the police will be. Surveillance is becoming the norm. Within ten years there could be a nationally integrated CCTV infrastructure with a national database providing instant image analysis and facial recognition.

For those concerned with civil liberties, many issues need addressing. For example, widespread surveillance infers that everyone being monitored is at least a potential suspect or likely criminal. The cameras make you guilty until you have proven yourself innocent by leaving the store without stealing anything. Maybe this does not matter: if you are a law-abiding citizen, the cameras and those watching the monitors will have little interest in you. On the other hand, should you trust either the people or the organisations doing the monitoring that our images or other information gained are not passed on to other parties or sold commercially or that mistakes of identification are not made? Should we have access to the data acquired on us if we wish it? Without a strict and enforceable code of conduct, CCTV controllers have the power to determine who has access and who is excluded from public spaces based on perhaps little more than their prejudices about what you look like. The cameras may be used to exclude social groups not perceived as belonging to a particular commercial space. When this occurs, crime prevention quickly turns into social control and manipulation.

It is not only through the lens that our habits and activities are analysed and evaluated. Our credit card purchases are, too, and even our email correspondence is open to state scrutiny under the provisions laid down in the Regulation of Powers Act 2000. Liberty has suggested the legislation could undermine the democratic process if no proper balance was struck 'between, on the one side, the protection of society from real threats to its integrity and, on the other, the need to preserve the very values that make a democratic society worth protecting: the rule of law, respect for individual liberty, and abhorrence of arbitrary or unjustified interference with citizens' rights.' A great deal of public opposition and criticism was voiced in 2002 when the government attempted to make these scrutiny powers operative.

The Human Rights Act 2000

The Human Rights Act means that all legislation (past or future) must be compatible with the European Convention on Human Rights.

Public authorities (local councils, the police, the courts, NHS and trust hospitals, etc.) must comply, in most instances, with the terms of the Convention. If they do not they will be acting unlawfully.

People who believe their rights have been violated may take legal action against public authorities in courts and tribunals. British courts may issue injunctions to prevent violations of rights, award damages and quash unlawful decisions. People may also use the Convention to defend themselves in criminal proceedings.

The Act incorporates only part of the European Convention on Human Rights. However, it does include all of the substantive rights:

- Article 2: the right to life
- Article 3: freedom from torture
- Article 4: freedom from slavery
- Article 5: freedom from random arrest and detention
- Article 6: the right to a fair trial
- Article 7: freedom from retrospective penalties
- Article 8: the right to privacy and family life
- Article 9: freedom of religion
- Article 10: freedom of expression
- Article 11: freedom of association
- Article 12: the right to marry and found a family
- Article 14: freedom from discrimination
- Article 16: restrictions on the political activity of aliens
- Article 17: prohibition of abuse of rights
- Article 18: limitation on use of restrictions on rights.

It does not incorporate Article 13: the right to an effective remedy.

In addition, the Act incorporates the rights in Protocol 1:

- Article 1: the rights to peaceful enjoyment of property
- Article 2: the right to education
- Article 3: the right to free elections.

Future issues

Article 8: Privacy

The development of new technology on listening devices, telephone taps (portable telephones, metering and pagers), keystroke surveillance (the monitoring of computer operatives' on-line activities by employers and others in authority) and CCTV may all create problems.

Respect for private life in a variety of circumstances is likely to raise new issues. Currently there is very little regulation of the privacy of employees. Those employees of public authorities will have a new right to respect for their privacy except where interference is justified once the Act comes into force. The right to family life may also be helpful to those wishing to challenge the ways that courts and local authorities deal with custody in divorce, care proceedings, adoption, the rights of other relatives to have access to the child (and vice versa).

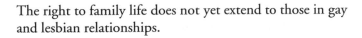

The right to family life does not yet extend to those in gay and lesbian relationships.

The enforced break up of families as a result of immigration decisions will need review.

Article 10: Freedom of expression

This will create realistic rights for journalists and the media, particularly in the protection of sources. It will also be very much harder for public authorities to obtain pre-publication injunctions.

Those in libel cases with a public interest issue will be able to rely on this to defend publication. Some of the technical rules on libel may need to be reconsidered.

Some minor public order offences relating to peaceful protest will be considered to be framed too widely to comply.

Substantive matters may be raised where the Convention may provide a defence to the criminal act. In many public order cases, e.g. those that have arisen from marches, demonstrations and protests, defendants are likely to want to argue that their right to freedom of expression, assembly or privacy would be violated by the conviction.

Article 10 includes the freedom to impart and receive information and is likely to affect Section 28 of the Local Government Act.

Finally, restrictions on political broadcasting on grounds of taste and decency may need to be reviewed.

Adapted from www.liberty.org.uk

> **?**
> 1) **Why do you think the government did not incorporate the right to 'effective remedy'?**
> 2) **How might this affect the way the Act is put into practice?**
> 3) **How might gay rights campaigners use the Act?**
> 4) **Why is freedom of expression important to journalists and ordinary citizens?**

Freedom of information and the Freedom of Information Act 2000

For centuries the liberty of the press and freedom of speech has been seen as a prior condition for any properly consti-

tuted democracy. A number of organisations such as the Campaign for Freedom of Information and Article 19 lobby strenuously against censorship, government intrusion and secrecy, and the invasion of personal privacy in order to protect civil liberties and human rights.

In a global society characterised by environmental risk, information blizzards, and moral and scientific uncertainty, the media, in all its forms, is more important than ever. Democracy requires informed citizens who are able to construct intelligent agreements, and disagreements, among themselves. This can only occur when there is free, equal and open access to a wide variety of opinions. As the American founding father James Madison said: 'a people who mean to be their own governors, must arm themselves with the power which knowledge gives'. For the political scientist John Keane, a **mass media** genuinely serving the public interest would support the development of democratic practices by challenging the arrogance of some political judgements and the inevitability of environmental risks or political abuses.

Democratic procedures combined with public service media can open up and render accountable the process in which citizens, experts and policy makers comprehend, estimate, evaluate and deal with the probabilities and consequences of risks. They are an indispensable means of rendering accountable those politicians and entrepreneurs who turn a blind eye to the environmental damage and 'normal accidents' ... which plague high-risk projects.

Keane, J (1991) *The Media and Democracy,* **Cambridge, Polity Press, p181**

Too often the media, particularly in America, seem to trivialise, sensationalise and anaesthetise people from the problems of others and of the world as a whole.

> **?**
> 1) **How important is the UK's Human Rights Act 2000?**
> 2) **Does CCTV protect or undermine a person's civil rights?**
> 3) **What institutions can best ensure that human rights legislation is adhered to nationally and internationally?**
> 4) **Why is the business of business not simply business?**

Freedom of Information Act 2000

The Freedom of Information Act 2000 will be phased in from 2002 and be fully effective to the whole public by 2005.

- The Freedom of Information Act 2000 received Royal Assent on 30 November 2000.
- The Freedom of Information Act 2000 provides clear statutory rights for those requesting information together with a strong enforcement regime. Under the terms of the Act, any member of the public will be able to apply for access to information held by bodies across the public sector.
- The legislation will apply to a wide range of public authorities, including Parliament, government departments and local authorities, health trusts, doctors' surgeries, publicly funded museums and thousands of other organisations.

The main features of the Act are:

- a general right of access to information held by public authorities in the course of carrying out their public functions, subject to certain conditions and exemptions
- in most cases where information is exempted from disclosure, there is a duty on public authorities to disclose where, in the view of the public authority, the public interest in disclosure outweighs the public interest in maintaining the exemption in question
- a new office of Information Commissioner, and a new Information Tribunal, with wide powers to enforce the rights created
- a duty imposed on public authorities to adopt a scheme for the publication of information. The schemes, which must be approved by the Commissioner, will specify the classes of information the authority intends to publish, the manner of publication and whether the information is available to the public free of charge or on payment of a fee.

http://www.lcd.gov.uk/foi/foiact2000.htm

See http://www.legislation.hmso.gov.uk/acts/en/2000en36.htm for detailed explanatory notes on the Act and its background.

The Act covers public bodies such as the government, local councils, education institutions, health service, police, etc. – all areas financed by the taxpayer. The Act took a long time before it was agreed and many still argue that it has not gone far enough. However, most commentators including the pressure group Campaign for Freedom of Information (www.cfoi.org.uk) agree that the Act is a good starting point towards full freedom of information.

ACTIVITY

Take a look at the Campaign for Freedom of Information's website.

1) What campaigns has it been involved in?
2) How does it operate?
3) What have been its major successes?
4) In what ways does it support active citizenship and democracy?

?

1) **What areas does the Freedom of Information Act cover?**
2) **How might the freedom of information enhance citizens' participation and influence in society on government/public bodies?**
3) **To what extent does the Freedom of Information Act ensure full freedom of information?**

Citizenship and the environment

Some people argue that we now have **environmental rights** as well as civic, political and social rights. We have a right to a clean rather than polluted environment. Animals have a right to be treated humanely. People throughout the world have a right to food, shelter, education and a decent quality of life. For most of us, however, the environment means the natural world of forests, fields, animals, rivers, atmosphere and wilderness. The first thing to recognise is that the natural world has been shaped for thousands of years by the activities of human beings. Our fields and woodlands are the result of agricultural changes; many of the world's deserts have been produced as a consequence of human activity. Our air quality (or lack of it) is the result of changing methods of production and tech-

Whitehall secrecy laws fall as information act bites

The government yesterday promised to repeal or amend 97 laws and review a further 200 that ban the publication of information held by Whitehall.

Some 79 laws are to be kept – mainly to protect information held on members of the public – in the biggest review of unnecessary secrecy undertaken for more than 20 years.

Yvette Cooper, the junior minister at the Lord Chancellor's Department, said the moves were the first stage of implementing the long delayed Freedom of Information Act, which will not come into force until 2005.

From Monday, every government department and Whitehall agency will have to list on its website all the types of publications that are available to the public on demand. The change will mean for the first time some ministries – notably the Department of International Development and the Lord Chancellor's Department – will publish the minutes of some of their top bodies and reports from advisers. Other bodies, including Parliament and the Ministry of Defence, are still keeping the minutes of their top executives' meetings secret.

Information kept secret will include personal details held on children with special needs, medical evidence on vaccine-damaged children, personal details held on child support claims, information held by MI5 and MI6, patent trade secrets and trade secrets on the composition of fertilisers and feedstuffs. The government will also maintain a ban on information held by the valuation office from personal visits to people's homes.

Still under review is how much information should be released on children involved in adoption procedures and on people who go to clinics treating sexually transmitted diseases. The Department of Health is keen to protect confidentiality in the area by a blanket ban on the release of information.

Maurice Frankel, director of the Campaign for Freedom of Information, yesterday welcomed the government's move to repeal a large number of laws banning the release of information. But he was disappointed that many of the publication schemes did not take the opportunity to release new information.

Information released will include:

- papers on one of the country's most celebrated supposed UFO sightings near a joint RAF and USAF base in Rendlesham Forest in Suffolk in 1980. The US released its papers on the sightings in 1983 under the American Freedom of Information Act
- a quarterly report on whether Clare Short, international development secretary, is on target in spending overseas aid properly. The current report says Britain has failed to reach targets on cutting child mortality but is ahead of targets in nine African countries in getting boys and girls equal access to schooling
- (from 2005) details on the safety of medicines currently kept secret to protect drug companies
- safety reports on big rail crashes, such as those at Ladbroke Grove and Potters Bar.

David Hencke, © *The Guardian*, **29 November 2002**

---

nology such as burning fossil fuels and extensive use of private cars. Even the animal world has altered shape because of selective breeding techniques and more recently, genetic modification. Towns, cities and sprawling urban areas have altered the way our country looks, the way we live our lives, and the time spent in traffic jams.

What environmentalists argue is that as citizens we must start taking responsibility for how our actions affect the wider environment and seek to alter our behaviour in a more environmentally friendly direction.

In 1987 the United Nations World Commission on Environment and Development recognised that it was impossible to segregate concern over the natural world from concern over the way we organise our societies, produce goods and services, trade with each other, govern ourselves and administer justice. The Commission's report, *Our Common Future*, offered a definition of a key concept, sustainable development, that has since informed policy making all over the world. Sustainable development is 'development that meets the need of the present without compromising the ability of future generations to meet their own needs'.

The report also recommended a set of legal principles including:

- all human beings have the fundamental right to an environment adequate for their health and well-being
- states shall conserve and use the environment and natural resources for the benefit of present and future generations.

1) What might be the rights and duties of environmental citizens?
2) How might these rights and duties be protected and fulfilled?

Exam questions

You must answer Question 1 and either Question 2 or 3.

1) Read **Sources A** and **B**, and answer parts (a) to (c) which follow.

Source A

> **A better kind of citizen**
>
> Classes should assist racial integration
>
> It is reported that the Home Secretary is planning to require new immigrants seeking British citizenship to take citizenship classes and language lessons. Citizenship classes will help widen understanding between communities and language lessons will give immigrants a better opportunity of reducing their social exclusion. Immigrants are entitled to know the rights and duties that come with British citizenship. The Home Secretary is right to make the granting of citizenship more than just a form-filling exercise.
>
> **Adapted from** *The Guardian,* **27 October 2001**

Source B

> **Caught in no-go areas**
>
> 'Inaccessible' healthcare services disadvantage disabled people
>
> A report from a leading charity says that disabled people (who account for 3% of the population) find it up to five times more difficult to use primary healthcare services than the able-bodied. The difficulties were most acute among the profoundly deaf – 56% of people in this category found doctors' premises inadequate or difficult to use.
>
> Six in ten disabled people said that feeling unwelcome and difficult access prevented them from taking part in common social activities.
>
> Among the able-bodied people the main reasons for not taking part in these activities were lack of interest, childcare responsibilities and shortage of time.
>
> **Adapted from** *The Guardian,* **17 April 2002**

Your answers should refer to the sources as appropriate but you should also include other relevant information.

(a) Explain **two** reasons why some citizens might find it difficult to participate fully in 'common social activities'. (**Source B**) (4 marks)

(b) Briefly examine some of the arguments for **and** against the proposed 'citizenship classes and language lessons'. (**Source A**) (10 marks)

(c) Critically examine how far the state protects the rights of citizens as employers **or** as consumers of state services. (16 marks)

AQA, 3 June 2003

2) (a) 'Citizens have duties as well as rights.' Assess this view, using examples. (20 marks)

AQA, 7 June 2001

3) (a) Explain **two** ways in which the Human Rights Act 1998 supports the liberties of British citizens. (10 marks)

(b) Assess the view that active citizenship is the basis of the modern state. (20 marks)

AQA, 15 January 2002

CHAPTER
2

Citizens and the Law

In this chapter you will explore the citizen and the law including:

- methods of resolving disputes; the courts and alternative dispute resolution (e.g. tribunals and the **ombudsman**)
- the rights of the police and the accused; the prosecution process
- the legal profession: who does what? The citizen's voice in the legal process
- contemporary debates about the nature of law enforcement within society.

The chapter is broken into six sections

Key terms

Alternative dispute resolution – methods of resolving differences without going through the court systems

Institutional racism – where racially prejudiced behaviour exists not necessarily knowingly, but as part of the culture of an organisation, e.g. insensitive policies on recruitment or racist language as the norm

Justice – is the idea that people's relationships with one another should be based on some understanding of fairness and impartiality

Laws – are the formally enacted rules of society by which citizens are bound

Ombudsman – an official with the power to investigate and check the proper workings of an organisation, e.g. compliance to financial regulations

Tribunals – often employment disputes resolved through special courts to hear employment disputes between employer and employee

Introduction

Down these mean streets

At 14, Max is tall and strapping and looks more able than most boys his age to take care of himself. But he has still fallen victim more than once to 'kid-on-kid' mugging. It first happened when he was 11. He and a friend were getting off a tube train when a group of older boys asked them for money. They said they didn't have any, so the boys attacked them. Adults on the platform stood by and did nothing while Max was being kicked in the head. [...]

National crime statistics published by the Home Office last Friday show that the number of street robberies rose by 28% in the year to March. When it comes to street crime, boys aged from ten to 17 are among the most vulnerable sections of society, much more vulnerable than pensioners. And most of those who prey on them are the same age as their victims.

Figures from the Metropolitan Police area, where the problem is at its worst, show that 65% of people accused of mugging and other street crime in London between April and November last year were between ten and 17 years of age. According to the Home Office, most offenders and half of all victims involved in thefts of mobile phones nationally were 15 or 16.

The official number of young muggers is rising: from 2545 in London between April and December 2000 to 3158 in the same period last year. There could be many more. Because the victims are other children, incidents frequently go unreported.

One problem is that today's schoolchildren walk around with a great deal more that is worth stealing than in the days when they had only their bus fare home. The Metropolitan Police's biggest bugbear is the mobile phone. 'If nobody carried mobile phones, you could probably reduce this kind of crime by 60%,' says Superintendent Simon Pountain. 'The most helpful thing schools could do is to tell children not to bring these phones to school.

'Young kids shouldn't have the most up-to-date mobiles, either. Someone should make a phone for school kids that is the equivalent of those standard NHS glasses of the 60s, something effective but so unattractive that nobody would want to steal it.'

Since February, the Met has been engaged in Operation Safer Streets, targeting street crime in 15 London boroughs, including hotspots such as Lambeth, Hackney, Southwark, Haringey, Brent, Westminster and Camden. The greater police presence should reassure parents that their children are safer, but somehow it does not. For one thing, the future of Operation Safer Streets is only guaranteed until the end of the financial year. After that, the Met's overstretched resources may have to be switched to the next political priority. [...]

Markham [Jehane] [writer and mother of three teenage boys in north London] and her husband, actor Roger Lloyd Pack, have given a good deal of thought to the subject because their middle son has been mugged five times in 18 months. Each time it was by boys his own age who were after cash and his mobile phone. Three of the incidents took place in daylight, with several adults around who did nothing to intervene; in fact, one group refused to phone the police and laughingly told the boy to go after his assailants himself if he wanted his phone back.

'I feel really angry about this endless persecution of boys,' says Lloyd Pack, who played Del Boy's lugubrious friend Trigger in *Only Fools and Horses*. 'What makes me particularly annoyed is the fact that adults can just sit by and watch it happen. As a society, we do not take responsibility for what is happening under our noses. We no longer feel we have to look after each other. People just watch and think, "It's nothing to do with me".'

Trying to think constructively about what could be done to safeguard children from mugging, Markham has come up with an ingenious idea. Parents at local schools could, she suggests, set up networks of 'safe houses' – one or two per street on popular routes home from school – where children know they could go if they were in danger.

© Sue Summers, *The Observer*, **14 July 2002**

ACTIVITY

1) Why are so many young people either victims or perpetrators of crime?
2) Why are mobile phones targeted so frequently by muggers?
3) Do you think Lloyd Pack is right when he says, 'we no longer feel we have to look after each other'? Give reasons for your answer.

Crime and the fear of crime

Crime and people's fear of crime is rarely out of the headlines. Newspapers frequently tell horror stories of serious crimes like murders, robberies, muggings, assaults, frauds and embezzlements. Vandalism, aggressive begging and other examples of **anti-social behaviour** worsen the quality of life in many urban and rural communities. Although the police have a role in enforcing the law and catching criminals to bring them to justice, the prevention of crime and the maintenance of peace and order in our communities is the responsibility of everyone living in them. This is an important aspect of citizenship.

Crime rates

For many people, the number of crimes committed show how healthy our society is, but crime statistics produced by governments and other bodies are open to criticism. They may not always represent a true picture of crime and disorder in British society. For instance, the number of crimes actually reported to the police are far fewer than the number of crimes actually committed. In the year March 2001–02, 5.5 million crimes were reported to the police, representing a 2% increase on the year before, the first rise in government figures since 1995. However, the British Crime Survey (BCS), published in July 2002 and interviews 33,000 people in England and Wales about their experience of crime, estimated that in the same period over 13 million crimes had been committed, representing a 2% decrease. The way in which crime figures are compiled may vary so it is not always easy for researchers and policy makers to make judgements about long-term trends.

Views on crime

People also have different ideas about why crime takes place and whether the law should always be obeyed. Crimes may be committed by people simply because some people are bad. On the other hand, crime and rates at which crimes are committed may be influenced by such things as poverty, unemployment and other aspects of social exclusion. This leads some politicians to talk about being 'tough on crime and tough on the causes of crime'. However, what research does tell us is that people's fear of crime, particularly burglary, street and violent crime, is only marginally affected by official statistics. One-third of those interviewed in the BCS believed crime had risen 'a lot' and one third thought it had risen 'a little'. The media may influence people's perceptions. 42% of those people who read tabloid papers such as *The Sun*, *The Mirror* and *The Mail* believed that crime is rising. Only 26% of readers of broadsheet papers such as *The Guardian*, *The Daily Telegraph* and *The Independent* felt that crime was on the increase. Many elderly people and many women feel vulnerable to street attack or burglary but elderly people are far less likely to be victims of crime than younger people. The population group most likely to be victims, and perpetrators of crime, are young males. It is this group that is least likely to fear being victims of crime. Many people in well-off areas feel unsafe and insecure. In many poor areas, with high levels of unemployment and low levels of business activity, people actually are unsafe and insecure.

1 English law and the court system

This section explores how the legal system applies to citizens and looks at:

- distinctions between criminal law and civil law, and the court procedure
- criminal courts: magistrates and Crown Courts
- civil courts: coroner's courts, county courts and the high court.

Distinctions between criminal law and civil law, and the court procedure

Criminal law

Criminal law is concerned with legal rules, the infringement or breaking of which can lead to the imposition of punishments (by the state) administered through the courts and criminal justice system. Such law breaking or crimes may include murder, robbery, assault and fraud. Punishment of offenders may include custodial sentences such as imprisonment or non-custodial sentences like **probation or community service**.

Civil law

Civil law concerns legal relationships between ordinary persons and between ordinary persons and public bodies such as local authorities and other government institutions, businesses, etc. Civil law deals with such issues as divorce (family law), contracts and property (business and land law), negligence and libel (tort). The infringement of civil law is known as a civil wrong.

Criminal acts and civil wrongdoings are usually heard in different courts where procedures and outcomes are different. In a civil court, a person may bring a claim against (**sues**) another person (**defendant**). If the court accepts the claim, it can award financial damages to the claimant, or:

- order the transfer of property from the defendant to the claimant
- order the defendant not to do something by imposing an **injunction**
- order the defendant to do something.

N.B. Scotland has its own legal system different to that of England and Wales.

Court procedure

A person charged with a criminal offence is known as the defendant. In a criminal court, the defendant is asked to plead either 'guilty' or 'not guilty' to the charge. If a 'not guilty' plea is entered, the lawyer, known as the prosecutor, will **prosecute** the defendant with a view to proving his guilt beyond all reasonable doubt. The defendant will usually, through his lawyer, attempt to prove the truthfulness of his case. This system is known as **adversarial**, for the two sides oppose each other and argue out the case in court. If found guilty, the defendant will be convicted and sentenced by the court.

Criminal courts: magistrates and Crown Courts

The magistrates courts

Magistrates in the magistrates courts deal with the vast majority of criminal cases. These cases tend to be relatively minor. The most serious cases are heard in the Crown Courts. What goes on in a magistrates court (the proceedings) and the powers magistrates have are regulated by Acts of Parliament. Offences may be classified in three ways. Their classification will determine what proceedings are adopted.

1 Some offences, e.g. careless driving or using threatening behaviour, may be tried instantly (summarily) by a magistrate.
2 Some offences, e.g. robbery, rape or murder, may be tried only on **indictment** before a judge and jury in a Crown Court.
3 Some offences, e.g. theft or dangerous driving, may be tried either in a magistrates court or in a Crown Court before a judge and jury.

When an adult is brought before a magistrate with an indictable offence, the magistrate's role is to confirm that what the person is charged with is an indictable-only offence. They also decide whether the defendant qualifies for financial assistance. Where it can go *either way*, and the magistrate is prepared to hear the case, the defendant has the legal right to decide where his case is heard – in a magistrates court or in a Crown Court before judge and jury.

If a defendant agrees to be tried by magistrates and pleads not guilty, the case will be put back to a later date. If a defendant opts for trial in a Crown Court, there will be a later date set for **committal proceedings** to take place. This involves all prosecution evidence being presented to the court in written form and the right of both defence and prosecution to make oral statements on whether the case should go to the Crown Court or not. Committal proceedings only take place for *triable either way* offences. The defendant will not be asked to enter a plea at this stage. If a defendant pleads guilty, he or she will be dealt with immediately.

When an offence is tried summarily, the magistrate may declare both verdict and sentence. Powers of magistrates include:

- the maximum custodial sentence of six months in prison
- the maximum fine of £5000 or up to £20,000 for cases involving issues such as pollution or health and safety
- transferring the defendant to a Crown Court if they feel the defendant deserves a higher sentence than they can administer.

Magistrates also have limited civil jurisdiction and powers but may, for example, order a violent spouse to leave the family home. A defendant in a criminal case may appeal to the Crown Court against his sentence and conviction if he pleaded not guilty. An appeal may also be made to the high court.

Recent reforms have been designed to speed up or 'fast track' criminal cases and reduce time spent dealing with offenders in magistrates courts. In looking at the circumstances of the offence, magistrates may reject a request for a jury trial. Critics have suggested that although such reforms may lead to greater efficiency and save public money, they may not be in the interest of justice. The human and legal right to trial by jury have existed in England since before King John signed the **Magna Carta** in 1215.

Magistrates may also sit at **youth courts** when criminal proceedings are brought against children between ten and 14, and young persons 14–17, except in cases where charges relate to serious offences such as murder or manslaughter. Magistrates may administer custodial sentences, e.g. detention in a young offenders institution, and non-custodial sentences, such as probation, community service orders, curfews and drug treatment and testing orders.

The Youth Justice Board and youth crime

The causes of youth crime are complex. Those at risk of offending are often the most socially disadvantaged. For its annual report for 2001, the Youth Justice Board commissioned some research on the causes of young offending. The researchers identified a number of risk factors making anti-social and criminal behaviour more likely. They include:

- aggressive behaviour, including bullying
- low achievement, beginning in primary school
- family history of problem behaviour
- alienation and lack of social commitment
- peer acceptance of problem behaviour
- family conflict or breakdown
- lack of commitment to school, including truancy
- peer involvement in problem behaviour
- availability of drugs.

The YJB Report concluded that the only sure way of dealing with youth offending is to deal with these risk factors in Britain's disadvantaged communities.

 Should crime only be tackled by the police courts and prison system?

Crown Courts

Crown Courts deal with serious criminal cases, where either a high court judge or a **circuit judge** will be in charge. Trial by jury is a feature of Crown Court proceedings.

Civil courts: coroner's courts, county courts and the high court

The coroner's court

Coroner's courts began in 1194 and are among the oldest English courts still in existence. Their job is to look into cases of violent, unnatural, sudden or suspicious death, to find out the identity of the deceased person, and the cause and place of death if unknown. The procedure is that of an inquest or inquiry and not a trial. No blame or responsibility is assigned. In cases of suspected murder or a death in prison or police custody, the coroner may summon a jury of between seven and 11 persons.

The county court

County courts deal with the less serious civil cases including contract, tort, land, debts and family matters. A single circuit judge is in charge and usually sits alone. The small claims court hears cases where financial claims do not exceed £5000.

The high court

High courts deal with the more serious civil cases dealing with issues such as personal injury and where the financial claims for damages could exceed £25,000. Any person who brings a case before a civil court has to prove to the judge or judges that any alleged wrongdoing took place on the **balance of probabilities**. This is easier to attain than that required in the criminal court. Many cases brought against the police are heard in civil courts.

2 Alternative dispute resolution

This section explores means of resolving disputes without going to court and looks at:

- mediation
- tribunals
- arbitration
- ombudsmen.

Not every legal infringement or dispute actually goes to court. Many are dealt with by tribunals or through mediation, conciliation or arbitration services. Judges in civil cases may actually recommend mediation (i.e. parties seek resolution of their dispute with the help of a neutral third party) but cannot enforce such a course of action. In 1997, the use of mediation was piloted in some divorce cases. Conciliation is a process whereby the neutral third party takes a more active role in seeking settlement. As with mediation, the dispute may not be resolved but rather the parties agree to continue the court case, known as **litigation**. The process of settling disputes outside of the court is known as alternative dispute resolution.

Mediation

Mediation UK

Mediation UK is a voluntary organisation that operates nationally. Its purpose is to develop ways to resolve conflicts that occur in communities. It offers practical help and support through a network of local mediation services, which include advice, training, consultancy, information and much more.

Victim–offender mediation refers to mediation within the criminal justice system. It involves the victims of crimes, others affected by crime, and occasionally offenders themselves. The aim is to find ways by which the offender can repair the damage done to the victim by his or her criminal act. The emphasis is firmly on meeting the needs of the victim. Victim–offender mediation is used within the probation services and local youth offending teams. Some police officers are also trained as mediators.

Tribunals

Administrative tribunals deal with disputes between a person and the state. People have many different social and welfare rights, e.g. the right to disability allowance or redundancy pay, which are not always honoured. Some deal with disputes between individuals.

Social security tribunal – appeals service

If, for example, a man feels he has been unfairly refused a social security benefit or has been awarded less than he is entitled to, he may present his case to a social security tribunal. For all benefits except incapacity benefit, an appeal is dealt with by a legally qualified chairman known as a 'legally qualified panel member'. This person normally sits alone. These tribunals are not independent and their decisions may be replaced by the Department of Social Security if a change of circumstances has occurred since the decision was made.

Employment tribunals

Employment tribunals have jurisdiction in cases relating to disputes over unfair dismissal, contractual disputes, redundancy, equal pay, and sex, race and disability discrimination. Tribunals consist of a chairman appointed by the Lord Chancellor and members drawn from two lay panels. If a sum of money is awarded to a claimant and not paid, the claimant may go to the county court to have the decision enforced. Hearings before employment tribunals are normally held in public.

Advantages of tribunals include the following:

- tribunals have detailed knowledge of their particular fields and localities
- procedures are simple and often cheaper than those in courts
- decisions are often made quickly.

Other tribunals

- Rent tribunals decide on whether or not a rent is fair.

- Immigration tribunals hear appeals on the right of immigrants to enter or stay in the UK.
- Mental health review tribunals decide if a mentally ill patient should continue to be detained in hospital.

Arbitration

Arbitration involves parties agreeing to let a third party make a binding decision. Frequently, commercial contracts include clauses whereby disputing parties are able to seek arbitration to resolve their differences. An arbitrator need not be a lawyer but a person who has detailed or special knowledge of the area under dispute. Arbitration can take a long time and be expensive. Parties involved in the arbitration are required to accept and abide by the arbitrator's decision. Arbitration proceedings take place in private and only in the commercial court, which is part of the high court.

Outside of the court system, arbitration is also used in industrial relations disputes, settling community and neighbourhood differences over issues such as noise, anti-social behaviour, boundaries, planning decisions, etc.

ACAS

The Advisory, Conciliation and Arbitration Service (ACAS) was established in 1974. It became a statutory body in 1975 with the passing of the Employment Protection Act. ACAS seeks to ensure good industrial relations and improve performance by finding means to settle disputes. ACAS states that there are four major elements to its work:

- it provides unbiased information and advice
- it resolves difficulties between employers and employees
- it settles issues concerning employees' rights
- it encourages peaceful and harmonious work relations.

Ombudsman

The ombudsman offers certain safeguards against bad government administration to citizens. In 1967 the Parliamentary Commissioner for Administration (ombudsman), now called the Parliamentary Commissioner and Health Service Commissioner, was created by an Act of Parliament to investigate complaints made about government administration, most notably in the Department of Social Security and the Inland Revenue. Since 2000, a member of the public is able to make complaints directly to the Commissioner who may examine administrative procedures. It is not able to take any action if correct

Collars, ties and T-shirts under spotlight at tribunal

Civil servant seeks compensation over 'unfair' dress code

A civil servant claimed yesterday that he had suffered sexual discrimination because he was forced to wear a collar and tie at work when dress rules for women were less restrictive.

'It may not be the convention for women to wear a collar and tie, but the point I am making is that a similar standard of business dress is not applied to women as it is to myself,' Matthew Thompson told an employment tribunal in Manchester.

'Women are allowed to wear T-shirts, they have logos on, and on at least one occasion they have worn football tops.'

Mr Thompson, an administrative assistant at a Jobcentre Plus office in Stockport, Greater Manchester, formerly worked for the benefits agency, where rules were more relaxed on neckwear. But when the agency was merged with the employment service, the Department for Work and Pensions introduced a new, more prescriptive dress code, which demanded ties and also banned denim, Lycra, leggings, shorts, crop-tops, trainers and baseball caps.

Much of the hearing, in which the chairman, Keith Robinson, wore a striped tie, was taken up with discussions of the distinction between 'conventionally businesslike' and 'smart casual' wear.

It emerged that Jobcentre Plus staff could wear Doc Marten boots with trousers, but not with summer dresses, and that a Hawaiian shirt (even with tie) was likely to fall foul of the rules.

There was also much discussion of what was the female formal equivalent of the collar and tie, with both Mr Thompson and his counsel, Karen Monaghan, arguing that it was the blouse.

Ms Monaghan asked Terry Moran, northwest director of Jobcentre Plus, to look at photographs of Mr Thompson's female colleagues taken at work.

The first wore a polo shirt, which Ms Monaghan said would not be acceptable on a man. Mr Moran said the shirt was 'casual but acceptable'.

The second woman wore a loose T-shirt not tucked in. 'That's casual isn't it?' asked Ms Monaghan. 'I think that's casual,' Mr Moran agreed. 'But I don't think it's a T-shirt. It's got a different kind of neck from any T-shirt I have seen.'

Another woman was shown wearing what Ms Monaghan described as a vest. 'She is wearing a smart sleeveless top,' commented Mr Moran.

'That would not be acceptable on a man, would it?' asked Ms Monaghan. 'Not in terms of collar and tie, no,' Mr Moran replied.

He added that the dress code was introduced to ensure all staff were dressed consistently and in a 'professional and businesslike' manner. 'It is really important that we present a professional service that employers see as credible and one that they can recognise.'

He accepted that women had a wider range of options in choosing their clothing, but added that there was no equivalent 'business convention' for female staff.

'It is difficult to stipulate what is businesslike convention for women,' he said.

Of the 90,000 employees, 25 men and two women are refusing to comply with the new dress code.

The hearing continues.

David Ward, © *The Guardian*, **25 February 2003**

---

administrative procedures have been followed, even if the decision in question is a poor or bad one. The ombudsman is not able to investigate personal matters or initiate an investigation. Despite these limitations, the Parliamentary Commissioner receives increasing numbers of complaints every year.

There are also:

- two commissions dealing with complaints made against local authorities
- a legal services ombudsman, examining complaints made against the legal profession
- a banking ombudsman
- an insurance ombudsman
- a building society ombudsman.

1) What is meant by alternative dispute resolution?

2) What is the role of the ombudsman?

3 The legal profession

This section explores the people involved in the legal profession, their roles and responsibilities, and ways that citizens can use the services. It looks at:

- what the people involved are called
- the judiciary and judges
- law officers
- social composition of the legal profession.

What the people involved are called

The legal profession consists of all those people who are concerned with administering the law. Many of these professionals are highly educated and paid to carry out a particular role. These include judges, magistrates, barristers and solicitors.

Judges

Judges are supposed to be independent of political and commercial interests but have sometimes been perceived as being subject to political control or influence. This has particularly been argued regarding government attempts to limit the freedom (discretion) judges have to determine sentences in serious criminal cases, particularly involving certain violent and sexual offences that aroused significant popular concern. The legal profession is also mainly white, middle class and male. The perception here is that it is largely socially conservative, pro-establishment and out of touch. However, there are a number of radical lawyers working in areas such as race relations and human and civil rights who frequently question the existing state of affairs.

Solicitors and barristers

The legal profession also consists of solicitors and barristers who are sometimes referred to generally as lawyers. Unlike other countries, Britain retains this clear professional distinction, with most of England and Wales' 80,000 solicitors working in smaller or larger practices in all towns and cities. Although some solicitors may specialise in a certain area such as divorce, business or land law, many work in general practices offering clients advice on a wide range of topics. Solicitors will meet with and interview clients, write letters, draft contracts, draw up wills and deal with the legal side of buying flats, houses, offices and land (conveyance). Until 1985, solicitors had the sole right to conveyance and until the passing of the Courts and Legal Services Act 1990 were not allowed to act as **advocates** and represent their clients in court. Today, most follow their traditional pre-trial functions of preparing a case, establishing the facts, making sure that witnesses turn up, ensuring necessary documents are available, and dealing with any disputes over costs awarded after a judgement has been given.

The Law Society

The Law Society is the professional association of solicitors responsible for:

- authorising the qualifications necessary to become a solicitor

- setting examinations
- issuing practicing certificates
- preserving minimum standards of behaviour (i.e. appropriate professional conduct in terms of fees charged, legal advice given, etc.).

Advocacy is the process whereby a lawyer will present a case in court and question witnesses, etc. By 2001, over 1000 solicitors had also qualified as advocates although this role is still mainly the work of barristers.

There are around 10,000 barristers in England and Wales, who as a group are known as the Bar. They are mainly self-employed but work within a number of chambers of roughly 15–20 individuals to share administrative expenses. Most concentrate on advocacy and many specialise in a particular legal area such as criminal or shipping law. Some barristers are directly employed by the Crown Prosecution Service (CPS). After ten years experience, a barrister may apply to the Lord Chancellor to become a Queen's Counsel (QC). These experienced lawyers have taken work on high profile and often difficult cases. As a result, many command very high fees. Some QCs earn up to £500,000 a year.

Cherie Booth QC

Increasingly more women are qualifying as solicitors and barristers. Just over half of new solicitors and just under half of new barristers are women. 20 years ago few women studied law at university or started a professional career in law. This is reflected in the fact that today only 7% of QCs are women. On the other hand, ethnic minority groups are quite well represented in the legal profession. Although making up roughly 6% of the UK population, about 8% of working barristers and 5% of solicitors are from minority backgrounds. Many of these are newly qualified and this may in part explain why very few people from ethnic backgrounds are QCs or judges.

The judiciary and judges

The judiciary is the collective term given to those individuals known as judges. Judges serve in both civil and criminal courts. Their role is to adjudicate in disputes ensuring that the law is applied in a fair, unbiased and reasonable manner. The head of the judiciary is the Lord Chancellor, who is appointed by the Prime Minister, and is a member of the government. He sits in the Cabinet and presides over proceedings in the House of Lords as speaker. As a member of the Lords, he also contributes to debates on the

Cherie Booth, the Prime Minister's wife, continued working up to a week before the birth of her last baby. Acting for the TUC in the high court, she challenged the government's ruling on parental leave. She said that the government's refusal to backdate a 1999 EU Directive deprived up to 3 million parents and young children of their rights

law and may introduce new bills connected with law and justice. He also sits as a judge in the House of Lords and has a very important role in the appointment of, and occasionally, dismissal of judges. The Lord Chancellor is a political appointment and will have to leave office if his party in government loses a general election. It is the present government's intention to abolish the post of Lord Chancellor and establish a Supreme Court similar to that in the USA. This is a controversial proposal signifying a fundamental change to Britain's constitutional and legal arrangements.

There are two types of judges known as superior and inferior judges.

Superior Judges

The Law Lords

The Law Lords are appointed by the Queen (on the advice of the Prime Minister) from the country's most senior judges. The Law Lords are made life peers. There are 12 Law Lords who, when sitting, make up the highest court in the UK known as the Lords of Appeal in Ordinary. They hear mainly civil cases but some criminal cases when there is a dispute over a point of law. Many cases are highly specialised and technical but others, particularly those dealing with human rights, attract a great deal of public interest and media attention as with the 'right to die' case of Diane Pretty.

The Lords Justices of Appeal

These lords hear both civil and criminal cases in the Court of Appeal. The Lords Justices must have had at least ten years experience as high court judges before being appointed by the Queen on the advice of the Prime Minister. Appeal court judges hear appeals about decisions, convictions and sentences in the lower courts. In 1988, the first woman, Elizabeth Butler-Sloss, was appointed an appeal court judge.

High court judges

High court judges are appointed by the Queen on the advice of the Lord Chancellor and are normally former barristers or circuit judges with ten years experience. They may sit in all three divisions of the high court (Queen's Bench, chancery and family) and in the Crown Court when hearing serious cases.

Inferior judges

Inferior judges are appointed by the Lord Chancellor and include:

- circuit judges who sit in both the Crown Court and county court
- recorders who are part-time judges normally sitting in the Crown Court
- district judges who hear mainly small claims and sit in the county court. Others, known as stipendiary magistrates, will sit in the magistrates court
- chairmen of tribunals.

Law officers

The government has a law officer department consisting of the Attorney-General, who is the government's chief legal advisor appointed by the Prime Minister from those MPs who are trained barristers, and the Solicitor-General, who is deputy to the Attorney-General. The consent of the Attorney-General is required before a prosecution can start in cases such as corruption or hijacking. He also has the power to prevent a prosecution case from continuing. In 2001, the first woman, Harriet Harman, was appointed Solicitor-General.

The Director of Public Prosecutions (DPP) is appointed by the Attorney-General to whom s/he is responsible. The Director heads the Crown Prosecution Service whose duties include, among other things, to take over the conduct of all criminal proceedings instituted by the police, to advise police forces on criminal offences, and to appear for the prosecution in some appeal cases.

Social composition of the legal profession

- In 2002, only nine out of 98 high court judges were women.
- Only two out of 35 appeal court judges were female. In November 2003 Dame Brenda Hale became Britain's first female Law Lord.
- Only 9% of circuit judges and 12% of recorders were female.
- No high court judges were from ethnic minority backgrounds.
- 1% of circuit judges and 3% of recorders are from ethnic minority backgrounds.
- Between 1997 and mid 1999, 85 judges were appointed. Of these, 73% had been to fee-paying public schools and 79% had been to the elite universities of Oxford and Cambridge.

Patriarchy and male dominance in the criminal justice system

The criminal justice system works towards legitimising and actively promoting the maintenance of a patriarchal society. In support of this claim, it is generally believed that as most of the decision-makers within the justice system are male (perhaps with the exception of the magistrates court), there is a tendency for them to adopt a more lenient approach towards women. This leniency is said to be based upon the chivalry hypothesis, which asserts that most males are likely to respond to female offenders in much the same way as they would respond to their wives, daughters or mothers.

Alcock, C, Payne, S & Sullivan, M (2000) *Introducing Social Policy,* **Prentice Hall, p297**

ACTIVITY

1) Could this quote be true?
2) How could you verify these claims?

Some critics of the British criminal justice system have pointed out that there seems to be a disproportionate percentage (18%) of minority ethnic persons in prison. This may suggest racial discrimination exists within the judiciary and criminal justice system. However, others have noted that part of this over-representation may be the result of the imprisonment of people of foreign **nationality** convicted of drug trafficking. Additionally, the black-British or Afro-Caribbean population is largely youthful, from working class backgrounds and lives in areas with high crime and unemployment rates. All these factors are statistically associated with high offender rates.

? 1) **What do judges, barristers and solicitors do?**
2) **Why might some people be concerned about the social composition of the legal profession?**

4 Ordinary citizen involvement in the legal system

This section explores the roles ordinary citizens have in the legal system and looks at:

- lay magistrates
- the jury system
- reform of the jury system
- restorative justice and victim satisfaction.

Lay magistrates

Normally, ordinary people's (lay) involvement in the legal system is as defendants, claimants, victims, and as members of a jury in criminal and occasionally civil trials. Ordinary citizen's involvement in the court system's decision-making process dates back to 1195 when Richard I appointed 'keepers of the peace'. In 1999, there were about 26,000 lay magistrates, also known as Justices of the Peace or JPs, in England and Wales. They usually sit to hear cases as a bench of two or three magistrates and have a wide ranging workload.

JPs do not have to have a qualification in the law although they do undertake some legal training. In 1988, the Lord Chancellor identified six essential personal qualities all JPs must exhibit. These include:

- good character
- understanding and communication
- social awareness
- maturity and sound temperament
- sound judgement
- commitment and reliability.

Appointments of lay magistrates are made by the Lord Chancellor on the basis of recommendations made to him by local advisory committees consisting of mainly retired JPs. JPs are frequently criticised for being middle class, middle aged, socially and politically conservative, and overwhelmingly white. Although 49% of JPs are women, there is under-representation of minority groups, young and particularly working class people. However, both Conservative and Labour governments have been concerned to open up the appointment system to secure a fairer social balance and greater public confidence in the legal process.

Lay magistrates are local people and hear local cases. One significant advantage of lay magistrates is their local knowledge and, for the government, another is that they are unpaid. One problem is that there seems to be vast differences in the sentences JPs administer where the same offence is concerned. In some areas, to drive a car when disqualified means imprisonment but in other areas prison sentences are never given. Youth courts in the north of England tend to administer tougher sentences than in the south. A study in 1991 showed that lay magistrates tended to be more lenient than stipendiary (paid) ones.

The jury system

Juries have been used in England for over 1000 years with a person's right to trial by his peers being confirmed by the Magna Carta of 1215. Since the mid seventeenth century, it has been unlawful for a judge to interfere in the deliberations of a jury. Juries have been a democratic cornerstone, guaranteeing fairness and impartiality by making the legal system more open. With certain exceptions, anyone aged between 18–70 years may be required to serve on a jury. Members of a jury should not be subject to outside influences or be connected to anyone involved in the trial.

Today, relatively few cases are heard by jury and recent governments have been keen to further restrict the right to trial by jury in order to speed up the judicial process and to ensure that more criminals are convicted and sentenced. Some people feel criminals are frequently let off by gullible juries or escape on a legal technicality. Juries are used in:

- Crown Court for serious criminal cases such as murder or manslaughter
- high court for cases such as defamation, fraud, false imprisonment or malicious prosecution
- county court for cases such as defamation, fraud, false imprisonment or malicious prosecution.

Less than 1% of criminal cases are heard by a jury as 97% are heard in magistrates courts and the defendant pleads guilty in many of those heard in Crown Courts. Juries are used in roughly 20,000 cases a year when the defendant pleads not guilty. Juries listen to the legal argument, witness testimony and other evidence, and deliberate in secret on the guilt or innocence of the defendant. Since 1967 juries have been able to enter a majority verdict, which means at least ten out of the 12 jurors must be in agreement. Juries are used very rarely in civil cases but when used they decide whether a claimant has proved his or her case or not. If s/he has, they will determine the size of the damages that will be awarded.

Issues and problems with the jury system

Juries sometimes have been known to acquit people even if they are legally guilty of the offence they have been charged with. For example, Clive Ponting leaked official secrets about the sinking of the Argentine cruiser *Belgrano* during the Falklands War to Tam Dalyell MP. The jury refused to convict him in 1984 because they believed he was right to do what he did even if he technically had, as the trial judge directed, no defence. Juries do not have to justify their verdicts. They are able to express popular conceptions of justice and a collective common sense, sometimes acting as a referee between the state and the ordinary citizen.

The pool of potential jury members can be vetted in order to check their eligibility for jury service. In some exceptional cases, it is possible for potential jury members to have their social backgrounds and political views examined. Juries have sometimes been criticised for being racially prejudiced because the selection process can produce an all white jury to try a defendant from an ethnic minority background. In 2000, the European Court of Human Rights ruled that this was a breach of Article 6 of the European Convention on Human Rights. Women and members of black and ethnic minority groups are generally under-represented on juries. Once called for jury service, an individual may only be excused if certain limited circumstances apply and then only at the discretion of a court official. Sometimes this leads to rushed verdicts because jury members want to go home or back to work. There have also been cases of jury members having been bribed or physically intimidated by people associated with the case being heard.

Jurors live in society and cannot be isolated from the outside world, particularly media influences, or not fully understand the arguments they hear. In 1996, the mass murderer Rosemary West appealed against her conviction claiming that press stories had prejudiced the jury against her. Some cases, particularly those involving fraudulent accounting practices, may be exceptionally complicated. Many critics believe that ordinary men and women are not in a position to understand long and complex cases. They may also be unable to understand detailed technical legal arguments or sometimes even court proceedings.

Reform of the jury system

The government's comprehensive proposals for reform of the criminal justice system was outlined in the white paper *Justice for All* in July 2002. Of the many proposals suggested, some were relating to trial by jury.

Delivering justice – fairer, more effective trials

We want cases tried in the most appropriate court, and when they come to trial, we want the process to convict the guilty and acquit the innocent, promptly and transparently. An individual is innocent until proven guilty and the prosecution must prove their case against the defendant beyond reasonable doubt. But the system should not become a game where delay and obstruction can be used as a tactic to avoid a rightful conviction.

We propose to:

- *overhaul the rules of evidence so that the widest possible range of material, including relevant previous convictions, is available to the court*
- *extend sentencing powers of magistrates from six to 12 months and require them to sentence all those they have found guilty, rather than committing some to be sentenced in the Crown Court*
- *allow defendants to have the right to ask for trial by judge alone in the Crown Court*
- *allow trial by judge alone in serious and complex fraud trials, some other complex and lengthy trials, or where the jury is at risk of intimidation*
- *strengthen youth courts to deal with more young offenders accused of serious crimes*
- *allow witnesses to refer to their previous and original statements and change the laws on reported evidence ('hearsay')*
- *introduce an exception to the double jeopardy rule in serious cases where there is compelling new evidence*
- *allow prosecution a right of appeal where the judge makes a ruling that effectively terminates the prosecution case.*

Justice for All, **Government white paper (2002)**

1) What is meant when we talk about trial by jury?
2) What are the arguments in favour of reforming the jury system?
3) Do you think a jury should know about the criminal record of a defendant?

Blunkett defends planned justice shake-up

The Home Secretary, David Blunkett, today defended his plans to drop the 'double jeopardy' rule and radically reform Britain's criminal justice system. Mr Blunkett said the proposals are intended to prevent the system being exploited by what he called 'the unscrupulous and avaricious'.

The Home Secretary argued that the white paper simply aimed to bring about a 'rebalancing of the whole system in favour of the victim'. Adding that 'the rights of the defendant to a fair trial' would be protected, he said the proposals were intended to fix failings in existing procedures. At present, he said, 'a third of all trials are declared to be what is called cracked, i.e. the trial literally disintegrates. We have got a whole series of ways in which people refuse to plead guilty until they get to the Crown Court, 57% of those who could have been sentenced at magistrates courts wait until the Crown Court, the lawyers get the money, they plead guilty. That is a complete distortion. What happens in the meantime, of course, is that witnesses and victims stop turning up, they become disillusioned, they won't play the game.'

A spokesman for the civil rights organisation Liberty said today that the jury is one of the cornerstones of British justice. 'Making it harder to duck jury service is a welcome step – measures to undermine those same juries are not.' He added: 'The scope for perverse verdicts is one of the things that endears the jury system to the public and inspires confidence.'

Julian Glover, © *The Guardian,* **17 July 2002**

1) Why does the Home Secretary want to reform the court system?
2) Why does Liberty praise the jury system's 'scope for perverse verdicts'?

Restorative justice and victim satisfaction

Restorative justice is the term used to denote a form of justice that requires active reparation by the offender to the victim of crime. It focuses on two key elements:

1 victim satisfaction: reducing the fear of the victim and ensuring they feel 'paid back' for the harm that has been done to them

2 engagement with the young offender to ensure they are aware of the consequences of their actions.

The Youth Justice Board has funded 46 new restorative justice projects working with over 6800 young people since April 2000. Restorative justice approaches are being used largely at the early stage of offending.

Outcomes for the offender

Evaluation results show that both the rate of offending and the seriousness of the offending were reduced. Reconviction rates showed a decrease of 2.1% and the average level of seriousness reduced from 4.0 to 3.6 – a statistically significant decrease.

Outcomes for the victim

The majority found the process a positive experience with 62% saying they would recommend the experience to others. 79% of victims said they were now able to put the offence behind them and 70% said they thought the offender understood better the impact of the offence on them.

Paul, 15, began getting into trouble while sleeping rough after walking out of his home. He was given a 12 month referral order after admitting theft and was remanded into local authority care as his mother refused to have him home. Both his mother and the foster carer attended the panel meeting. The victim's views were presented and, at first, Paul was not very forthcoming and his mum was very negative. But, with help from the Youth Offender Panel members, Paul was able to express his feelings. The meeting also gave Paul and his mother a chance to talk about why their relationship had broken down.

It was agreed that Paul would carry out 25 hours reparation, write a letter of apology and see the education welfare officer and the drugs worker. He was also referred to the local mentoring scheme. Paul's mum accepted the offer of parenting support. Paul has complied with his contract fully, talks to his mum on the phone every day and they are currently working towards overnight visits, with a view to him returning home permanently.

Adapted from the Youth Justice Board's annual report for 2002

> **?** 1) **What advantages might restorative justice have over the court system?**
> 2) **What problems might the system of restorative justice confront?**

5 Police powers, justice and law enforcement

This section explores the role and power of police and looks at:

- police authority and power structures
- debates about justice and law enforcement.

The ordinary citizen has a number of legal rights which are enshrined in various Acts of Parliament such as the Race Relations Act 1976 and 2000, the Disability Discrimination Act 1995, the Equal Pay Act 1970, the Health and Safety at Work Act 1974, and the Human Rights Act 1998. People are able to move around the country freely, express themselves freely, join political organisations or trade unions, say or write what they like (so long as this does not break the law, e.g. is not libellous or likely to incite racial hatred or violence to others).

Police authority and power structures

The police are financed through public taxation, organised into a number of regionally based forces, e.g. West Yorkshire. They are accountable to a local public committee known as the police authority with their chief officer, known as the Chief Constable, answerable to the Home Secretary. The role of the police is to maintain public order, to prevent crime from occurring and where it does to detect and apprehend the offenders in order to bring them before the courts for trial. The police have a number of rights, or powers, that enable them to fulfil this duty. These powers are clearly laid out in Acts of Parliament of which the most important is the Police and Criminal Evidence Act 1984, frequently referred to as PACE. Some of these powers include the following.

Powers to stop and search

Police have the right to stop and search people and vehicles in public places such as streets, car parks and even private gardens if an officer has reasonable grounds for believing a person is in possession of stolen goods, weapons or tools that could be used in burglaries or thefts. The number of stop and searches rose from around 100,000 in 1986 to 850,000 in 1999–2000, rising to over a million in 1998. Despite a code of **practice** that states that a person's hairstyle or skin colour should not be the main motivation for a stop and search, some evidence suggests that young black males are far more likely to be stopped than other social groups. Police also have the right to stop and search a person if they believe s/he is in possession of illegal drugs or is suspected of terrorist involvement. Before 1999, only 10% of people stopped and searched by the police were actually arrested.

Powers to search premises

The police can enter and search premises without the owner's permission if they have been issued with a **warrant** by a local magistrate who is satisfied that a serious arrestable offence has been committed and that evidence relating to the offence is likely to be found on the premises. The police also have the right to enter premises if there is a need for them to deal with or prevent a breach of the peace.

Powers of arrest

The police have the power to arrest someone if they believe they have committed or are about to commit an arrestable offence which may include any act that carries a sentence fixed by law, e.g. murder, burglary or driving a car without the permission of the owner. Ordinary people also have the power to lawfully exercise a citizen's arrest in many circumstances. When a person is arrested, the arresting officer must tell him or her that s/he is being arrested and why. There is no set formula of words although police dramas on television often give the impression there is.

Powers of detention

Once arrested, a person can be held in police custody for a maximum of 24 hours before being either released or charged. For serious offences, a person may be held up to 96 hours but only with the permission of the magistrates court.

Rights of suspects

All police interviews with the arrested person must be tape-recorded and in most cases, the arrested person has the right to have a solicitor present. Information cannot be extracted from the arrested person by means of intimidation, which is legally defined as including torture, inhu-

man or degrading treatment, or the threat of or use of violence. Other rights include:

- having someone informed that the arrest has taken place
- the right to legal advice – an arrested person may use their own solicitor or a duty solicitor provided free of charge
- if the arrested person is under 17, mentally ill or handicapped, they have a right to have an appropriate adult present at the interview.

Until 1994, the suspect had a right to silence. This meant that the arrested person could refuse to answer questions without having any negative inferences drawn as to his guilt if the case came to court. Since 1994, a defendant can still keep quiet but the trial judge has the right to suggest that this silence may be seen as evidence against them. The judge, however, can only do this if the defendant is over the age of 14.

Once arrested and at the police station, the custody officer may search, finger print and collect 'non-intimate' samples from the suspect such as body hair or saliva. Only senior officers can authorise an intimate body search.

Rights of redress

If the police are believed to have abused their authority, a complaint may be made to the police authority. If the complaint is serious, it may be referred to the Police Complaints Authority. If the police have committed a criminal offence in the execution of their duty, e.g. assault, criminal proceedings may be taken against them. If civil rights have been ignored or breached, e.g. false arrest or malicious prosecution, then civil proceedings may be brought against them.

Debates about justice and law enforcement

Fairness in the law

It is important that the law is fair, that it works and is administered equally and justly. Many groups and some individuals feel that the law and the application of police powers in some instances do not conform with the principles of justice or of civil and human rights. Britain does not escape the criticism of **Amnesty International** in its annual reporting of human rights abuses. Deaths in police custody, ill treatment of prisoners and police handling of racist killings receive attention that challenges automatic belief that no human rights abuses occur in Britain.

The experience of racism

My son was murdered nearly four years ago; his killers are still walking the streets. When my son was murdered the police saw my son as a criminal belonging to a gang. My son was stereotyped by the police, he was black then he must be a criminal and they set about investigating him and us. The investigation lasted two weeks: that allowed vital evidence to be lost. My son's crime is that he was walking down the road looking for a bus that would take him home. Our crime is living in a country where the justice system supports racist murders against innocent people.

The value that this white racist country puts on black lives is evident as seen since the killing of my son. In my opinion, what had happened in the Crown Court last year was staged. It was decided long before we entered the courtroom what would happen, but the judge would not allow the evidence to be presented to the jury. In my opinion, what had happened was the way of the judicial system making a clear statement saying to the black community that their lives are worth nothing and the justice system will support anyone, any white person, who wishes to commit any crime or even murder against a black person, you will be protected, you will be supported by the British system.

...There needs to be changes for the future; the establishment needs to have in place a system that will allow all crimes to be treated in the same way and not to be investigated, or to be investigated in the same way regardless of who the victim, of who the perpetrators might be, not to have one rule for the white and another for the black people who just happened to be in the investigation into the murder of Stephen to that of a white boy who was killed in Kings Cross.

Mrs Lawrence's deposition to the MacPherson Inquiry (her deposition to the Inquest took place in 1997; the MacPherson Inquiry was published in 1999).

Stephen Lawrence

In April 1993, Stephen Lawrence, a black A level student, and his friend Dwayne Brooks were attacked in south east London by a gang of white youths. Their attack was thought to be racially motivated. Five men were arrested in May. Proceedings against two of them were dropped after the Crown Prosecution Service had discussed the case with the senior investigating officer and concluded there was insufficient evidence to proceed. In 1994, the CPS again decided not to prosecute on the basis of insufficient evidence. Stephen's parents Neville and Doreen Lawrence then decided to institute a private prosecution but the case was dropped at the committal stage. Exactly three years after the murder, three of the five men eventually stood trial for murder at the Old Bailey but the jury was ordered to find the defendants not guilty after the judge decided Dwayne Brooks' evidence was unreliable.

A legal rule known as double jeopardy, which dates from Roman times and has been part of English law for 800 years, means that those accused of Stephen Lawrence's murder cannot be tried for the same crime twice. Fresh witness statements made after the trial allowed detectives investigating the murder to cast fresh doubt on the alibis of the prime suspects. In February 1997, the Coroner's Inquest into Stephen's death resumed after being adjourned in 1993 and several times in 1994. It ended with the Coroner explaining to the jury that there was no doubt that Stephen Lawrence was murdered but they also had a duty to explain the circumstances of his death. After 30 minutes deliberation, the jury confirmed Lawrence had been unlawfully killed adding that he had died 'in a completely unprovoked racist attack by five white youths'. This was a direct reference to the young men arrested and then acquitted in the Old Bailey but still widely believed to be guilty.

Immediately following this verdict the *Daily Mail* published the names and photographs of the young men on its front page with a banner headline 'Murderers' and a challenge to the young men to sue the paper for libel if they felt the accusation was false. A civil action requires a judgement as to the truth or otherwise of a claim to be based on a balance of probabilities. No civil action resulted.

Institutional racism

In 1999, Sir William MacPherson headed a public inquiry into the Stephen Lawrence case. He noted that the police investigation had been fundamentally flawed 'by a combination of professional incompetence, institutional racism and a failure of leadership by senior officers'. The lengthy and detailed report led to a general acceptance of the need for human rights legislation, changes in the law (notably the passing of the Race Relations Amendment Act 2000), and a reform of police procedures and training. The Act makes it unlawful for any police officer to discriminate on racial grounds when executing police functions such as carrying out stop and searches, arresting and detaining suspects, assisting victims and controlling demonstrations. Chief Constables are now liable for all acts of discrimination perpetrated by any officer under their command unless they can show that they have taken all reasonable steps to prevent the discrimination. Individual officers who discriminate will also be liable. The Act also places a new positive duty on public authorities, including the police, to tackle institutional racism.

On racism, the MacPherson Report had concluded:

At its most stark, the case against the police was that racism infected the MPS [Metropolitan Police Service] and that the catalogue of errors could only be accounted for by something more than incompetence. If corruption and collusion did not play its part then, say the critics, the case must have been thrown or at least slowed down because officers approached the murder of a black man less energetically than if the victim had been white and the murderers black.

We have examined with anxiety and care all the evidence and have heeded all the arguments both ways. We do believe that institutional racism is apparent in those areas described. But we do not accept that it was universally the cause of the failure of this investigation, any more than we accept that a finding of institutional racism within the police service means that all officers are racist. We all agree that institutional racism affects the MPS, and police services elsewhere. Furthermore, our conclusions as to police services should not lead to complacency in other institutions and organisations. Collective failure is apparent in many of them, including the criminal justice system. It is incumbent upon every institution to examine their policies and the outcome of their policies and practices to guard against disadvantaging any section of our communities.

The testimony of Mrs Lawrence at the 1997 inquest into her son's murder illustrates the personal consequences of racism, itself an abuse of human rights, and a criminal justice system that is far from colour-blind. The efforts of the family in seeking truth and justice shows the lengths some people need to go in order to secure the most basic of rights.

Hate crimes

Racist hate crimes are crimes committed not only against the individual but against the community to which that individual belongs. They may be seen as being perpetrated on behalf of another community. No one wants to see the police prevented from stopping crime or capturing criminals, but policing methods must not make worse sensitive situations where the trust of often poor or black communities in the police and criminal justice system is already extremely fragile. Home Office research shows that a much higher proportion of black defendants choose a jury trial than whites. Blacks believe they have a better chance of acquittal in a Crown Court rather than in front of magistrates who are perceived to be on the side of the police. Magistrates send a higher proportion of black defendants to prison than they do whites.

Professor Bridges of Warwick University has written that stop and search is relatively ineffective in combating robbery and street crime with which black people are most commonly associated. There are serious implications for civil and human rights if stop and search is used indiscriminately, but many people are willing to limit civil liberties to prevent the rise of crime and ensure law and order is maintained. In 2002, some people from black and ethnic minority groups have argued that stop and search is an important police power that, if used wisely, can reduce the growth of a gun and associated drug culture developing within some inner city minority communities.

1) What are the main powers of the police?
2) Why did the MacPherson Report say the Metropolitan Police were institutionally racist?
3) What is meant by institutional racism?
4) What is meant by hate crimes?

6 Law and order in communities

This section explores law and order in communities and looks at:

■ neighbourhood watch
■ the problem of youth crime
■ legal services and citizen action.

Neighbourhood watch

The problems of domestic burglary, anti-social behaviour, vandalism and other forms of crime and disorder have been subject to a number of initiatives that have attempted to engage people in crime prevention activities. In the 1980s, neighbourhood watch schemes were established in many locations. These schemes invite individual members of a local community to become active citizens and help prevent crime in their neighbourhood. They can do this by looking out for signs of suspicious or criminal behaviour and informing the police if any is observed. Most of these schemes exist in middle class areas where crime is perceived as coming from outside and where there exists a high degree of trust in the police. In poor often racially mixed inner city areas with relatively high levels of social housing and where crime rates are higher, neighbourhood watch schemes are less popular. In these areas, the perpetrators of crime and disorder frequently live in the locality themselves and crime victims may consequently have little trust in their neighbours, fearing intimidation if they go to the police. They may also feel the police would do little if they were called.

Neighbourhood wardens

In some of the poorer areas, neighbourhood wardens are now being employed by the local council or housing association to patrol an estate, consult with residents, gather information about crime and disorderly conduct, and to generally improve the quality of life on the estates. These wardens only have the powers of ordinary citizens and evidence of criminal behaviour or anti-social behaviour is reported to the local authority, Housing Association, or the local police. The neighbourhood warden scheme is a key element in the Labour government's National Strategy for Neighbourhood Renewal. In 2000, 85 schemes were established employing 450 wardens. Sheffield City Council now employs city ambassadors to offer both protection and advice/support to the people in the city centre. The ambassadors have fewer powers than police, are dressed in purple and offer a symbol of authority much like the presence of a police officer on the beat.

Observing and reporting

Two wardens were on patrol in the Caldmore Green area of Walsall when they stopped a young man from entering an unoccupied building because they thought it was dangerous. The young man became aggressive, pushed one of the wardens into the road and threatened to bite off the nose of one

of the wardens. The wardens walked away from the situation after again telling the man that he could injure himself in the building. One of the wardens pressed her phone's panic button to alert the control room. The police arrived shortly afterwards and arrested the man, who turned out to be a local drug dealer. Thanks to their calm handling of the situation, neither of the wardens was hurt.

Neighbourhood and street wardens annual review, 2000–01, www.neighbourhood.gov.uk

The problem of youth crime

The problem of youth crime has long been a central issue for both Conservative and Labour governments. In 1998, the Labour government's Crime and Disorder Act proposed a comprehensive reform of community and youth justice. Juvenile offenders were now to be dealt with by a number of agencies working together in a multi-agency partnership. These included:

- community safety teams
- youth offending teams
- drug action teams
- crime reduction partnerships
- the probation service
- the police force.

The Act and consequent legislation introduced a range of court orders that would seek to prevent crime and punish offenders. Many of these new orders are applicable to both young and older people and include the following.

Anti-social behaviour orders (ASBOs)

The police or local authority can obtain an ASBO from a magistrates court when a person's (over the age of ten) behaviour has caused 'harassment, alarm or distress' and it is necessary to protect others from further anti-social behaviour by that person. An ASBO lasts for at least two years and any breach is a criminal offence, which can attract penalties of up to five years imprisonment.

Child curfew schemes

These apply to unsupervised children under ten, prohibiting them from specified public places between 9 p.m. and 6 a.m. The police can remove children breaching a curfew from the street and take them home or to a safe place. Applying to establish a local child curfew scheme is optional for local authorities.

Detention and training orders

These are applied to persistent offenders aged 12–18 and comprise of a mixture of 50% detention in secure accommodation, such as a young offenders institution, and 50% in supervised community supervision. The minimum sentence is four months and the maximum is two years.

In addition to the above, the Powers of the Criminal Courts (Sentencing) Act 2000 sets out five community orders which can be used in sentencing offenders over 16 years of age.

1 Community rehabilitation orders place offenders under the supervision of a probation officer for a period of between six months and three years.
2 Community punishment orders requiring the offender to work for between 40–240 hours on a project organised by the probation service, e.g. painting a school building or working on an environmental conservation project.
3 Curfew orders whereby an offender is required to remain at a fixed address for between two and 12 hours. This may be enforced by electronic tagging.
4 Drug treatment and testing orders apply only to those offenders who agree to drug treatment.
5 Exclusion orders aim to keep offenders away from specific areas, e.g. shoplifters from shopping centres.

British prisons are full to capacity with over 71,000 people currently in jail. Many argue the need for more creative and effective ways of dealing with offenders, particularly those committing minor offences or engaging in anti-social behaviour. The purpose of the criminal justice system focuses on punishing offenders but there is also a need to rehabilitate them so they later become sound members of society and do not re-offend. The criminal justice system may even be said to have a welfare role because a number of offenders are mentally ill or addicted to hard drugs and therefore need looking after as well as or instead of punished. There is a growing moral problem as some people are seen as having 'dangerous and severe personality disorders' which make them prone to re-offending. Although psychiatrists say these individuals are not medically ill, the government has suggested that some of these individuals should be detained in secure (psychiatric) units in case they commit an offence in the future. It is issues like this that pull together concerns about community safety, crime prevention, civil liberty and human rights.

Legal services and citizen action

Using the law can be costly, frightening and time consuming, but many people do so to uphold their rights or to fight against something they believe to be wrong, or for something they believe to be right. Those who do frequently remark on the learning experience it produces. Before embarking on any legal action some basic knowledge is necessary, e.g. the difference between civil and criminal law, or a county court and a high court, and the nature of a criminal prosecution or a judicial review. It is also important to consider whether recourse to law is going to be worthwhile and whether the time or the money exists to follow the action through. It is always a good idea to seek advice maybe from a friend who knows something of the law, or from a local community law centre, the Citizens Advice Bureau or the Legal Services Commission before any action is undertaken.

Community Legal Service

The Community Legal Service (CLS), which from 1 April 2000 replaced the old civil scheme of legal aid, brings together networks of funders (e.g. local authorities) and suppliers into partnerships to provide the widest possible access to information and advice. Everyone who provides help or advice within the CLS has to be approved by the Legal Services Commission (LSC). Charges vary and some services are free. There is a CLS fund which may help with some costs and some people may receive support from the fund if the problem is related to:

■ divorce
■ housing matters (e.g. rent or eviction)
■ welfare benefits
■ credit, debt
■ immigration
■ nationality or asylum
■ discrimination at work.

The CLS funds a range of civil legal services including initial advice and assistance with a legal problem, help in court in the form of a solicitor or advisor, approved family help or mediation, and legal representation in court. Funding is available for cases in the county court, high court and appeal court, but not for tribunal hearings. Financial assistance is dependent on the level of a person's disposable income and capital, the type of case (priority being given to child protection cases and those that involve loss of life or liberty), and whether or not a case is likely to be successful. People on income support or income based jobseekers allowance automatically qualify for financial assistance.

Citizens Advice Bureau

Gives free general advice on welfare and some legal issues. Many have arrangements with solicitors who may hold legal surgeries. All will have lists of solicitors who offer free legal advice or do legal aid work. There are 1000 in the UK.

Law centres

Law centres have expanded considerably in recent years. They are usually funded by local authorities and offer advice on community issues such as housing, planning, environment, immigration, discrimination and employment.

Accident Legal Advice Service (ALAS)

This is a scheme run by the Law Society in which solicitors offer free legal advice on whether a person has a case worth taking further.

Criminal Defence Service

This is run by the Legal Services Commission and aims at ensuring individuals involved in criminal investigations or proceedings have access to proper legal advice. Local solicitors operate a rota in which a 24-hour legal service is provided for virtually every police station. The service is free.

www.justask.org.uk

A Community Legal Service website designed to help people get legal advice.

ACTIVITY

In small groups, discuss the criteria you would use to identify the justification of spending taxpayer's money on legal aid.

1) Would you give it to all cases as a matter of universal principal or to specific worthy cases where a case seems genuine?
2) Would you restrict or limit legal aid to those on a certain income, e.g. no legal aid to those in the highest income brackets?

The Commission for Racial Equality

Pressure groups frequently use the law and not only on high profile cases involving expensive barristers and expert witnesses of various descriptions. The Commission for Racial Equality, a publicly funded non-government body, works in both the public and private sectors to encourage fair treatment and promote equal opportunities for everyone, regardless of their race, colour, nationality, or ethnic origin. It has statutory powers under the Race Relations Act 1976 to:

- advise or assist people with complaints about racial discrimination, harassment or abuse
- conduct formal investigations of companies and organisations where there is evidence of possible discrimination. If the investigation does find discrimination, the CRE can oblige the organisation to change the way it operates
- take legal action against racially discriminatory advertisements and against organisations that attempt to pressurise or instruct others to discriminate, such as employers instructing employment agencies not to send them applicants from ethnic minorities, or companies instructing their workers to discriminate in the way they provide goods or services.

Local environmental groups and ordinary people frequently use the law to stop polluters, further a campaign, or influence planning decisions on road building, the location of waste incinerators, the building on green field sites and many other issues. In this respect, local environmentalists or other campaigners are seeking to recruit the judge or magistrate to their side. One book giving advice to campaigners states:

It is the judge who will or will not stop the bulldozers, and no amount of smart law work will count unless the judge is persuaded that not only does the law support your campaign, but that it is also worth their time and reputation intervening. The efficacy of both judicial review and criminal prosecutions relies on the gravity with which the judge or magistrate views the case. It is not enough simply to win the legal argument. You must impress on them that the case matters.

Gilligan E & Watson, A (2000) *How to Win: A Guide to Successful Campaigning,* **London, Friends of the Earth, p90**

A judicial review provides the means by which judicial control of administrative action is exercised. It is concerned with the legality of decisions made by magistrates, government departments or public bodies. As Lord Chief Justice Woolf has stated:

Judicial review is all about the balance between the rights of the individual to be treated fairly and the rights of government at a local and national level to do what it has been elected to do.

1) How might ordinary citizens get involved in community safety initiatives?
2) What are the main elements of the Crime and Disorder Act 1998?
3) What are the main sources of legal advice?

Exam questions

You must answer Question 1 and either Question 2 or 3.

1) Read **Sources A**, **B** and **C**, and answer the questions which follow.

Source A

> **Law Lords dash hopes of human rights appeals**
>
> Dozens of convicted criminals who hoped to sue the Human Rights Act to get their convictions quashed were dealt a severe blow by the House of Lords.
>
> In an appeal by a man convicted of drug offences, the Law Lords decided that the Act did not apply to those convicted before it came into force. This will be a setback for dozens of people pending appeals who were convicted before the Human Rights Act came into force.
>
> **Adapted from** *The Guardian*, **6 July 2001**

Source B

> **Law Lords make ground-breaking ruling**
>
> In a ground-breaking ruling, the Law Lords held that the law which puts the burden of proof on a defendant in a drugs case to prove that he was unaware he was carrying drugs goes against the assumption of 'innocent until proved guilty' guaranteed by the European Convention on Human Rights. For only the second time, the House of Lords used new powers in the Human Rights Act to rewrite an Act of Parliament to make it comply with the Convention.
>
> **Adapted from** *The Guardian*, **6 July 2001**

Source C

> **All teenagers to be forced to do community work**
>
> Ministers are to compel the 3 million pupils in state secondary schools to do voluntary work from next year. Children from the age of 11 will be expected to spend time helping others in

ways such as cleaning out ponds or improving communal playgrounds as part of the citizenship programme that all secondary schools will be required to provide. The government is keen on schemes designed to rebuild a sense of community and citizenship.

> **Adapted from** *The Guardian*, **1 July 2001**

Your answers should refer to the sources as appropriate but you should also include other relevant information.

(a) Explain briefly the relationship between the European Convention on Human Rights and the Human Rights Act 1998. (**Source B**) (4 marks)

(b) Explain **two** of the changes introduced by the Human Rights Act 1998. (**Sources A** and **B**) (10 marks)

(c) Consider how projects such as that described in **Source C** support the government's policy promoting 'active citizenship'. (16 marks)

AQA, 28 May 2002

2) (a) The UK is unusual in having two legal professions. Explain the role of **both** barristers **and** solicitors in representing citizens in criminal courts. (10 marks)

(b) 'Court hearings are not the only means of resolving disputes.' Evaluate the suitability of alternative methods of dispute resolution which are available to the citizen. (20 marks)

AQA, 7 June 2001

3) (a) Briefly explain how the jury system provides opportunities for active citizenship. (10 marks)

(b) 'The law claims to balance the need for the police to have sufficient powers to investigate crime with the need to protect the liberties of the citizen.' Assess how far this balance has been successfully achieved. (20 marks)

AQA, 3 June 2003

The Welfare of the Citizen

In this chapter you will explore issues of welfare including:

- debates about the role of the state in the provision of welfare
- themes of welfare in relation to housing, healthcare and provision for older age
- the role of the private and voluntary sector in the context of community and individual responsibilities for welfare
- citizen's charters, their aims and effectiveness, looking at specific charters relating to citizen rights and action as public service consumers.

The chapter is broken into four sections

Key terms

Citizen's charters (now called **service first agreements**) – statements by an organisation published to indicate the basic standard of service from that organisation to the consumer and what ways are available to the consumer to influence the level and standard of the service

Ideology – a set of ideas that underpin policies of government or state

The state – sections under the government and legal profession responsible for making and carrying out policy and law on behalf of citizens

Taxation – moneys acquired from citizens and businesses for government spending purposes

Welfare – the life-chances of an individual or group, reflecting their economic, health, mental and social status

Welfare state – a state whose primary objective is to promote and protect the economic, health and social status of its citizens often through direct involvement

1 Models of state welfare

This section explores how the state and individual rights and responsibilities towards welfare provision have evolved over time. It looks at:

- the emergence of the **welfare state**
- the **New Right**
- the Third Way
- radical models of welfare.

Most of the last century saw debate between the main political parties about the role the state had in the provision of welfare. By the 1970s and 1980s, the debate revealed a fundamental difference between the main political parties emerging. For about 30 years after World War II a temporary consensus was considered to have dominated government welfare policies. This is usually referred to as the post-war consensus. The post-war consensus involved a broad agreement between both Conservative and Labour governments that the state had a primary role in and responsibility to ensure full employment and adequate provision of health, housing, education, social security/unemployment and pensions for retirement. The term 'welfare state' became dominant indicating the fundamental belief that the state had responsibility for the social welfare of its citizens.

It is important to explore how state and individual rights and responsibilities have evolved over time.

The emergence of the welfare state

Towards the end of the nineteenth century and the earlier part of the twentieth century, the welfare state evolved through an acceptance by the state of responsibility for guaranteeing a basic standard of living for all. Strongly associated with the welfare state's role in delivering this guarantee was the social research of William Beveridge who, over a ten-year period, developed his model for the role of the state which was published as The Beveridge Report in1942. The report was the product of a series of papers presented to an Inter-Departmental Committee on Social Insurance and Allied Service. Beveridge identified five giant evils which were socially divisive and economically costly in British society. These were:

- disease
- idleness
- ignorance

- squalor
- want.

Many argued that sympathies with fascism grew in the 1920s and 1930s in many parts of the industrialised world and emerged because of the extreme poverty, ill health and unemployment of that period. If such divisions and inequalities persisted, then Britain's sliding economic prosperity would continue to suffer. Beveridge's prescription for society to avoid the rise of social, economic and political unrest was to tackle the five giant evils head on.

Following Beveridge's report many policy makers and academics argued that the state had to accept primary responsibility for:

- guaranteeing working people's social insurance
- guaranteeing a basic standard of living
- providing adequate housing for all by demolition and re-building
- providing free healthcare for all
- ensuring full employment
- providing adequate social security payment in the event of unemployment
- expanding and guaranteeing a minimum pension for retirement.
- ensuring free education was provided for all up to the age of 14.

The central role of the state was to ensure individual social and economic welfare and to accept responsibility for it.

The New Right

The New Right's ideological argument in the 1970s that the state should reduce and limit its responsibility for full employment and welfare provision, began to gain support. These arguments did not suddenly emerge in the 1970s but were dominant in the eighteenth and nineteenth centuries. They had since fallen out of favour. The older arguments in favour of a more liberal or restricted role of the state began to re-emphasise contrasts between the main political parties in the 1970s, 1980s and beyond.

Academics and politicians, such as Sir Keith Joseph and Hayek, began to question the effectiveness and the morality of a state that had such close involvement with aspects of employment and welfare, which ultimately influenced individual lives and lifestyles. The term 'neo-liberalism' was used to label and describe this emerging and reforming ideological approach. Such neo-liberal ideology was adopted and adapted to fit a revised policy approach by the Conservative Party and sympathetic academics. As a result, the New Right ideology was established.

Towards and during the 1970s, the role of the state (the post-war consensus) was challenged. The idea that individuals had more responsibility than they were currently accountable for took hold. Terms such as 'nanny state' were and are used to describe the state's intrusion into individual social welfare and responsibility. The 'nanny state' took care of everything – like a nanny who knows best! The Conservative Party became largely associated with the arguments challenging the post-war consensus and Mrs Thatcher's Conservative government became identified with the break-up of the so-called post-war consensus after their election in 1979.

The Third Way

More recently in the 1990s onwards, some politicians and many academics, such as Giddens (1993) and F Field (1995), argued that a blend of state and individual responsibility for social and economic welfare must be forged in order to balance individual and state responsibilities. Consequently, approaches to welfare involve individuals fulfilling strict responsibilities before state intervention is permitted. For example, the government's welfare to work programme allows unemployment benefit (called job-seeker's allowance) only if an individual proves he or she is actively seeking work and training for work.

This state–citizen partnership of responsibilities, obligations and rights is consistent with the Communitarian Third Way approach to welfare. For example, as UK citizens, by right we expect the state to ensure a basic provision of free education up to the age of 19. But, as a result of this right, our obligation is to go to school and, if not, be prosecuted for truancy. We have no right not to go to school unless we have arranged home schooling for which the parents/carers must be registered. Further illustration of the concept of citizen obligation in return for state provision are home-school contracts under which parents/carers can be prosecuted for not making every effort to ensure their children attend school. In this system, the parent's responsibilities are emphasised and expected in return for state education.

The box below identifies differing approaches by Western European countries and other capitalist states to the issue of welfare. The differing approaches to the role of the state reflect differing ideologies.

CASE STUDY: Esping-Andersen's three models of welfare capitalism

Neo-liberal (USA)

Low level of state intervention in welfare provision which is/was largely the responsibility of the individual and local community to insure against. State intervention is mainly restricted to regulation of the market to preserve free and fair trade, e.g. control of monopolies.

Corporatist (France/Germany)

Primary responsibility of the state is to preserve economic stability and regulation of the financial markets with some state responsibilities for welfare according to economic affordability.

Social Democratic (Scandinavia)

State intervention in welfare involves direct provision. Also, direct state intervention in market regulation. The citizen rights of welfare provision and redistribution of wealth are a primary commitment of the government.

Adapted from Esping-Andersen (1990) *The Three Worlds of Welfare,* **Baldock, J (ed)** *Social Policy* **(1999) OUP**

ACTIVITY

Which of the models would be closest to the Third Way? Or would you need a fourth box? Explain your choice.

Radical models of welfare

Although Esping-Andersen's categories of contrasting welfare models is useful, their focus is within capitalist societies. In contrast to these models, the **Marxist** theory suggests that our economic and social order is based upon inequality of ownership. A minority possess control of the majority of the wealth and power in society. As a natural consequence, redistribution in capitalist societies is not possible without a fundamental re-structuring of the capitalist system. To make genuine steps towards equality in welfare we need to promote equality of ownership, which requires changing society from a capitalist to a more communal system.

This is a radical alternative to welfare capitalism. Any attempts to promote fairness and to redistribute resources and wealth will fail as long as the inequality at the heart of capitalist society remains.

Feminists

Radical feminists argue that society is based upon **patriarchy** and that all systems of welfare have not fully considered the issues as relate directly to women. For example, models of welfare payments for income support in the past have assumed the male is the main breadwinner and that females will look after the children. Some radical feminists believe a state which is truly attempting to promote freedom and greater equality through welfare should pay for free childcare and encourage women to work for paid employment rather than to be housekeeper and child carer. Other feminist criticisms of the welfare systems that have operated in the past have stated that women's health issues, for example, are neglected by a system more preoccupied with disease associated with male issues. Again there needs to be a change of culture in our system of welfare from focusing primarily on men to women's priorities.

> **?**
> 1) **Explain how the Third Way draws upon other approaches to welfare.**
> 2) **Explain how the Third Way differs from other approaches to welfare.**
> 3) **How does the feminist perspective on welfare differ from other approaches?**
> 4) **Define and explain the term 'nanny state'.**

2 The citizen, state welfare and society

This section explores the relationship between the citizen or consumer of welfare from state, with specific reference to aspects of welfare. It emphasises the relationship between individual responsibility for welfare and that of the state. It looks at:

- paying for the welfare state and redistribution
- housing
- the welfare state and elderly citizens
- healthcare: the structure of the NHS and healthcare reforms.

Paying for the welfare state and redistribution

Many argue that social, political and economic inequality must be challenged in order to allow maximum numbers of individuals to participate in public affairs. Many individuals have restricted life-chances largely due to, among other things:

- poor educational achievement
- racial, disability and gender prejudice or discrimination
- low incomes
- unemployment.

As a consequence, some citizens have differing opportunities to take a full and active part in society. Being unable to participate in decision-making processes slows down the development of active citizenship in society.

Most government welfare systems whether they be in money or goods/services are **means tested**. This means that you are entitled to claim for benefit or government welfare provision depending on your level of income. For example the state will increase your income if it falls below a certain level (**income support**). The state will pay your rent and council tax if you are below a certain level of income. Also dependent on income the government will pay some or all of your children's fees for nursery if they attend. Prescriptions are free if you are pregnant or fall below a certain income. However some state welfare provision is paid to everyone regardless of income – **universal welfare**. For example child benefit is paid for every child regardless of the level of income of the parent/parents. Also legal aid is paid to everyone regardless of income as long as the case is worthy of consideration by the courts. However if the case is found against you the costs may have to paid back!

Themes of welfare can be explored through a series of questions and case studies. For example, a central question is the relationship between state and individual in welfare. What is the balance of responsibility between the state and the individual for the welfare and social security of citizens? What priorities should governments observe in spending taxpayers' money?

Taxation

In capitalist society's welfare models, the state taxes individuals so that this money can be channelled towards the needs of poorer sections of society. Taxation refers to governments taking a proportion of income from groups to be used in areas it sees as important. It comes in three main areas:

- direct (from people's earnings)
- indirect (from addition to the cost of goods, e.g. value added tax)
- corporate (company profits).

A separate tax called national insurance is taken to pay for pensions and social security including the National Health Service.

As emphasised earlier, government spending on social welfare could be targeted towards the relief of poverty, provision of housing, education spending or insurance for older age. Alternative approaches from the New Right suggest that taxation should be reduced wherever possible with corresponding reductions in state spending as a result. With reduced emphasis on taxation and state spending the idea is that individuals themselves have the choice as to how to spend their money, whether it is on insurance against older age and illness or a new set of golf clubs. From this New Right perspective, morally the state has less authority over spending citizen's money than the individuals themselves.

FLOW CHART OUTLINING THE THEORY OF REDISTRIBUTION

Taxation

↓

Treasury spending

↓

Improved life-chances and living standards for all

↓

Further tax revenue is raised as employment increases

↓

Further spending

↓

Further improvement to living standards

GOVERNMENT EXPENDITURE 2001–02	
Department	**Expenditure (£ billion)**
Social security	109
Health	72
Housing and the environment	18
Defence	24
Education	50
Law and order	23
Transport	10
Total	306

www.parliament.uk

ACTIVITY

If you were the Chancellor of the Exchequer, would the above spending reflect your priorities? Revise the spending according to your own priorities.

Housing

Housing and the state

For those that have accommodation there are a number of housing statuses in Great Britain as is the case in most societies.

- Owner-occupiers, who own outright or are buying their house or flat with a loan (which is known as a mortgage).
- Private tenants, who rent their house or flat from a private landlord.
- Council house tenants, who rent their dwelling from the local council.
- Housing association tenants, who rent from housing associations (shown as 'other' on the table of housing tenure below).

Housing is an area where state intervention affecting citizen's social welfare has been extensive. The state has taken a major role in influencing housing developments for well over 200 years but especially since 1945. However, over the last century, especially since the 1980s, there has been a shifting emphasis from state ownership and tenancy in private property to owner-occupation.

The table below indicates the transition in Great Britain from privately rented and council rented accommodation to owner-occupied housing.

HOUSING TENURE IN GREAT BRITAIN, 1914–96 (%)

Year	Home-owner	Public rented	Private rented	Other (housing associations)
1914	10.0	1.0	80.0	9.0
1938	25.0	10.0	56.0	9.0
1951	29.0	18.0	45.0	8.0
1961	43.0	27.0	25.0	6.0
1971	50.5	30.6	18.8*	–
1981	57.1	30.6	10.1	2.1
1991	66.0	21.3	9.6	3.2
1996	66.9	18.7	9.8	4.6

* Includes other

The noticeable increase in public renting tenants up to 1981 illustrates the increased role of the state in taking responsibility for housing citizens. The thinking is and was that if the state owns the house and individuals rent, then the state can subsidise rents. It can allow those with lower incomes to afford to live in a house or flat dwelling without having the major expense of borrowing money to buy a house. The shift in government thinking by the mid 1970s and 1980s (the end of the post-war consensus) led to a shift in resources spent by government from council housing to private owner-occupation, e.g. 'the right to buy' legislation (1980).

The idea that individuals themselves will be able to decide the kind of home they need and how to maintain the property was central to the shift in social policy to encourage owner-occupation. Such thinking, which dominated in the 1980s, is a classic illustration of the changing views about the role of the state and its relationship to the individual. The result has been a dramatic drop in the number of houses and flats owned by local authorities as individuals buy them from the local authority.

According to Baldock (1999) and many other commentators there are two main problems emerging from the council house sales and shift to owner-occupancy.

1 *The most attractive council owned property is inevitably sold first and often as a consequence the less attractive property is left in council hands, which costs more to upkeep and proves less attractive to council tenants.*

2 *A growing gulf has developed between those households who are owner-occupying and households in council*

houses. From 1963–93 the proportion of households in council owned housing in England with no earners (unemployed or pensioners) increased from 7% to 63%, whereas the same category of households as owner-occupiers rose but far less steeply from 19% to 28%.

Baldock, *Social Policy,* **p416**

ACTIVITY

1) What do you think will be the impact on individuals with low incomes and little chance of securing a mortgage now that local authorities have greatly reduced numbers of housing units?
2) What would you consider the most suitable use of the money received by local authorities from council house sales?

Housing stock in England

- The total number of dwellings in England is 20.9 million. Of these, 68% are owner-occupied, 11.1% rented from the private sector, 15.9% rented from local authorities, and 5% rented from registered social landlords, e.g. taking DSS claimants.
- Over 842,840 individuals are in housing registered on council house lists in the England region.
- There are 1.4 million unfit dwellings in the England region. 173,490 are local authority owned, 11,610 are registered social landlord owned, and 1.2 million are privately owned.

Adapted from www.shelter.org.uk

CASE STUDY: The right to buy

It is 20 years this month since Margaret Thatcher's dream of turning Britain into a nation of property owners – and Conservative voters – was enshrined in law. The Housing Act 1980, which gave council tenants the right to buy their homes, was at the time hugely controversial. Today, it hardly merits a second thought.

Flagged as the 'sale of the century', the right to buy was introduced in a £600,000 blaze of publicity, with Thatcher personally visiting some of the proud new home-owners. It forced reluctant councils to sell properties at a price considerably below the open market value. And to add insult to injury, they could only reinvest 25% of the capital they raised on refurbishing remaining housing stock.

Many councils fought it, while some members of the white-collar public sector union Nalgo (now part of Unison) refused to process right-to-buy applications. Sheffield Council took advertisements in its local papers explaining why it did not want to sell. Norwich went all the way to the high court in protest against then Environment Secretary Michael Heseltine, who was implementing the policy. Norwich lost.

It was in October 1980 that the Conservative government introduced its policy, giving 5.5 million council tenants a chance to own their homes. Before then, you could only buy your council home if your local council agreed: many did not.

Gone, for people who chose to buy the homes they rented for years, are the days when they had to abide by rules and regulations about what they could change in their house. Gone are the restrictions on moving to another part of the country, either for a job or in retirement. But what has been left in its place?

Alan Murie, professor at the School of Urban and Regional Studies, Birmingham University, believes right-to-buy has in part been responsible for the increased divide between the haves and have-nots. 'It has been good news for most people who bought, but is a one-dimensional policy,' he says. 'This government is having to deal with the consequences of that.'

Right-to-buy can now be seen to have underpinned a fundamental change in society, breaking down the divide between the 'working class' – for which read council tenants – and those with middle class aspirations, who bought their own homes. Now, having an address on a council estate does not automatically earn a working class tag. In many places, nobody any longer knows who is 'council' and who is not. More often than not, nobody really cares.

'You've got the Social Exclusion Unit talking about urban renewal. One of the contributory factors in that has to be the right to buy, which meant people with the fewest choices are concentrated on these estates. There is a greater concentration than there was before; a greater polarisation of society.'

Although only 90,000 families bought in the first year – fewer than had been expected – the numbers gradually picked up, peaking in 1989 at 216,043. In 1997, only 70,961 homes were sold. But over 20 years, in England alone, a total of 1.4 million homes passed into private ownership.

In July last year, Newcastle Council was selling homes for a nominal 50p in the notoriously difficult North Benwell area, in the hope of attracting young owner-occupiers who would spend money improving the properties.

High hopes, low points

Even in the affluent southeast, where most people who bought their council homes have made a handsome profit, some people have had their fingers burnt.

In Grays town centre, Essex, the local council recently bought back 38 high-rise flats at a total cost of £950,000 after the owners found they could not sell them. Building societies were refusing to give potential new buyers a mortgage. Now the council is letting tenants-turned-owners revert to tenants again.

Lynn Eaton, © *The Guardian Unlimited,* **18 October 2000**

1) How far is the state responsible for provision of housing?
2) Should the government, through local authorities, build more council housing?
3) Alternatively, should the government encourage private housing associations through subsidies?
4) Given the large number of unfit and empty dwellings, how may local authorities improve housing stock without new build?
5) Describe the differences between the following housing statuses:
   - owner-occupier
   - private tenant
   - council tenant
   - housing association tenant
   - homeless.
6) Explain the main purpose of the right to buy government policy. Evaluate its effect.

The welfare state and elderly citizens

Healthcare and the elderly

In an ageing population such as that of Britain, there is a growing demand for healthcare services from older people. The danger is that we see the elderly as 'dependant' and a 'drain' on resources, especially the health service. Whilst it is true that the elderly are more likely to need healthcare than younger people as a whole, there is no reason to suggest that the elderly are less productive in society. In our society we tend to consider the worth of an individual according to their economic productivity. However, the older generations can be equally as productive in modern society as the young. More individuals that are elderly are working beyond retirement and are more likely to possess greater economic worth in terms of assets than any other generation.

Two major issues emerge with regard to healthcare and the elderly. Firstly, many elderly people are denied healthcare because of their age. Many services are not administered to the elderly because of their age. 63% of women with breast cancer are 65+ but women of this age group are excluded from automatic screening (which is encouraged among younger women). Early detection is the most effective challenge to breast cancer. Older people have less chance of organ rejection and a better survival rate than young people, yet two thirds of kidney patients aged 70–9 are rejected for dialysis programmes or transplants.

Secondly, the evidence above leads Henshaw and Howells (1999) to argue that healthcare is denied to older people not because of clinical decisions but because of a cultural perception of older people, which assumes older people are seen as ill, retarded, useless, decayed, soppy and slow. Only now, as the older population begin to outnumber the younger and so achieve more political, social and economic influence, are we recognising the issues of prejudice and discrimination the elderly face in the healthcare services and in society as a whole.

The chart below shows the spending on different age groups by the NHS.

NHS SPENDING ON DIFFERENT AGE GROUPS			
Age	**£ millions**	**Age**	**£ millions**
0–4	1147	65–74	3277
5–15	1365	75–84	3600
16–44	4757	85+	2063
45–64	3942		

NHS Handbook, **1998**

ACTIVITY

1) Work out the percentage spending on 45–64 year olds and compare this to the spending on the 65–85 age group.
2) There is no doubt the elderly do receive a large section of the spending on health. It is clear, if we are lucky, that we will all be part of the 'elderly' age group one day. Comment on this in relation to the justification for healthcare spending by age group.

Retirement, pensions and the elderly

Another area where the state supports elderly citizens is the state pension. Started in the first decade of the twentieth century, the government guaranteed a basic state pension for all elderly retired individuals.

The state pension is paid to every retired individual (now 65 for men and 60 for women) and is drawn from payments wage earners make to national insurance throughout their working life. The idea is that the government will take a proportion of your wages and pay this back to all pensioners at retirement age. As the population has grown older, the government have argued there are insufficient funds and taxpayers to fund the basic state pension for all. Reforms have been introduced mainly in order to reduce the cost to the taxpayer of the basic state pension.

One such reform in 1997 was to increase the state pension in line with increases in **inflation** and not earnings. It is very likely that earnings will always increase faster than inflation and so the state pension will not rise as fast as other people's earnings increase.

Reforms to the pension scheme have proved controversial. Many argue that the government is attempting to avoid the true extent of their responsibilities towards the elderly and pensioners by indirectly reducing the state pension. This has particular problems for people with private pensions who have retired early (often due to redundancy) and are reliant on a pension, which has not proved as large as planned. Premature departure from work means they may qualify for income support, but the state system for pensions only applies to those above 65 years of age. Recently the government announced it was trying to encourage people to delay retirement until 70 before they start to claim the state pension. The pressure is very high from the government in encouraging, perhaps forcing, individuals to take responsibility for their own financial stability after working age.

CASE STUDY: Basic pension, is it enough?

What is a basic pension?

Not enough to live on, according to virtually everyone. There are millions of pensioners living in poverty. Pensions start at 60 for women and 65 for men. Single pensioners get £67.50 and married couples £107.90 a week. There is a safety net for the very poor: anyone who does not get income from another source like a private pension gets a minimum of £78.45, but this is still not enough by anyone's standard.

If everyone agrees it's too little to live on, why not put pensions up a lot?

The country simply cannot afford it. People are living longer, the working population is shrinking. There are already 11 million pensioners. There is just not enough money being paid into the national coffers to keep on increasing pensions. A lot of people have private pensions, incomes from savings or investments, etc., so paying big pensions to everyone is not the answer.

Labour want to 'target' benefits by giving heating allowances and free television licences. In the long run, the government wants the entire workforce to pay into private pension funds and not rely on the state to keep them in their old age. Eventually, it hopes that only those unable to work, or very poor for other reasons, like long-term unemployment or low-paid jobs, will need top-up state pensions.

So, the welfare state is on its uppers?

Yes, well at least it's heading that way, but this is a very sensitive subject politically. The government temporarily has a lot of money in the coffers because the economy is doing well and people are paying lots of tax. The trouble is putting the pensions up means having to keep paying out forever. The trouble for politicians is that pensioners are becoming the largest group of voters. Make them very cross by appearing mean and losing the next election is a real possibility.

What do the other parties think?

Hague is being attacked from all sides for being opportunistic, fiddling his figures, jumping on bandwagons and generally acting like a politician. Social Security Secretary Alistair Darling argued that his plans would leave the oldest and poorest pensioners worse off. Pensioners on the minimum income guarantee (£78.45) with no second pension would lose the winter fuel payment and free TV licence, but get no benefit from increasing the basic state pension because income support is higher than the basic state pension.

Liberal Democrat Social Security spokesman Steve Webb said: 'No one trusts the Tories on pensions. All but 70p of this money would have gone to pensioners anyway under existing plans.'

Paul Brown and Gideon Spanier, © *The Guardian Unlimited,* **24 May 2000**

ACTIVITY

1) Does the individual have responsibility for insuring a reasonable standard of living in older age or should the state guarantee a basic standard of living for all? Or should there be a mixture of both? Explain your answer.
2) Should the annual increase in state pensions be decided by:
   (a) increases in average earnings, or
   (b) increases in cost of living, i.e. inflation?

See Chapter 7 for further details on the state pension system changes and social exclusion/inclusion of the elderly.

Healthcare: the structure of the NHS and healthcare reforms

The National Health Service (NHS)

The National Health Service is considered the pride of post-war Britain. Politicians are very aware of the importance the public place upon it. However, there have been extensive changes in the structures of the health service since the late 1980s, throughout the 1990s to the present day. Controlling the growing cost of the National Health Service whilst maintaining and improving the service has been a constant dilemma for the current and previous governments.

1) How should we meet the challenges of an ageing population?
2) How do we exploit, if at all, new, expensive medical technologies, e.g. genetic engineering?
3) How does public accountability apply to the health services?
4) How should we direct resources towards (a) prevention, and (b) cure?
5) In what ways does the National Health Service work with the private sector (if at all) to deliver services?

The first table below illustrates the increasing costs of the National Health Service and the increased importance placed on the NHS (in terms of spending) since the middle of the last century. The second table below gives a comparison with EU member states.

TOTAL HEALTHCARE EXPENDITURE IN THE UK (% OF GDP*)	
1960	3.9
1965	4.1
1970	4.5
1975	5.5
1980	5.6
1985	5.9
1990	6.0
1995	6.9

*Gross Domestic Product

TOTAL HEALTHCARE EXPENDITURE BY EUROPEAN COUNTRY (% OF GDP)	
Austria	8.5
Belgium	8.0
Denmark	6.5
Finland	8.2
France	9.9
Germany	9.6
Greece	5.3
Ireland	8.0
Italy	7.7
Netherlands	8.8
Norway	7.3
Portugal	7.7
Spain	7.6
Sweden	7.7
Switzerland	9.7
UK	6.9

Both tables adapted from *Office of Health Economics* (**1997**) **c. Baldock,** *Social Policy*, **pp321–2**

In the year 2000 the Chancellor of the Exchequer Gordon Brown announced 'huge' spending increases (£25 billion) in the NHS in an attempt to bring UK spending in line with the average European country's expenditure of about 8% of GDP. Such a move indicates the central political significance of the NHS. The spending emphasis is in return for targets of reform. The relationship between changing ideological approaches and government spending policy is clear when we consider the following quotation from Tony Blair.

We decided to make an historic commitment to a sustained increase in NHS spending. Over five years it amounts to an increase of a third in real terms. Over time, we aim to bring it up to the EU average. In doing so, we offered the nation and those in the NHS a deal. We would spend the money if, and only if, we also changed the chronic system failures of the NHS. Money had to be accompanied by modernisation, investment, by reform. For the first time in decades we had to stop debating resources and start debating how we used them to best effect.

From Prime Minister Tony Blair's foreword to the government's reforms of the NHS: *The NHS Plan: A Plan for Investment, a Plan for Reform* (**July 2000**)

ACTIVITY

1) Explain the sentence in the quotation above that starts 'For the first time in decades...'
2) Explain the implied message from the cartoon below.

Structure of the NHS

Below is an outline of the mechanisms the National Health Service adopts to ensure consultation and community influence upon NHS services. It must be noted that other social services such as education and social care services link into the health service in a range of welfare areas.

- Health Authority Trust
- Patient Advocate and Liaison Service
- Primary Care Trusts.

At each stage of the bureaucratic structure the public must be consulted and their views taken into account when establishing spending and resource priorities. Patient/community consultation is crucial for decisions on, for example, where to build a new hospital, whether or not a hospital should be closed, and what health resource needs there are in a locality or particular community.

Given that resources are not endless, there will always be a need to decide where resources are to be allocated. Areas not considered a priority over others will lose out.

The cartoon image illustrates how government spending on the NHS is not a mere handout, but strings are often attached

One may believe that illnesses caused by smoking should be treated as a lower priority after the health difficulties caused by illnesses which are not in the control of the victim. The difficulty here is where the cut-off point is made in determining whether resources are allocated. How is the decision made so that the best interests of all citizens and the specific needs of the community are considered?

ACTIVITY

You are the chief executive of a health trust and seek to re-think services according to your own moral value stance. What priority would you give to the following?

- Illness caused by smoking
- Illness through alcohol abuse
- Illness caused by drug abuse
- Illness caused at work
- Illness resulting from birth defects
- Infertility.

Patient Advocate Liaison Service (PALS)

The Patient Advocate Liaison Service (PALS) is a forum for patients and user groups in communities and the health trusts to establish what services and healthcare priorities are needed in their locality. Community organisations are encouraged to take part in the liaison groups and most meetings are open to the public. If, for example, there was a local industrially related illness which was particularly acute in one community, the liaison group should be able to identify this and advise the trust in the medical needs of the community and so determine where resources should be directed. For example, rural areas may have a high instance of back problems associated with land work. In mining communities there may be a high instance of respiratory illnesses. It is such local needs and community priorities that the liaison groups should identify.

Overview of the PALS structure ('new patient advocacy service')

When patients are concerned that the NHS is not delivering for them, they should get their concerns addressed.

By 2002, an NHS-wide Patient Advocacy and Liaison Service will be established in every trust, beginning with every major hospital, with an annual national budget of around £10 million.

Patients need an identifiable person they can turn to if they have a problem or need information while they are using a hospital or other NHS services. Usually situated in the main reception areas of hospitals, the new patient advocate team will act as a welcoming point for patients and carers and a clearly identifiable information point. Patient **advocates** will act as an independent facilitator to handle patient and family concerns, with direct access to the chief executive and the power to negotiate immediate solutions.

Patient advocates will be able to steer patients and families towards the complaints process where necessary. The Patient Advocacy and Liaison Service will take on the role of supporting complainants and will work with other organisations, such as the Citizens Advice Bureau, to ensure additional support for people complaining.

Patients' Forum

A Patients' Forum will be established in every NHS trust and primary care trust to provide direct input from patients into how local NHS services are run. For the first time patients will have direct representation on every NHS trust board – elected by the Patients' Forum. The Patients' Forum will have half of its members drawn from local patients groups and voluntary organisations. The other half of the Forum's members will be randomly drawn from respondents to the trust's annual patient survey. The Forum will be supported by the new Patient Advocate and Liaison Service and will have the right to visit and inspect any aspect of the trust's care at any time.

The reforms will bring patients and citizens into decision-making at every level. A tier of elected government in England other than in Whitehall will be involved in examining the local NHS. It will enhance and encourage the involvement of citizens in re-designing the health service from the patient's point of view.

Adapted from the government white paper *The NHS Plan: A Plan for Investment, a Plan for Reform* **(July 2000)**
www.nhs.uk

ACTIVITY

Evaluate the extent to which you think the new PALS will benefit service users. Note that some areas of health spending are covered by different structures and form trusts in their own right. For example, the areas of mental health services are covered by Care in the Community legislation, which is linked to the social services.

?
1) Identify some of the main government changes to the NHS and their purpose.
2) How can citizens influence the NHS?
3) How has the government sought to promote modernisation of the NHS?

Private healthcare

The cost of private medicine is very high and is therefore only available to people able to afford it. Those unable to afford private healthcare are reliant on the NHS, which has long waiting lists in many areas caused by lack of resources to meet the demands for service from a large population. Consequently, one's level of affluence determines the standard of available healthcare. However, the state could purchase health services from the private sector (paid for through taxation) and make them available to everyone through the NHS. Such arrangements are called public/private partnerships.

?
1) Should those with private healthcare be told they cannot use the NHS? What do you think would happen to NHS services if this were done?
2) Define 'means tested'. (See page 48.)
3) If means testing was used in the health service, should those not using the service be allowed a tax rebate for the money they do not receive in services?
4) Using examples, refer to either housing, pensions, health or work, and explain how the state seeks to promote welfare security.
5) Explain how citizen participation can be promoted through state intervention.

3 The voluntary sector and welfare of citizens

This section explores the role the voluntary sector has in support of and delivery of welfare to citizens and looks at:

- charity based forms of welfare
- volunteering
- examples of community/voluntary organisations
- the informal sector.

The voluntary sector includes organisations and individuals providing care funded through donations to charities and good will from families, friends and communities.

Charity based forms of welfare

Charity based forms of welfare are a crucial aspect of social inclusion and the promotion of participation and active citizenship. Governments are frequently criticised for neglecting their responsibilities and leaving chunks of provision to the charity organisations. However, many argue from the New Right perspective that charity is a more effective source of welfare than the state as it focuses on specialist areas with voluntarily supported financial backing.

The New Right approach

Given the New Right's view that the state should reduce its intervention in social welfare, preferring instead to leave individuals to insure their future and well-being, charity based forms of welfare have a central role.

The communitarian approach

It is the case that other ideological approaches also recognise the crucial role of charities in the provision of welfare. The communitarian view emphasises the role of the state in supporting charity activity and promoting charity activity in terms of time and money/resources. Many aspects of welfare provision are contracted out to charity organisations such as ChildLine, which is run by the Children's Society, and has joint funding from government and charity. Such public/voluntary schemes are promoted by the current government, which is considered to be strongly influenced by communitarian ideas towards welfare.

The voluntary sector includes charities such as:

- Barnardos
- Child Poverty Action Group
- National Society for the Prevention of Cruelty to Children (NSPCC)
- The Autistic Society
- The Terrence Higgins Trust
- Salvation Army
- Shelter.

These charities fund their work through donations and grants. Charities rely heavily on the donations not just of money but of volunteers' time in order to deliver their services. The charities by definition are not for profit but instead ensure all funds are directed into services. The work of charities includes meeting needs where the NHS and social services are unable to provide resources for such services. They also act as **pressure group**s and champions of a particular group in society and their needs. For example, the NSPCC provides services to support families and children and apply pressure through advertising to promote the issue of child abuse among public and government.

Barnardos

As the country's largest children's charity, Barnardos works in communities through 300 services throughout the UK. It employs over 5000 full- and part-time workers, co-ordinating some 427,000 volunteers to fundraise and provide services to more than 47,000 children, young people and their families. Barnardos' work also includes championing the rights of children and campaigning for better childcare in society.

Barnardos has an annual income of about £100 million, 40% from voluntary sources, e.g. Barnardos charity shops, and 45% from the government, i.e. local authorities and social services. 10% of the income comes from other sources such as donations. Barnardos spends 88 pence in every pound on children's services, conferences and publications and 12 pence in every pound on fundraising and administration.

For more information on the work of Barnardos go to www.barnardos.org.uk

Adapted from www.barnados.org.uk

Volunteering

Much community work is voluntary and many organisations rely upon volunteers for their services to run effectively. Oxfam, Scope and others run high-street retail outlets designed to raise funds from donated goods. The people staffing the shops do so largely on a voluntary basis. Volunteering can involve an international dimension, broadening our perception of community. Individuals can volunteer for the Voluntary Services Overseas organisation or for CAFOD (Catholic Agency for Overseas Development), Christian Aid and other church-based charity organisations. Given the wide range of organisations through which individuals can engage in community volunteering, the government, in conjunction with the National Centre for Volunteering, have encouraged initiatives such as Cares Incorporated (www.caresinc.org). This organisation was launched in November 1999 as an employee volunteering initiative and aimed to recruit 100,000 volunteers by 2002.

Along with Cares Incorporated, the government has funded and supported an initiative called Time Bank, which is an electronic database where volunteers state their time commitment and area of special interest. It is then matched to need in their locality. There is also a scheme called Millennium Volunteering, which is a government attempt to encourage young people aged 18–25 to pledge and undertake voluntary action. The initiative has gained much public support from well-known figures in the entertainment business such as some of the cast of the BBC soap opera *EastEnders*. There were national awards presented at the Millennium Dome on 2 March 2000 to encourage more voluntary activity.

> **?**
> 1) Identify some factors that may influence the type of voluntary activity of a citizen.
> 2) Identify factors that influence some to volunteer more than others. Why do some people give more time to voluntary work than others?
> 3) Assess the likely impact of some of the measures introduced to encourage more voluntary participation.

Examples of community/voluntary organisations

Groundforce

This is an organisation set up to connect social disadvantage, environmental **regeneration** and community involvement. The group brings together various organisations to tackle youth and long-term unemployment, general economic depravation, whilst engaging issues of responsible urban environmental regeneration.

ONE20

Jane Tewson describes the charity as one that attempts to encourage individuals of all kinds to bring their skills together voluntarily. The charity follows the philosophy that all individuals, no matter what their circumstances or background, have something to offer. The skills brought together can then be harnessed to tackle social problems of all kinds, e.g. community support groups of Asian women who have

suffered domestic violence. ONE20 functions as an advisory group who can also publicise a local organisation's work and they serve as a skills resource to support charities.

FARE (Family Action in Rogerfield and Easterhouse)

This organisation has six staff who arrange activities and facilities to support local people and communities where few resources exist, commercial or otherwise. The group fundraise and have been supported by the National Lottery. The group's activities are used by over 300 children and parents each week, including a breakfast club, a café, and education classes for adults. They encourage community action by the local residents themselves who are best placed to determine their own needs.

Adapted from Carpenter, A *et al* (2000), *Community Links 2000: Fifteen Visions of Change for Britain's Inner Cities*

>
> 1) Identify three charity organisations and outline their main area of activity.
> 2) Using examples, describe how charity activity contributes to citizen welfare.
> 3) Describe why the link between volunteering and charities is so important.

The informal sector

The voluntary sector also includes activities of support to dependants from family members and friends, e.g. neighbours and communities. Care for dependants such as children, the elderly and dependant adults with, for example, learning or physical disabilities, often takes place within the family through the efforts of family members. It is important to note that although all family members are involved many argue that the majority of the 'burden' is taken up by women.

Often the state supports the informal sector for care. For example, the recently introduced carers allowance provides financial support for named family carers of dependants. This means the role of the informal sector in care is increasingly recognised as a vital means of welfare for citizens.

Care in the community

The government policies of care in the community was and continues to be designed in order to allow as much care and support for dependants as possible. This care is to be provided in the community and the family instead of hospitals and specifically designed institutions. An assessment is done by social workers and health workers who determine how much support is required and how this is to be provided. If a family member was to be providing the support, that family member will be entitled to financial support. They also get support through services such as home help and respite care where carers are given a break by a paid professional taking over the responsibility for as much as three weeks each year.

Criticisms of care in the community

The approach to care in the community is criticised by many who argue the government are exploiting the system to get cheap healthcare. Also critics argue the government are not providing enough resources to deliver the 'care packages' the clients require. Despite these criticisms, most agree with the main idea behind the Act. Underlying the Care in the Community policy was the belief that care was best provided by and in families and the communities where dependant people lived, rather than in an institution such as a hospital. A hospital is more able to provide emergency and intensive care but not the best place to recover from long-term illness. Nor are hospitals considered the best place to support the long-term needs of individuals with mental health problems and learning difficulties. Such ideas are strongly supported by the New Right and more recent thinking about the welfare state and healthcare from New Labour.

CASE STUDY: Young people as involuntary carers – the forgotten 50,000

Many young people, who themselves are vulnerable to the pressures of adolescence, care for dependant relatives. The young carers do not receive the support many feel is necessary and are a forgotten group of a vital source of welfare for society's dependants. The young people have to live lives as students, as young people and as carers all in one day, involving responsibilities beyond what many consider normal for a young person whose priority should be education. Some of the carers' duties may be helping relatives to eat, cooking, lifting and cleaning, e.g. changing beds. There are often emotional difficulties associated with the care of relatives and young people are not best equipped to deal with these, especially as they have many anxieties of their own.

In response to the growing number of young carers (some estimate 51,000 carers are under 18 and the vast majority aged between 13–16 years old), some voluntary services such as the Children's Society have set up young carers groups to support the needs of young people caring for dependant relatives, which are varied and complex, often requiring co-ordination with the whole family as well as the young person/people involved.

Adapted from *Young People Now*, 26 February to 4 March 2003
www.ypnmagazine.com

The vulnerability of young carers

It is not possible to be precise on figures of young carers because of the private nature of most households. However, some estimates suggest 60% of young carers live in one-parent households and 65% of young carers suffer illness themselves, usually emotional and stress related. Most young carers are unaware of where to go for help and information.

Dependant individuals may be elderly, young children or family members with learning or physical disabilities requiring care beyond that which the individuals themselves can provide. Childcare is excluded because it is care considered to be a normal expectation of family members.

WEB ACTION

Search the Internet for **www.childrenssociety.org.uk** and links to young carers. Find out what you can about available support for young carers.

ACTIVITY

1) Using the above material on young carers, assess the balance in welfare provision between state, charity and informal family support. Do you feel the balance is right with regard to young carers? Bear in mind that the initiative above is charity based but also supported by some government funding.
2) The Children's Society Young Carers Initiative lists lobbying government as part of its activity to support young carers. What would you prioritise as a focus for challenging government to improvements for young carers?

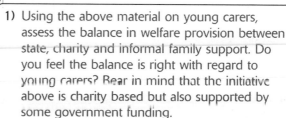

4 Citizen's charters and service first agreements

This section explores citizen's charters and the emergence of the charter concept. It looks at:

- background to citizen's charters
- an example of a charter
- criticisms of the Citizen's Charter
- two case study examples of charters.

Background to citizen's charters

Britain in the 1980s witnessed a period of great social, economic, political and cultural change. Many publicly owned industries declined, such as coal, or were privatised, such as gas and electricity, and later in the 1990s the railways.

A culture of dependency

Unemployment and inequality increased and the National Health Service, education and social security were perceived as placing increasingly unacceptable burdens on the public finances. Many people felt that a culture of dependency had developed whereas what was needed was a culture of individual initiative and enterprise. Instead of continuing to claim unemployment benefit, it was more important for the unemployed to look for work. When in work it was important to work hard and earn money, which should then remain yours to dispose of as you thought right. High taxation deterred hard work and enterprise. Successive governments under Margaret Thatcher and John Major pursued policies that placed increased responsibilities on the individual citizen to actively create their own material successes and through private insurance (against ill health or unemployment) to look after themselves. The Thatcher–Major years saw more social inequality, individualism and consumerism, which consequently undermined the social rights that had characterised the formation of the welfare state.

Active not passive

The intention was to create active citizens who would be self-reliant economically and socially but who would share the same values, loyalties and obligations. In this way, citizens actively involved in their local neighbourhood watch scheme would take some pressure off the police. Those who became involved in their local Parent Teacher Association would share responsibility for their children's education with the teachers. Active citizenship would restore basic moral values to a society that had become lazy and passive. By giving council tenants the right to purchase the homes they rented from the local authority, they would be given a stake in society and responsibility to maintain their own homes rather than wait for the council to effect repairs and moan when nobody turned up or did a bad job.

Not everyone in the 1980s had a job and could afford to become a property owner or contribute to a private health or pension plan. Many coalfield communities were destroyed by the closure of the mines after the miners' strike. Active citizenship, where it existed, seemed to be the preserve of an affluent few who increasingly cared for themselves first and last.

The Citizen's Charter

In trying to address this issue, Prime Minister John Major launched the Citizen's Charter in 1991 which emphasized the right of choice, downplaying the worst excesses of Thatcherite activism and individualism. As one commentator wrote:

The government was keen to ensure that people's duty to pay tax was balanced by a right to good and prompt service, so that citizens should have increased and more accessible information about public services. Citizens should be empowered by government to make choices in an environment of public service that was accountable to the people.

Faulks, K (1998) *Citizenship in Modern Britain*, **Edinburgh University Press, p134**

Rights did not come without responsibilities. The market was introduced into areas where it had previously been excluded. If schools delivered a bad service to pupils and parents, they could ultimately be forced to close. Standards, known as performance **indicators** and often expressed as pupil exam success, were set. Schools would have to publish their results and be graded in league tables. If teachers did a bad job, they could lose their jobs. If they did a good job, they might get a pay rise. If a council offered a poor service or was not considered value for money then that service, e.g. household refuse collection, could be provided by a private contractor. The citizen was now a consumer of public services such as education, health and refuse collection. If the citizen–consumer did not like what s/he got, s/he could go elsewhere or demand improvements. The Citizen's Charter aimed to:

- provide better quality and greater information and access to public services
- create a more efficient public service helped by more information about government spending
- introduce market choice and competition in many areas.

The Local Government Act 2000 has made local authorities duty-bound to provide **best value** to their customers for the services they provide.

Following the introduction of the Citizen's Charter, many other smaller charters were developed and published so that there are now:

- student's charters
- patient's charters
- rail traveller's charters
- tenant's charters
- jobseeker's charters

and a whole host of consumer charters.

An example of a charter

The Charter for Further Education

What this charter promises you

Part 1: Students

If you want to become a full time or part-time student, you have the right to expect:

- reliable and impartial advice about the choices available, given at the right time
- clear and accurate information about: courses, qualifications, facilities and entry requirements
- information on how courses will be taught and assessed, and how your learning will be managed
- college's policies and arrangements for students with learning difficulties or disabilities
- accommodation if you will have to live away from home
- information on how well colleges are doing, including published reports on the quality of what they provide.

You can also expect:

- to have your application for a place handled fairly and efficiently
- to be shown where you would be taught and the facilities available for students
- to be told about the fees and other charges a college makes, and any financial help that is available.

Once you are accepted as a student, you have the right to expect:

- prompt payment of grants and access fund payments if you are eligible
- high quality teaching and effective management of your learning, subject to independent inspection
- regular information on your progress and achievements
- access to reliable and unbiased careers advice and other guidance and counselling.

At all times you have the right to be treated equally regardless of your sex or ethnic background, and to have any learning difficulties or disabilities taken into account.

Adapted from www.dfee.gov.uk

Criticisms of the Citizen's Charter

For many, particularly those on the left, the charter concept was seen as an attack on the social rights guaranteed by the state. The various charters differed and still differ in what they offer the citizen–consumer in terms of redress or compensation if the service fell short. The charters emphasise individual rather than collective or community rights. A whole community and not just pupils and parents are concerned about the success or failure of a school. The whole concept of the citizen as consumer failed to address the reality of social inequality, exclusion, racial discrimination and other limits on people's choices.

These criticisms have not brought an end to citizen's charters but they have forced governments to realise that there is a difference to what is written on a piece of paper and what people actually experience in the real world. A school in a poor working class and perhaps racially mixed area with high rates of unemployment and crime will find itself confronted with problems that do not affect schools in more affluent middle class areas. Schools and colleges differ in what they offer and in what they specialise. The league tables and performance indicators do not tell the whole story. The information they offer the consumer/parent/student/citizen is actually quite limited. This means that although the rights of parent and child to education may be formally the same wherever they live, the way those rights are made real, their substantive realisation, may be very different. Schools in poorer areas tend to get poorer results than affluent ones.

The Charter Mark award

Accountability for service standards and commitments to service users are spelt out in citizen's charters now referred to as service first agreements. The idea became established in 1993 and the concept remains a central aspect of the public sector contract between provider and service user. Charters were statements of service standard by the provider to the consumer or client. The service provider may be the government or a contracted organisation, e.g. Rail Track, or the learning and skills councils. After a provider has set out its charter, they are then eligible to apply for the government Charter Mark award. The award is an indication of standard of service to the client or consumer. Eventually, the Charter Mark spread beyond the public sector to incorporate the private sector.

Given the charter statements, consumers of public services then have a measure to assess service provision and a basis upon which to hold the provider or government to account.

Many argued that charters and charter marks are simply statements of intent of little significance in terms of empowering citizens because there is no legal basis to them. In response to these criticisms, the last government reformed charters and re-named them service first agreements. Two main themes were introduced to make the Charter Mark more credible.

1   The charter commitments must be made after public consultation with the service users. In this way, the charters would reflect the actual wishes of the users. Many argued the problem with the old citizen's charters was that they were a 'top down' – statements defined by the provider *not* the user.

2   The government Charter Mark scheme was to be strengthened so that organisations would be stripped of the award if their service fell outside the service first agreement. Such a move occurred with the British Passport Agency when in 1999 the backlog of passport applications waiting for processing was so high that it broke the service first agreement and the agency was stripped of its award. The passport agency had to improve before the award was re-instated.

1) Get a copy of your school or college charter and ask your head to explain how the students were included in the writing of the charter.
2) How might you use a charter as an active citizen?

Two case study examples of charters

Below is an extract from the Arriva Trains Northern Network Passenger's Charter, February 2002. Every train station ticket office in the country should be able to give you a copy of their passenger's charter.

CASE STUDY: Arriva Trains Northern Network Passenger's Charter

This charter is a statement of our commitment to provide the safe and high quality service you have the right to expect. We publish it so that you know the standards we are determined to achieve. We will monitor how well we are doing by measuring our performance and by carrying out regular surveys of your opinion. We will publish the results and review our standards at least once a year. This charter applies to around 40 million customers every year.

Short-distance services (punctuality)

We aim that at least 91 out of every 100 trains will arrive within five minutes of the time shown in our timetables.

Long-distance services (punctuality)

We aim that at least 91 out of every 100 trains will arrive within ten minutes of the time shown in our timetables.

All services

We aim to run at least 99 out of every 100 trains.

Every four weeks we will publish and display posters at our main stations, showing how well we are performing against these standards. The figures are independently audited.

If we fail to reach our standards on a route that you use regularly, you may be entitled to a discount or extension on your season ticket.

Adapted from www.arrivatrainsnorthern.co.uk

1) How far do the points in the above charter guarantee a standard of service?

2) How (if at all) does the above charter improve the rights of citizens using Arriva Trains Northern?

CASE STUDY: Kirklees Housing Association Tenant's Charter

The Tenant's Consultation and Participation Charter

We rely on a representative structure of dedicated volunteers of about 120 tenant and resident associations to keep us in touch with the views of tenants. Tenants are involved with:

■ participation in decision-making: by sitting on neighbourhood housing committees and housing management committees

■ community initiatives: people living in council housing are encouraged to put their own ideas and plans for change forward and these must be considered by any decision-making body

■ consultation on ideas: by asking tenants to respond directly to proposals and ensuring tenants' views are heard and considered

■ information: being open about all policies and procedures, of the council dates of meetings and developments as affect tenants of the council

■ monitoring: fully include tenants in the monitoring of effective services. For example, the mystery shopping initiative allows tenants to access and assess the effectiveness of any council service and report on the standard of its delivery to the Housing Management Committee.

Extract from *Kirklees Neighbourhood Housing* **(2002), fourth edition (Kirklees Metropolitan Council)**

1) Comment on the title of this charter with reference to the terms 'consultation' and 'participation'. What do they actually mean?

2) Assess the extent to which such measures may encourage participation and consultation in the Kirklees Housing Association.

1) **Explain what citizen charters or service first agreements seek to achieve.**

2) **Explain how taxation and spending can redistribute wealth in society.**

Exam questions

You must answer Question 1 and either Question 2 or 3.

1) Read **Sources A**, **B** and **C**, and answer the questions which follow.

Source A

> **Blunkett hints at an end to unemployment benefit**
>
> David Blunkett, the Secretary of State for Education and Employment, said that the state might no longer pay people who are out of work.
>
> He said that the state should provide equality of opportunity and a fair and decent society.
>
> 'But it is not possible for the state to have responsibility for paying people,' he said.
>
> He argued that the key to creating an efficient welfare state was to make the system more flexible. It had to update its role as a safety net.
>
> He said that the welfare system had to be a means of helping citizens to help themselves. It should provide 'a hand up, not a hand out'.
>
> **Adapted from** *The Independent*, **8 June 2000**

Source B

> **The indifference produced by the welfare state**
>
> The present stage of growth of the welfare state has identified a further group of difficulties. Some people argue that higher wages, social insurance, full employment and the advent of the welfare state have meant that citizens are not as politically active as they once were. This results in loss of influence of private citizens.
>
> **Adapted from** *Social Dimensions of Law and Justice*, **Julius Stone: Stevens**

Source C

> **Categories of welfare benefit**
>
> The benefit system is broadly divided into three types of benefit:
>
> **1** *Contributory benefits* are based principally on the claimant's national insurance contribution, or in some cases, that of his/her spouse.
>
> **2** *Non-contributory benefits* are based broadly on the element of need, and not on national insurance contributions.
>
> **3** *Income related benefits* are based on a means test related to a person's income and savings.
>
> A claimant may well be receiving benefits of all three types at the same time.
>
> Some benefits do not fit into any of these categories.
>
> **Adapted from** *Welfare Benefits Resource Pack*, **Child Poverty Action Group (April 2000)**

Your answers to Question 1 should refer to the source materials as appropriate but you should also include other relevant information.

(a) Explain briefly what is meant by the welfare state providing a 'safety net'. (**Source A**) (4 marks)

(b) Using the sources and your own knowledge, discuss whether the welfare system should provide a 'hand up, not a hand out'. (**Source A**) (10 marks)

(c) Evaluate the extent to which the Citizen's Charter has improved the provision of welfare. (16 marks)

AQA, 7 June 2001

2) (a) Using at least **one** example, explain how the voluntary sector contributes to the welfare of citizens. (10 marks)

(b) Assess the view that 'the Citizen's Charter is both unnecessary and unsuccessful'. (20 marks)

AQA, 28 May 2002

3) (a) Using **at least one** example, briefly explain how the state provides for the welfare of its citizens. (10 marks)

(b) Explain what is meant by the term 'active welfare state' and consider whether there is an active welfare state in Britain today. (20 marks)

AQA, 3 June 2003

CHAPTER

4

Representative Democracy

In this chapter you will explore representative democracy including:

- the functions and levels of government – local, devolved, central and European
- theories and forms of representation – elections, **manifesto**s and the **mandate** elected representatives
- the powers and main responsibilities of parish, district, county/unitary councillors, MPs, MEPs, AMs, MSPs and NIAMs, and their interaction with the media.

The chapter is broken into five sections

Key terms

Authority – when an individual or group have the support from the people who are going to be influenced by the decisions made on their behalf

Direct democracy – where the citizens make decisions that directly shape policy or law (most often through referenda)

Government – the organisation responsible for making and carrying out policy/legal decisions on behalf of citizens

Politics – the process of debate before agreement or making a decision which requires the use of power

Power – when you are able to impose your will on someone else perhaps even against their best interests or consent

1 Politics and power

This section explores the relationship between power and politics and addresses the themes of authority and use of power. It looks at:

- what is politics?
- power in society.

What is politics?

Politics is not simply about people arguing and failing to agree, nor is it the sole preserve of governments. Many people could be forgiven for believing that politics is about middle-aged men (usually white and middle class) shouting at each other across the floor of the House of Commons or arguing on news programmes about irrelevant issues in confusing language. Such activity is a narrow definition of politics. Any behaviour that seeks to impose a point of view and/or to influence decisions is a political act. Politics is about making decisions and the processes influencing those decisions.

Where politics takes place

Politics takes place when differences of opinion are held and one or both parties seek to establish that opinion as the basis for a decision. Politics has a power dimension. It is the ability of individuals, or groups, to achieve aims or further the interests they hold. Power is a major aspect of all human relationships. Politics happens all around us in both subtle and more obvious forms. It can happen in the privacy of the home where power may be exercised unequally on gender or age lines, or in more public arenas such as the local council chamber. All societies have systems for decision-making and so upon this basis all societies have a political component, i.e. a process through which decisions are both made and influenced. However, the systems adopted do vary enormously from one society to another. In Britain, it is local councils and principally the government accountable to Parliament that make up the formal political institutions. On a broader scale, there is the European Union and international bodies such as the World Bank and the United Nations.

Political influence

Voting or lobbying representatives directly, as well as public campaigning, e.g. letters to the press, tend to be conventional ways of influencing the political process. Other forms of activity intended to exert political influence could be forms of **direct action** which may be confrontational, e.g. marches, occupation of trees and organising strikes. There are consequently a number of options available to the citizen when seeking to influence decisions. In choosing action, people need to ask a number of questions such as:

- what is morally or legally sound?
- what approach is most effective or possible?
- how much will it all cost?

Definition of politics

Politics involves any attempt to get your point of view heard and to make it influence another person or group. At the heart of politics is power.

Definition of power

Some amount of power is held by everyone. We all have some influence over others but some have more influence than others. Some people have relatively small amounts of influence (power). As power is at the heart of politics then the more powerful the individual the more political influence s/he has. In order to be more effective, one must seek a more powerful position from which to make a case. This may be by gaining support from others, gaining a recognised position of power (e.g. a seat on the student council if you have one), or by exploiting whatever resources are available to make your case more effective (e.g. by using the media, leaflets, etc.).

Definition of authority

Possessing authority means having the backing of the people whom your decisions influence. You have the justification for exercising power over the people affected by your decisions. Sometimes teachers lose authority. This is because the students or the school organisation have withdrawn their consent to be influenced by that teacher.

Power in society

1) For each of the following categories, list them in order with the ones you consider the most powerful first.

Who is most powerful?
The Pope · Richard Branson · Tony Blair · Steven Spielberg · Robbie Williams · Eminem · Bill Gates · the Queen · Harry Potter · David Beckham · Victoria Beckham · George Bush junior · controller of the national power grid · chairman of United Tobacco

Who is more powerful?
Dusty the bin man · Gill the GP · a parent of a young baby · Bill the police officer · a young baby · Emma, a renowned drug dealer · Justin, a journalist for *The Sun* · George, a journalist for *The Guardian* · Maurice, the popular and prolific novelist · Lawrence the lawyer

Which is the most powerful?
Microsoft Word · McDonalds · television · cinema · radio · money · BT · knowledge

What is most powerful?
Monogamy · alcohol · tobacco (nicotine) · romance · private property · justice · freedom · social class · love · fear · the afterlife · comedy/satire

Which dead people are more powerful?
Diana, Princess of Wales · Elvis · Marilyn Monroe · Gandhi · Jesus · Muhammad · Mother Theresa · a close relative

2) Compare your answers with the other members of your group. Do they differ?
3) As a group, decide on a single order for each category.
   (a) Did you find difficulty agreeing?
   (b) Which individual in your group was most persuasive of their choices?
   (c) Would you change your approach if it were repeated?
   (d) If the activity were repeated with a different group, would you have behaved in any different ways?
4) From the same lists of categories above, which individuals are valued most by society? Think in terms of earnings, direct influence on government, influence in terms of respect from communities and their potential power.
5) Find a measure of your own power in relation to the following:
   ■ a middle class, married, heterosexual, employed male (on average income)
   ■ a gay 16-year-old homeless male
   ■ a female law student addicted to heroin
   ■ a baby girl of two months old
   ■ an asylum seeker from Central Europe.

Dimensions of power and political influence

Power takes many forms and has a major impact upon politics and citizens' influence in society. For example, without knowledge of the effects of global warming, it is difficult to argue an effective case to stop the causes.

■ Knowledge
■ Technology
■ Physical presence
■ Sexual power
■ Social standing (status)
■ Wealth
■ Connections (friends and acquaintances)
■ Communication skills
■ Traditions
■ Where you live
■ Age.

1) Describe briefly how each of the above dimensions of power can affect your capability to influence a decision.
2) Can you think of any more dimensions of power other than those above?
3) Discuss the extent to which your influence may vary according to the following social groupings:
   - age
   - gender
   - ethnic group
   - religion
   - where you live.
   It may help to think about a specific issue or challenge, such as winning the next 'Pop Idol'.

1) Explain what is meant by 'politics'.
2) Describe how variations in levels of power affect political influence.
3) Identify and explain how status and power takes various forms.
4) Define 'government'.

2 Democracy, elections and the mandate

This section explores the concept of democracy, direct and indirect, elections and the mandate. It looks at:

- citizenship and democracy
- elections and the mandate
- turnout in elections
- electoral reform and debate on Jenkins' proposal.

Citizenship and democracy

The meaning of the word 'democracy' is 'rule by the people'. It was first used in the fifth century BC by the Greek historian Herodotus, combining the Greek word *demos*, meaning 'the people', and *kratein*, meaning 'to rule'. The literal interpretation of this word refers to the involvement of the whole population in major decisions of state.

Such a process would rarely be possible in a state that has nearly 60 million citizens. For this reason, in Britain, democracy is by a process where elected representatives are sent to decision-making bodies such as the House of Commons to debate policy on our behalf. This is known as representative democracy. A constitution, written or unwritten, forms the basis for government power and the rights of elected representatives. This means the government can and should be kept in check. Our democracy incorporates a number of essential liberal freedoms of free speech, freedom of association and freedom to stand for public office. Sometimes our system is also referred to as being a **liberal democracy**.

Democracy and technology

Democratic accountability and democratic structures are being fundamentally changed with the development of **information and communication technology**. Community action may have an immediate global dimension when we consider the capabilities of electronic campaigning and information sharing. Already power and influence is being exercised over large corporations by individuals who possess no more than access to a computer with email. Candidates can communicate with vast numbers of people very quickly and cheaply allowing numerous benefits including an effective and efficient fundraising mechanism. Environmental groups campaigning on global issues such as climate change often organise email campaigns to lobby politicians and big corporations.

Despite the huge advances technology brings, some social barriers to effective democracy remain, such as poverty and social exclusion.

1) Define 'democracy'.
2) Define 'representative democracy'.
3) Identify some of the ways democratic activity is changing.

Elections and the mandate

The referendum

Sometimes a local or national government body may feel the need to consult the people on specific issues that it does not feel authorised to or mandated for. For example, the government has decided that a **referendum** (a popular vote in which electors, rather than Parliament, determines the outcome of a given issue) will be held on whether or not to change the electoral system. A referendum was held in 1975 on whether or not Britain should remain a member of the European Economic Community, as it was then called. Referendums have also been held in Wales and Scotland on devolution – whether they should have national parliaments or assemblies of their own. There has also been a referendum on the question of regional government (assembly) in London and 30 other council areas had referendums of directly elected mayors. Such matters are thought of such unique importance that special debates should take place outside the context of a general or local election. Thus, a government does not feel able to act without public authorisation or special **mandate**.

It must be remembered that in the UK, referenda (plural of referendum) have been held but the results have not legally bound the government to act accordingly. The referenda have been consultative not mandatory.

There are a number of other ways in which government may consult with the public. See the sections below on citizen's juries with specific reference to Leeds City council.

The area a person elected represents is a geographical region referred to as a **constituency**. The person elected must represent all the people in that region whether or not they voted for them. In order to ensure voting is fair, voting takes place in secret and no one needs to tell anyone whom they voted for.

Mandates and manifestos

The person who is elected as a representative has a mandate or is mandated to implement their policies written in a manifesto presented to the electorate during the election campaign. The term 'mandate' refers to the endorsement of the policies and the victorious individual candidate made by the electorate. It forms a justification to use power to implement the set of policies laid out in the manifesto. Manifestos are published by political parties and groups standing for election. The theory is that the voters or electorate can read these policy frameworks and make an informed choice. During an election campaign, the candidates of any one **political party** will be asking people to vote for them on the basis of the party manifesto. In practice, only a few hundred thousand copies of the manifestos are sold and people look to the media to summarise the party manifestos. However, the manifestos are published in full on all political party websites. If a party wins an election, it can state it has a mandate to carry out the policies it set out in its manifesto, which was voted on in the election.

Recently, forms of proportional representation have been used to elect some representative bodies, e.g. European Parliament elections, the Scottish and Welsh Assemblies, and the Greater London Assembly.

In Britain, we have traditionally used a system of voting known as 'first past the post' for general elections. The candidate with more votes than his/her nearest rival wins even though his/her votes may constitute a minority of the votes (i.e. less than half) cast. The example below illustrates how a Member of Parliament can be elected by a minority of voters and where the sum of the votes cast for the other parties standing is greater than the votes cast for the elected MP.

Leeds North West [359]

TOTAL ELECTORATE	% TURNOUT	CANDIDATE	PARTY	NUMBER OF VOTES	% OF VOTES CAST
72,945	58.2	Best, H	Lab	17,794	41.9
		Pritchard, A J	Con	12,558	29.6
		Hall-Matthews, D	LibDem	11,431	26.9

Results of general election 2001

By-elections are single constituencies who for a number of reasons have lost their representative councillor, MP, MEP, MSP or AM, e.g. he/she dies, goes bankrupt or resigns. By-elections are often tests of voter feelings between general elections about the government and often the election produces shock results.

NUMBER OF SEATS WON BY EACH PARTY AT THE GENERAL ELECTION 8 JUNE 2001

Labour	412
Conservative	166
Liberal Democrats	52
Ulster Unionists	6
Ulster Democratic Unionist Party	5
Scottish National Party	5
Plaid Cymru	4
Sinn Fein	4
Social Democratic and Labour Party	3
Independent	1
The Speaker	1*

*stands as 'speaker seeking re-election'; is not associated with a political party

www.parliament.uk

Turnout in elections

Turnout in UK general elections since **1945** (%)	
1945	72.7
1950	84.0
1951	82.5
1955	76.7
1959	78.8
1964	77.1
1966	75.8
1970	72.0
1974 (Feb)	78.7
1974 (Oct)	72.8
1979	76.0
1983	72.7
1987	75.3
1992	77.7
1997	71.5
2001	59.4

The lowest turnout ever was in 1918, with 58.9%.

■ It seems likely that more people will fail to vote than will vote for the Labour Party, which has secured a second consecutive landslide victory.
■ Public apathy means that Labour may secure the support of just one in four people eligible to vote.
■ The lowest turnout so far has been recorded in the safe Labour constituency of Liverpool River in 2001, where just 34.1% of the electorate voted – a massive drop of 17.5% on 1997. The highest turnout, 71.8%, has been recorded in the constituency of Brecon and Radnorshire, where the Liberal Democrats held the seat.

Home Secretary Jack Straw said it was possible that the low turnout reflected the 'politics of contentment'. He told the BBC:

What I have been finding on the doorsteps is that an awful lot of people are saying 'Yes I am with you, of course I would turn out if it really mattered, but I think it is already won.' We will find after the election there are loads more people who wanted a Labour victory than actually turned out to vote.

However, Education Secretary (at the time) David Blunkett warned that there might be a growing feeling of disenchantment with representative democracy, particularly among young people. He said: 'If we have won a majority greater than Margaret Thatcher's in 1983 we have got to rejoice and be happy, but then draw breath and decide how to engage with people.'

The BBC polled people who decided not to vote. Some 77% said there was no point in voting because it would not change a thing, while 65% said they did not trust politicians. Just over half said it was obvious that Labour would win anyway. Among the 18–24 age group, just 38% said they planned to vote. The figure for the 25–34 age group was 45%, and for the 35–64 age group, it was 62%.

The five constituencies with lowest turnout in the 2001 general election were:

■ Liverpool Riverside, 51.6%
■ Manchester Central, 51.7%
■ Hackney North, 52%
■ Sheffield Central, 53%
■ Leeds, 54.2%.

Adapted from BBC News 8 June 2001, 'Turnout "at 80-year low"'

Following the low turnout in the 2001 general election, the government asked the Electoral Commission, the body responsible for running and organising elections, to explore ways of increasing turnouts in elections and to re-engage the electorate. Suggestions included:

■ reducing the voting age from 18 to 16
■ allowing an option on the ballot paper 'none of the above': this will allow voters to abstain
■ allowing electronic voting
■ placing polling stations in frequently visited places such as supermarkets.

Some of these ideas were piloted in the June 2001 general election and in the local elections of 2003.

ACTIVITY

1) Evaluate the likely impact of each strategy above on turnout at elections.
2) What do the five lowest turnout constituencies all have in common? Why might the turnouts be lowest in such areas?

WEB ACTION

Changing the ways we can vote
Go to www.electoral-reform.org.uk and using their search facility type in 'pilots on electoral reform'. Here you will find details on the pilots and some of the benefits and problems they experienced.

CASE STUDY: All-postal ballots

In the May 2003 local elections there were 32 all-postal ballots and four of these constituencies also had some form of electronic voting pilot, e.g. text voting and Internet voting. The average voter turnout in the 32 constituencies was 49% – 15% higher than the average of previous local elections without all-postal ballots. Most constituencies' turnouts increased by more than 10%.

Adapted from www.electoral-reform.org.uk

ACTIVITY

1) Why might all-postal ballots enhance citizen participation in voting at elections?
2) Evaluate the impact of all-postal ballots on turnouts in elections. (Note that 49% average is still below half of those eligible to vote actually doing so.)

?

1) Define the following terms:
   ■ mandate
   ■ manifesto
   ■ turnout
   ■ liberal democracy
   ■ referendum
   ■ constituency.
2) Explain some of the reasons for falling turnouts at elections.

Electoral reform and debate on Jenkins' proposal

There are presently a number of proposals to replace first past the post with a more proportional voting system. The Jenkins Report, commissioned by the government, on electoral reform, recommended a system known as 'additional vote plus' (AV+).

Additional vote plus (AV+) explained

The additional vote refers to voters having two votes. One is cast for the candidate they choose who is standing in a constituency, the other is cast for the party a voter prefers. The candidate in a constituency wins by a simple majority of votes cast. The second votes (for the party) are added up and the parties share out the number of list candidates according to the number of votes each party secures (polls). The number of candidates for each regional list varies from election to election. It may be between two and six. The illustration below shows the procedure at work. The AV+ is used for the Welsh Assembly, Scottish Parliament, the Greater London Assembly and the European Parliament elections.

Jenkins' proposal

1 Every voter gets **two** votes under a new system called alternative vote top-up. One vote goes to the constituency candidate, the other goes to a top-up MP. Voters would number candidates in order of preference.

Constituency vote

This vote will help decide who the constituency MP is for Westbury*. Rank the candidates in order of preference (1 for the highest, 2 for the next, then 3 and so on). Rank as many candidates as you wish.

Second vote

This vote will help decide the total number of seats for each party in the county of Purfordshire. You may vote either for one party or, if you wish, for one of the listed candidates. A vote for a listed candidate will also be counted as a vote for that candidate's party.

Example

First vote (constituency MP). Rank the candidates in order of preference, 1 being the highest and so on.

Collins (Conservative)	5
Crosby (Liberal Democrat)	2
Morgan (Labour)	1
Newman (Green Party)	3
Quine (Independent)	4

*fictional constituency

continued

Second vote (county MPs). Either place a cross against the party or a party candidate.

Conservative	Anderson
	Coleman
	Smith
Labour	Baxter
	Franklyn
	Jones
Liberal Democrat	Newton
	Hussain
	Morison
Green Party	Delany
	Franks
	Shab

2 Any candidate getting 50% of the vote would automatically be elected. But where no one reached the halfway mark, the least popular candidate would be eliminated and their supporter's second preference vote would then be taken into account.

Example

Result: Labour	48%
Conservative	45%
Liberal Democrat	7%

The Liberal Democrat would be eliminated and the second preference votes taken into consideration. This means that the Conservative candidate could win although s/he came second in the first preference votes.

3 Between 80–85% of MPs would be constituency MPs. 15–20% would be county MPs – so called top-up MPs – chosen to represent a county or city. The new system allows the proportion of votes cast to be more accurately reflected in MPs in the House of Commons.

Adapted from AQA, *Social Science: Citizenship Teacher's Support Guide* **(1999), p59**

?

1) Why does having a constituency vote and a vote for your party (or candidate of that party) allow for greater representation of votes cast in the House of Commons?
2) Describe how the vote for the constituency MP under Jenkins' proposal is more proportionate than first past the post.
3) If second preference votes are considered in the final analysis, which is often likely to be the case, what might this do to candidates when they campaign? Will they just look to persuade people to vote for them as first choice?
4) You may dislike a candidate on the list of county top-up MPs but still support the party. How does the system allow for your choice between candidates within a party?

- Parties do not get seats in Parliament in proportion to their share of the vote.
- Turnout is dropping as many people realise that as many as two out of every five votes will not help elect an MP.
- Many MPs are elected with the support of less than half the voters.
- There are very large areas where one party is not represented at all, for instance there are no Conservative MPs in Scotland or Wales and no Labour MPs in Surrey, despite the fact that they have many voters there.
- No government since 1935 has had the support of a majority of voters.
- In 1929, 1951 and February 1974, the party with the most votes actually lost the election.

Benefits of AV+

- MPs will have the support of the majority of local electors.
- Nearly every elector will have a real chance to elect an MP from their favourite party for the first time. There will be no 'no-go' areas.
- Elections will no longer be fought just in marginal constituencies. Parties will have to campaign in every part of the country.
- Each party will have a fairer share of MPs based on their real support, not on the electoral arithmetic.
- Every MP will have been chosen by voters, not just parties.
- AV+ will generally produce majority governments when there is clear desire from voters for such an outcome, but will force politicians to work together when voters choose not to give a clear advantage to one party.

Debate on electoral reform

There has been much controversy over the issue of electoral accountability at Westminster.

What is wrong with our existing voting system?

First past the post (FPTP) has a number of disadvantages:

Arguments to keep first past the post

- FPTP usually gives clear decisive results.
- Proportional systems cause weak government because they rarely give a clear majority for one party.
- The FPTP system is simple to understand, but the proportional systems including AV+ are complex and may confuse voters.
- A proportional system may allow extremist parties a foot into the electoral system which may cause extreme right-wing and left-wing groups/candidates to get elected and so cause instability in some communities.

ACTIVITY

1) Do you agree the FPTP system is failing to deliver fair representation?
2) How might a proportional system allow extremist groups/candidates to gain electoral support under AV+ or any proportional system?
3) How does FPTP cause elections to be focused in marginal constituencies?
4) To what extent do you agree with the argument that AV+ is confusing and is therefore a reason for rejecting it?

?

1) Define 'first past the post'.
2) Explain how the FPTP system can be described as 'unfair representation'.
3) Outline the case for and against electoral reform.

The list system in action

The Scottish parliamentary elections 1 May 2003

The Scottish Parliament elects MSPs (Members of the Scottish Parliament) by an additional vote top-up system. 73 MSPs are voted for in the normal way to represent the 73 Scottish constituencies. There is then a second vote to elect 7 MSPs from each of the eight Scottish regions, making 56 'list' MSPs. Voters can vote for the party or for a candidate. It causes arguments for some candidates who are placed low down on the list and so, unless the voters vote for the candidate on the regional list rather than the party, that candidate has less chance of winning.

How are Scottish MSPs elected?

The advent of the Scottish Parliament introduced a new electoral system to Scottish democracy (which was used for the first time on 6 May 1999). There are two methods of electing Members to the Scottish Parliament:

1. 73 constituency members are elected, based on the UK Parliament constituencies, using the first past the post system.
2. A further 56 regional members, seven for each of the eight regions (based on the regions used in the European Parliament elections). These members are elected using the additional members system. This is a form of proportional representation using party lists, which ensures that each party's representation in the Parliament reflects its overall share of the vote.

This means that every Scottish resident is represented by one constituency MSP and seven regional MSPs. This makes the Scottish Parliament different from other parliaments where only one elected member represents the local area (e.g. the UK Parliament).

Adapted from www.scottish.parliament.uk

The total seats won by the Labour and Liberal Democrat parties was 67. The total won by all of the other parties added together is 62. The Labour Party and Liberal Democrat Party have formed a coalition and will be able to pass their legislation as together they have an overall majority. But the Labour Party could not govern without constant threat of the other parties getting together and voting down their proposals. Many argue that this makes for a better democratic process because the Labour and Liberal Democrat parties have to compromise on both sides to form a government where their policies are agreed. This makes for a larger spread of MSPs' views being incorporated into Scottish law. Others argue that this destabilises the clarity of a government's policies, as compromise is necessary.

ACTIVITY

Referring to the data in the table below, illustrate and explain how the regional list system helped the smaller parties win MSPs in the Scottish Parliament.

RESULTS OF THE SCOTTISH PARLIAMENTARY ELECTIONS 1 MAY 2003			
Party	Seats	List	Total
Conservative	3	15	18
Green Party	0	7	7
Labour	46	4	50
Liberal Democrat	13	4	17
SSP	0	6	6
SNP	9	18	27
Other (Independant)	2	2	4
www.scottish.parliament.uk			

CASE STUDY: A spinning mess

Jo Moore resigned as press officer as did her boss Martin Sixsmith (director of communications at the Department of Transport) in May 2002 after it emerged they had been infighting and leaking damaging sometimes untruthful stories about each other to the press. Martin Sixsmith had said to the press that Jo Moore had sent another email saying this time Princess Margaret's funeral was a good day to bury bad news. This proved to have been made up and was intended to further undermine or damage Jo Moore.

The Prime Minister and Alistair Campbell intervened and the Secretary of State was told to sort out the feud as it was damaging the government. Stephen Byers then told the House of Commons that both had resigned from their posts. Jo Moore had, but Martin Sixsmith had not. Stephen Byers was then found out to have misled Parliament. The Prime Minister had had enough and after a catalogue of bad decisions and media stories about Stephen Byers over the last year or so he was sacked.

Misleading Parliament is one of the most serious offences an MP or Prime Minister can make.

ACTIVITY

1) Why do you think the Electoral Commission believes paid political advertising should remain banned?
2) What do you think Jo Moore meant by her email?

MPs on the Internet

Many MPs now have websites for information on their activities and ways through which to contact them. The political parties and local councils also have websites. The Internet is becoming an increasingly powerful tool for politicians, political parties, local and national government, and the active citizen.

The media can educate citizens on the political process and on campaigns. The BBC, Channel 4 and _The Guardian_ newspaper all have websites devoted in part to political literacy and information linked to other sites about political issues. They are increasingly important sources of knowledge and political interaction for citizens.

?

1) Using examples, describe how the Internet can be a tool for government and political parties to communicate with the electorate.
2) Discuss the impact a candidate's image in the media may have on his/her chances of getting elected.

Social characteristics of elected representatives

The social characteristics of elected representatives show a group identity towards male professionals, mainly white, and usually over the age of 50. It is noticeable that elected representatives could be said to reflect a narrow range of identities in society and that representation of many sections of the community is thin.

ACTIVITY

1) With reference to the table below, which groups are over-represented and which are under-represented in relation to their populations in the country as a whole?
2) How far does the profile of local councillors reflect the population as a whole?

After the 2001 general election, 541 MPs were male and 118 were female. To be successful in politics and to get elected in the first place it would appear, apart from being a member of a major political party, you should be middle aged, university educated, white, male, and in a professional occupation.

In 1979, 16.5% of MEPs were women and this figure has risen steadily over successive parliamentary terms, reaching 27.5% on 1 January 1996 and 29.7% after the 1999 elections.

PERSONAL CHARACTERISTICS OF COUNCILLORS, ENGLAND AND WALES 1997–8

Characteristic	% of adult pop	All councillors	Cons	Lab	LibDem	Ind
Male	49	73	74	74	66	78
Female	51	27	26	26	34	22
Ethnic minority	6	3.1	0.9	5.5	1.1	0.5
Under 25	8	*	*	*	*	*
25–34	21	4	3	5	4	*
35–44	19	14	8	18	14	5
45–54	18	28	21	30	33	18
55–64	13	30	33	27	29	35
65–74	14	21	31	17	18	34
75+	7	4	5	3	2	7
Managerial	17	33	53	23	30	48
Professional (tech)	17	28	26	28	32	23
Teacher/lecturer/academic	4	12	4	16	15	4
Admin/clerical/secretarial/sales	22	13	11	14	14	13
Manual/craft	30	14	7	19	9	13

Adapted from Wilson, D and Game, C (2002) *Local Government in the UK,* **Palgrave, pp240–1**

ACTIVITY

1) Look at the 4 images of two of the most successful Prime Ministers since the second world war. How far do their images as males and females differ?

2) What are the necessary characteristics of a Prime Minister that you can identify from the pictures?

Margaret Thatcher after the Conservative Party's general election victory in May 1979. Margaret Thatcher was leader of the Conservatives and became Britain's first female Prime Minister

Margaret Thatcher launching the Conservative Party's European election manifesto in May 1989

Tony Blair after his conference speech in Blackpool to the Labour party, October 1994

Tony Blair in Belfast, Northern Ireland, October 2003

4 Local government

This section explores the various structures and roles of local government in the UK and their relationship to citizenship and communities they serve. It looks at:

- types and patterns of local government
- the Greater London Assembly (GLA)
- local council reform.

There are a number of elected decision-making bodies at local (e.g. Metropolitan Council), national (e.g. House of Parliament), and supranational level (e.g. the European Parliament).

Types and patterns of local government

In England from 1 April 1998, there were:

- 34 county councils
- 47 unitary councils

- 36 metropolitan councils (seven Met authorities in West Midlands; five in Merseyside; ten in Greater Manchester; four in South Yorkshire; five in West Yorkshire; five in Tyne and Wear)
- 33 London boroughs
- 238 district councils.

The Guardian Local Authority Directory (**2000**), **p11**

Town/parish councils

There are about 10,000 town, parish and community councils in England, Scotland and Wales. A significant number of town and parish councils carry out a range of functions (especially the larger ones) and many employ staff.

The Guardian Local Authority Directory (**2000**), **p11**

These bodies are elected once every four years. Parish and town councillors are unpaid. Their job is to represent the views of their constituents in the town or parish on areas such as plans set out by the county and district authorities on house building or public transport.

Town and parish council views must be incorporated into any scheme that influences their localities. Some have revenue raising powers allowing them to increase the overall council tax. This additional revenue raised may be used by the town or parish in any legitimate way it sees fit. However, most town and parish councils represent small areas and do not have revenue raising powers. For example, a town like Otley in West Yorkshire, with a population of around 10,000 people (about 8000 voters). Although it falls within the metropolitan area of Leeds, Otley also has a town council made up of one councillor for every 500–600 voters. The town is separated into **wards** or areas of about the same size with about 1500 voters. Each ward has three councillors. In Otley, five wards equals 15 councillors on the town council.

The councillors sit on the full council committee and the sub-committees of the full council. Town councillors are also invited to sit on outside bodies such as the Citizens Advice Bureau, school governing bodies, etc.

Councillors communicate with the people they represent, explaining council decisions and listening to the concerns of the people they represent, e.g. on proposals for a new leisure centre. Communication between councillors and the population also happens through the local papers and other media.

Single-tier authorities

These are responsible for all local services. Some are called unitary authorities such as Peterborough, Stoke on Trent and Milton Keynes. Others are called metropolitan areas such as Manchester, Stockport, Birmingham, Newcastle upon Tyne and Sheffield, and are in major urban cities. The third type of unitary council is the London boroughs such as Barnet, Harringay, Southwark and Islington. Scotland, Wales and Northern Ireland only have single-tier local governments called unitary councils. There are 47 unitary councils in England, 36 metropolitan councils and 33 London boroughs.

These single-tier bodies are elected once every four years. Three councillors are elected for each section of the authority that includes about 7000–10,000 people (wards). The councillors serve for four years and they will be paid a part-time salary of about £7000.

Two-tier authorities

These are usually in rural areas and have county councils and district councils. The populations are more dispersed and the needs of one area of the county may be very different to an area 30–40 miles away elsewhere in the county. For example, Cambridgeshire County Councils cover north and south Cambridgeshire including a more rural district council, Fenland, Cambridge (a city) district council, East Cambridgeshire district council, and South Cambridgeshire district council. The county council has responsibilities for the major services but district councils have many powers and responsibilities devolved from the county councils to better administrate on a local level. There are 34 county councils in England covering 238 district councils. The councillors are also elected once every four years but on a different year to unitary authority elections. They also get a part-time fee of about £7000.

WEB ACTION

1) Search for your local council website by using a search engine and explore what parts of the council are responsible for education, the police, transport, trains, refuse collection and recycling.
2) What is the political balance of your council?
3) How many independent councillors are there, if any?
4) Using the same website, explore the council structure and how the council is organised. You may find the council has a mayor leading a cabinet or you may find a chief executive as the leading figure on the council.
5) Write or email your local councillor or council asking for an explanation leaflet on how the council structure works and why this system was introduced. You will get a leaflet from the council explaining the structure.

Local government in the UK

THE DIVISION OF RESPONSIBILITY

Functions	Metropolitan areas		Shire areas		London area	Northern Ireland	Scotland	Wales
	Metropolitan district councils	County councils	Unitary councils	District councils	London boroughs, incl. City of London	City, borough and district councils	Unitary councils	Unitary councils
Education	•	•	•		•		•	•
Housing	•			•	•		•	•
Planning (applications) and building control	•		•	•	•	+	•	•
Strategic planning	•	•	•		•		•	•
Transport planning	•	•	•		•		•	•
Highways	•	•	•		•		•	•
Police (indirectly)	•	•	•		•		•	•
Fire	•	•	•		•		•	•
Social Services	•	•	•		•		•	•
Libraries	•	•	•		•		•	•
Leisure and recreation	•		•	•	•	•	•	•
Waste collection	•		•	•	•	•	•	•
Waste disposal	•		•		•	•	•	•
Environmental health	•		•	•	•	•	•	•
Local taxation (collection)	•		•	•	•		•	•
Trading Standards	•	•	•		•		•	•

+ Enforcement of building regulations only

Adapted from *The Guardian Local Authority Directory* (**2000**), p13

Local council communication with constituents and communities

In carrying out the duties listed above, local councils must consult with the citizens in a number of ways set out in the DETR [Department of Environment, Transport and the Regions] guidelines for local authorities, *Local Democracy and Leadership 1997*, including:

- citizen's juries
- focus groups
- visioning conferences
- opinion polling
- citizen panels
- community/area
- interest group and user group forums/committees
- local referenda.

?
1) Identify and describe some of the main differences between town/parish councils and metropolitan/district councils.
2) Explain some of the ways councils consult with their communities/electorates.
3) Define the term 'ward'.
4) Identify and describe some of the roles councillors perform.

The Mayor of London, Ken Livingstone

Payment of councillors

Many argue that the job of a councillor is very complex and so important that it should be paid as if it were a full-time job. Councillors are at present paid a part-time salary. The argument in favour is that if people were to be encouraged to stand for election to council they should not have to take a wage cut in order to do this. If there is a loss in wages, there may be a disproportionate number of wealthy or retired councillors elected because they have more time and money to consider it. Once councillors are elected, they may be appointed by the mayor or council executive to be the leader of a cabinet department such as transport or environment. This job is paid a better wage to reflect the higher rate of responsibility and time commitment.

Arguments against suggest that paying councillors mean there will be professional politicians squeezing out the local candidate who wants to campaign independent of political parties and who is not so well trained in campaigning.

ACTIVITY

Make a list of the points for and against elected councillors being paid, encouraging them to approach the role not voluntarily as a public service but as professional politicians.

The Greater London Assembly (GLA)

As part of the government's local government reform, the decision on London was that it was a commercial and cultural area of Britain. It was unique to any other area needing consideration for transport, housing, social services and environmental policy of its own. Given that the central and Greater London area was deemed to have a specific identity and set of policy priorities, it required a separate government body called the Greater London Assembly (GLA).

The body was first elected in May 2000. Ken Livingstone was the first elected Mayor of London. The assembly has 25 members. Following the May 2000 elections, nine were Conservative, nine were Labour, four were Liberal Democrat, and three Greens.

What does it do and how?

The GLA has strategic responsibility for:

- transport
- policing
- fire and emergency planning
- economic development
- planning
- culture
- the environment
- health.

The London boroughs, of which there are 32, such as Haringey, Lewisham and Tower Hamlets, retain responsibility for mainly:

- education
- housing
- social services
- local roads
- libraries and museums
- refuse collection
- environmental health.

However, the GLA holds power over aspects that cut across all boroughs affecting the whole of London.

The Mayor appoints members of four functional bodies:

1 transport for London
2 Metropolitan Police Authority
3 fire and emergency planning
4 London development agency (responsible for promoting employment, economic development and **regeneration**, which is similar to the eight English regional development agencies).

Rather like the committees on local councils, the GLA also has a committee responsible for overseeing policy and making recommendations to the Mayor.

The GLA is mainly funded by central government, but 11% is funded through Londoners themselves. The total budget in 2001–02 was £3.7 billion.

Adapted from Wilson and Game, *Local Government in the UK*, **p77**

Political parties, candidates and elections, and representation

Issue 1

The government proposed a London mayor and Greater London Assembly in a consultation paper (green paper) called *New Leadership for London* (1997) and then a white paper called *A Mayor and Assembly for London* (1998). The paper proposed a referendum in Greater London on whether it wanted a London mayor directly elected and an elected assembly. The turnout was 34% and 72% voted in favour of a London mayor and assembly.

ACTIVITY

Evaluate the extent to which the referendum on the issue of a London mayor and assembly was a conclusive and clear mandate.

Issue 2

Ken Livingstone is the Mayor of London and is standing again in the local elections of 2003. Ken Livingstone was not elected by his party to be the official candidate. In fact, Frank Dobson, the former Health Secretary, was elected as the Labour Party candidate. The main reason for Livingstone not being selected by his party as the official candidate was that he was considered by the Labour Party leadership as someone who could not be trusted to follow party policy. Despite the narrow decision by the Labour Party to select Frank Dobson as the official candidate, and knowing it would result in his expulsion from the Labour Party, Livingstone decided to stand.

The rules of any political party are that you cannot be a member of that political party and stand against its officially selected candidate. Consequently, Ken Livingstone was expelled from the Labour Party and stood as an independent candidate.

The Conservative Party also had their own candidate problems. The initial Conservative Party candidate was Lord Archer (now Jeffery Archer) who was sacked after media revelations that he had paid prostitutes for sex. He sued for libel against the newspaper making the allegations, but after the trial they were upheld and he was sent to prison. He was replaced by Stephen Norris as the Conservative Party candidate.

ACTIVITY

Given the issues above, discuss the significance of party politics for selection and election of candidates.

Issue 3

The turnout at the election for the mayor and GLA was 33% and Ken Livingstone won after the count of the second preference votes. Elections for the mayor are by proportional representation system (supplementary vote – a second preference), by numbering the preference of candidates from 1 (being the first preference) and 2 (the second). After the first count, the official Labour candidate came third and was eliminated. After the second preferences were counted, Ken Livingstone had 776,000 votes and Stephen Norris 564,000. Ken Livingstone is said to have a huge mandate from the electorate given no other elected member of any UK government has secured so many votes. However, the turnout was low and Stephen Norris also secured a huge number of votes.

MAYOR RESULTS LONDON WIDE

Name	Party	1st pref	%	2nd pref *	%	Final **
Ken Livingstone	Independent	667,877	39.0	178,809	12.6	776,427
Stephen Norris	Conservative	464,434	27.1	188,041	13.2	564,137
Frank Dobson	Labour	223,884	13.1	228,095	16.0	–
Susan Kramer	Liberal Democrat	203,452	11.9	404,815	28.5	–
Ram Gidoomal	Christian Peoples Alliance	42,060	2.4	56,489	4.0	–
Darren Johnson	Green	38,121	2.2	192,764	13.6	–
Michael Newland	British National Party	33,569	2.0	45,337	3.2	–
Damian Hockney	UK Independence Party	16,324	1.0	43,672	3.1	–
Geoffrey Ben-Nathan	Pro-Motorist Small Shop	9956	0.6	23,021	1.6	–
Ashwin Kumar Tanna	Independent	9015	0.5	41,766	2.9	–
Geoffrey Clements	Natural Law Party	5470	0.3	18,185	1.3	–

* 2nd preference votes are only used if no candidate receives more than 50% of 1st preference votes

** If no candidate receives more than 50% of 1st preference votes, the top two receive 2nd preference from remaining candidates

ACTIVITY

In the light of the result for the mayoral election of London, discuss the extent to which it (Ken Livingstone) has secured a clear mandate.

party they belong to) and a second vote for the party of your choice or another named candidate. The second votes are counted and the seats are allocated to the party winning a majority of the votes (FPTP).

Issue 4 Voting System for the Mayor and the GLA

Supplementary vote (SV) for the Mayor of London

The supplementary vote is similar in method and purpose to the alternative vote, the key difference being that, under SV, voters are limited to indicating a first and second preference. Where candidates receive more than a half of first preference votes cast on the first count, they are deemed elected. If not, all but the top two candidates are eliminated and their second preferences redistributed. The candidate with the greatest share of the resultant vote is elected. In the majority of cases, but not necessarily, this will be with more than half of the votes cast.

The AV+ system for the GLA

The additional vote system (AV+) is used to elect members of the European Parliament and the Scottish and Welsh Assemblies, as well as the Greater London Assembly. The system allows two votes: one for the named candidate (alongside the name is also the political

LONDON ASSEMBLY RESULTS MAY 2000

Constituency results

Constituency name	Party elected
Barnet and Camden	Conservative
Bexley and Bromley	Conservative
Brent and Harrow	Labour
City and East	Labour
Croydon and Sutton	Conservative
Ealing and Hillingdon	Conservative
Enfield and Haringey	Labour
Greenwich and Lewisham	Labour
Havering and Redbridge	Conservative
Lambeth and Southwark	Labour
Merton and Wandsworth	Conservative
North East	Labour
South West	Conservative
West Central	Conservative

Top-up votes

Results Greater London Assembly Election May 2000

	Constituencies	Top-ups	Total seats
Labour	6	3	9
Conservative	8	1	9
Liberal Democrat	0	4	4
Green	0	3	3
LSA	0	0	0
UKIP	0	0	0
Other	0	0	0

An example of a local assembly constituency with the result for mayor, the result for the candidates, and the result for the party (additional vote).

Barnet and Camden

Mayor

Name	Party	1st pref	%	2nd pref *	%
Ken Livingstone	Ind	51,649	38.8	13,368	12.0
Stephen Norris	Con	36,826	27.7	14,858	13.4
Susan Kramer	LD	17,096	12.8	33,144	29.8
Frank Dobson	Lab	16,978	12.8	17,125	15.4
Darren Johnson	Grn	3564	2.7	16,621	15.0
Ram Gidoomal	CPA	2336	1.8	3649	3.3
Michael Newland	BNP	1451	1.1	2285	2.1
Geoffrey Ben-Nathan	PMSS	1055	0.8	2865	2.6
Damian Hockney	UKIP	972	0.7	2832	2.6
Ashwin Kumar Tanna	Ind	708	0.5	2938	2.6
Geoffrey Clements	NL	397	0.3	1388	1.2

	Total votes	%
Turnout	133,032	35.0

* 2nd preference votes are counted if no candidate receives more than 50% of 1st preference votes

ASSEMBLY

First past the post

Name	Party	Votes	%
Brian Coleman	Conservative	41,583	32.9
Helen Gordon	Labour	41,032	32.5
Jonathan Davies	Liberal Democrat	22,295	17.6
Miranda Dunn	Green	14,768	11.7
Candy Udwin	London Socialist Alliance	3488	2.8
Magnus Nielsen	UK Independence Party	2115	1.7
Diane Derksen	Maharishi's Natural Prog	1081	0.9

	Total votes	%
Majority	551	0.4
Turnout	136,384	35.0

TOP-UP SEATS (LONDON-WIDE)

Name	Votes	%
Conservative	37,795	29.4
Labour	37,352	29.1
Liberal Democrats	19,376	15.1
Greens	16,789	13.1
Christian Peoples Alliance	3258	2.5
London Socialist Alliance	2421	1.9
British National Party	2217	1.7
UK Independence Party	2037	1.6
Peter Tatchell	1908	1.5
Campaign Against Tube Privatisation	1517	1.2
Pro-Motorist Small Shop	1381	1.1
Socialist Labour Party	1115	0.9
Natural Law Party	677	0.5
Communist Party of Britain	632	0.5

	Total votes	%
Turnout	127,475	35.0

All tables from BBC News website

Issue 5 Power of the central government versus GLA tested

The GLA, led by Ken Livingstone, want the London underground system renewed and updated to be more efficient and safe and so does the government. However, the debate rages about how this should be paid for. The central government argue that a mixture of private and public (government) money should be used to build a better, safer and more effective underground transport system. The GLA argue that the public/private partnership will cause under-funding and shortcuts on safety that may lead to danger on the underground trains. The question is, who has the power to enforce their view? If the central government have their way, they will be undermining the GLA, which it set up to represent the voters of London. If the GLA get their way, the government is seen as weak and simply playing along with whatever the GLA says. If the GLA and Ken Livingstone get their way, the government will face a much higher bill for transport in London than they (and the taxpayers) are willing to accept.

WEB ACTION

Where do you stand on the issue? Research the archive of *The Guardian Unlimited* to explore post newspaper articles on the issue and devise an argument for and against the GLA/Ken Livingstone position of a mainly public money and ticket-price funded transport system with the preferred government alternative of a public/private funded system.

ACTIVITY

Discuss the extent to which the GLA should be able to make decisions without central government intervention.

Local council reform

Local Government Reform Act 2000

Many argue that local government has been under constant reform throughout its life. In 2000 the New Labour government set out its Local Government Reform Act with the main aims of:

- better connections between local government with the electorate
- making the decisions more accountable
- making the system clearer and more efficient
- attempting to integrate greater scrutiny of decisions and decision-making by citizens.

Before the Act, most local government involved a series of committees branching out from a central committee, often called policy and resources. The problem with this system was that it was considered confusing and complex and it was difficult to identify who had made what decision.

Under the Local Government Reform Act 2000, all councils in England and Wales, except shire districts with populations of less than 85,000 people, were required after consultation with their local residents to choose one of three systems. All of the three options were designed to make the decision-making separate to the carrying out of policy execution. Each option was intended to make the system simpler to citizens.

Below is a brief outline of the three main options available to councils to select. Although councils have three options, they must abolish their existing systems and select one of the three.

Option 1: Leader and cabinet executive

A leader elected by the full council (often in effect the largest party) plus between two and nine councillors with specific powers and responsibilities for council policy.

Council elections would happen as normal and then the elected councillors would elect a small number of senior councillors to become the cabinet. One of them would be elected as the leader. The remaining councillors would sit on committees chaired by the elected cabinet. Others would sit on scrutiny committees who would check that the procedures and policy of the council were being followed correctly.

Arguments in favour of Option 1

- Speeds up decisions since the cabinet is a smaller single body making decisions.
- Cabinet members would become locally well known.
- Non-cabinet members would no longer be tied down to a series of committees and would be able to communicate and work better with their constituents on, for example, residence committees.
- The scrutiny of the council is rigorously applied by the scrutiny committee.

Arguments against Option 1

- Alternative systems (e.g. mayor directly elected) would be a quicker system of decision-making.
- The council is still complicated by a large number of committees.
- It is not very different from the existing system.

Option 2: Mayor and cabinet executive

Mayor directly elected by the whole electorate who appoints between two and nine councillors as executive members, much the same as with Option 1.

All voters elect a mayor and all committees are abolished. The mayor selects a cabinet from the elected councillors. The remaining councillors scrutinise the council decisions and actions and are released for constituency work.

Arguments in favour of Option 2

- Simple recognisable system where an individual becomes the focus for council policy and work, giving focus for public interest and elections.
- Decisions are quick and responsibility is clear.

Arguments against Option 2

- Too much power given to one person in choosing his/her cabinet and in decision-making about policy.
- Other elected councillors should have more say in decisions and policy.
- No guarantee it will increase citizen involvement and interest.

Option 3: Mayor and council manager

Mayor directly elected by the whole electorate with an officer provided by the council to action the policy decisions of the council as defined by the mayor.

Mayor elected, as with Option 2, and s/he would appoint a council manager and junior managers to run services.

Arguments in favour of Option 3

- As with Option 2, except it would be even simpler and quicker with only two main people identified and responsible for decisions.
- Councillors are free to work outside committees with their constituents directly.

Arguments against Option 3

- Too much power to only two people, one of whom is not elected and therefore less accountable.
- Limited role for other elected councillors.
- Probably less open system for decision-making since most decisions would be made behind closed doors with no open council meetings for decision-making/ debate.

The scrutiny committees can ask for policy decisions to be re-examined by the executive, whether that be the mayor, mayor and cabinet, or leader and cabinet. The scrutiny committee also has powers to ensure that no decision is made without having followed the correct procedure of being made in consultation with the residents. They also suggest, through reports and recommendations, areas for policy development that the council should consider.

 To what extent do you believe directly elected mayors encourage voting and participation with local government?

The government were very keen on elected mayors when they set out the Act, but the general public seemed less convinced, although some areas did seem to support the idea strongly. The Department for Transport, local government and the regions (as it was called at the time) commissioned a survey which found, among other things, the likelihood of people voting in an election for a mayor rather than an election for a local councillor:

- more likely   31%
- less likely   13%
- no difference   54%.

As for the great majority of the councils, by May 2002 the leader–cabinet system was adopted (Option 1).

Which model to adopt?

The decision as to which model a council should adopt is made by the council themselves. However, they must show evidence that they have consulted their citizens by referendum, questionnaire, public meeting or focus group. If a community wanted a referendum on the issue of a directly elected mayor, they needed to secure a petition from 5% or more of the constituents who fall within the council area. If secured, then a referendum of all citizens would have to be carried out. If a majority were in favour, then the mayoral system would have to be adopted by the council.

By December 2002, 30 councils held referenda, some of which were:

- Lewisham
- Doncaster
- Hartlepool
- Middlesborough
- Brighton and Hove
- Sedgefield.

Most were done by postal ballot. There was also a referendum in Greater London on the mayoral issue. Of the referenda, 11 supported a mayoral system and 19 rejected it.

WEB ACTION

Find your local council website by using a search engine and explore what type of council structure applies to it and you.

 1) **Which of the three options would you consider most democratic?**
2) **Assess the argument that more decisions in local government should be carried out through referendum of all constituent citizens.**
3) **Imagine you are elected as leader of a cabinet by the elected councillors. How far would you be free to select your cabinet from all the councillors elected if a) your council has a majority from one political party, or b) your council has no overall control (balanced)?**

4) The Local Government Reform Act does not require electoral reform. Discuss the extent to which electoral reform to implement a system of proportional representation for local elections would a) enhance and encourage both voting itself, and b) include in council policy all constituent citizens.

Example of a council connecting with citizens in decisions

The revised Leeds City Council will have a leader with a cabinet selected from the councillors elected rather like the national government from the House of Commons. The full council will meet less frequently and the old committee structure has given way to a more streamlined process for agreeing policy. Councillors in each ward will work together to set up **Community Involvement Teams** (CITs). These teams will incorporate local councillors, groups and organisation representatives, such as church leaders, to establish a community plan identifying priority areas for spending and council policy in general.

An example of a council using a citizen's jury comes from Leeds City Council's review and monitoring of the council reforms. A group of Leeds citizens form a representative sample of citywide opinion on the reforms being implemented.

For the first time, the Council has recruited a representative sample of 1000 Leeds residents to form a citizen's panel to act as a sounding board to test views on key issues. Citizen's panels, along with CITs, are attempts to extend councils into communities and, in theory, they will increase citizen participation in civic affairs.

Community Involvement Teams

Community Involvement Teams is an attempt to change the working of local councils so that the views and priorities of the citizens–constituents are brought closer together in the work councillors and the council do. Below is an example of a Community Involvement Team for an area of Leeds City Council – the Otley and Wharfedale constituency.

?
1) How do the CITs allow decision-making at a more local level?
2) To what extent does asking citizen's views promote greater participation and accountability of representatives?
3) What is a citizen's jury?
4) Why has the government told councils to set up Community Involvement Teams?

5 National and European government

This section explores the role and function of governments at national level and international level (the European Union). It looks at:

- the House of Commons
- the House of Lords
- reform of the House of Lords
- devolved assemblies and the Scottish Parliament
- regional government
- European Parliament
- debate on enlargement of the EU.

The House of Commons

This body is elected once every five years or earlier if the Prime Minister decides otherwise. It operates on a national level and comprises of 659 Members of Parliament (MPs), a ratio that roughly means one MP for every 70,000 voters or 100,000 constituents. MPs are paid a full-time salary of £56,358 and have an administration support budget to cover the expenses of the office and two or three staff. The functions of the House of Commons include the following:

- representation of the constituencies and considering constituents' grievances
- legislation: all laws must be passed by the Commons
- scrutiny and criticism of government policy
- operates as a forum for national debate
- finance: authorises and controls the raising and spending of money
- recruitment of a government (usually) from the majority party.

Adapted from Coxall and Robbins (1998), *Contemporary British Politics* **(3rd ed) Macmillan, p300**

See www.explore.parliament.uk for further details on the work of the House of Commons and the House of Lords.

WEB ACTION

Go to the UK Parliament website at **www.parliament.uk**. Explore through the list of MPs websites and what MPs do in Parliament. Not all MPs have websites so you will have to scroll down the list.

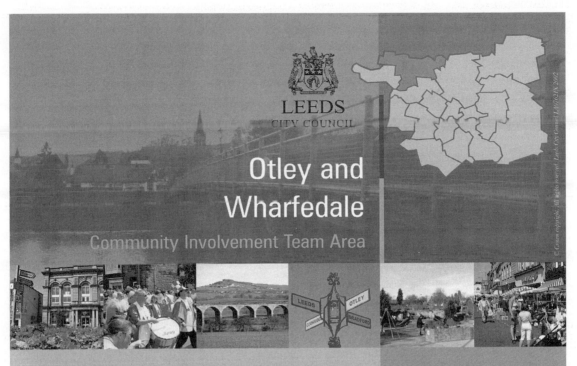

LEEDS
CITY COUNCIL

Otley and Wharfedale

Community Involvement Team Area

Actions in Your Area

This leaflet tells you about some of the things we've been doing in your area to improve local services and facilities.

Last year we produced a Community Plan for your area and sent information to every household about it. We've reviewed the plan and this leaflet describes some of the actions and our priorities for the year ahead. It also tells you about the Community Involvement Team (CIT) which is your local committee of the City Council.

Please take the time to read this leaflet and answer the questions attached. Your views will help us to build on the work we've done so far and ensure we focus on the things that matter to people in your area.

Improving Services

We are looking at ways to develop the work carried out by the CITs over the last three years. We are planning to bring some of our priority services and decision making closer to local areas through new area committees and area management arrangements. But first, we would like to know what you think.

With this leaflet you'll find information on the Council's proposals for area committees and a few questions.

We would also like your views on three important service areas which you've told us are high priorities:

- the street environment (such as rubbish and roads),
- things for young people to do, and
- ways to cut crime and make people feel safer

A Community Involvement Team (CIT) oversees activity in your area and checks the action being made. It meets six times a year to discuss issues of local importance. The CIT covers the whole of the ward (Otley and Wharfedale) and includes local councillors and advisory representatives from across the area

WEB ACTION

Go to **www.leeds.gov.uk** to find further details of the CIT activity in Otley and Wharfedale. Find your local council website and explore the role of CITs in your area.

The Houses of Parliament includes the House of Commons and the House of Lords

Diary of an MP

Siobhain's diary, 2001–02

In addition to her parliamentary work as MP for Mitcham and Morden, Siobhain enjoys a busy schedule of visits throughout the constituency. This is a selection of her activities in the past year.

January 2001

Toured renovation and demolition work at Pollards Hill. Took part, with residents, in a public meeting on **anti-social behaviour** in Lavender. Tea and coffee mornings at St Marks Family Centre and Colliers Wood Community Centre.

February 2001

Presented prizes at Sherwood Park School Adult College. Held House of Commons Reception for first-time voters in Mitcham and Morden, guest of honour Tony Robinson (Baldrick from *Blackadder*).

March 2001

Opened new Post Office in Colliers Wood High Street. Held meetings with South London Irish Association and Mitcham Garden Village.

April 2001

Opened the Alleygaters scheme in Pollards Hill and held meeting with residents about graffiti. Also meetings with developers about the future of Merton Abbey Mills, with Colliers Wood Residents Association and Mitcham Police Working Party.

May–June 2001

General election campaign. Presented awards for child-care at the Red Hut. Opened St Barnabas' Church Summer Fair. Merton Chamber of Commerce reception.

July 2001

Visited Malmesbury Middle School and Morden Farm Middle School. Toured improvements at Colliers Wood Tube. Held tea and coffee morning in Longthornton.

Siobhain McDonagh, MP for Mitcham and Morden. For more information go to www.siobhainmcdonagh.org.uk. (Copyright of this extract remains with the original author, Siobhain McDonagh)

ACTIVITY

Refer to Siobhain McDonagh's diary extracts and describe the range of constituency-based activities an MP may get involved in.

Met Association of London Government to discuss possible legislation on quality of life issues.

August 2001

Worked throughout August in constituency office, continuing advice surgeries each Friday. Opened St Marks Family Centre community garden. Took part in launch of neighbourhood warden scheme in Pollards Hill with Secretary of State Stephen Byers.

September 2001

Took part in inspection of Mitcham Common. Held meeting with DVLA in Wimbledon to discuss tightening law on abandoned cars. Met British Telecom to discuss vandalism of phone boxes. Met Community Health Council.

October 2001

Labour Party Conference. Attended reception for General Federation of Trade Unions. Attended Association of London Government conference on environmental crime. Exhibited Elvis at Parliamentary Dog of the Year – he didn't win! With Health Select Committee, visited PFI hospitals in Carlisle and Durham.

November 2001

Attended prize giving at Rowan School. Met with Health Minister John Hutton, re: St Helier and St Georges Hospitals. Met Lord Falconer, re: Merton housing. Met with South West London Community NHS Trust. Opened Hall Place for the homeless.

December 2001

Visited Learning and Skills Council for South London. Attended Guides and Brownies Christingle Service. Grenfell Housing Association open day. Site meetings, re: abandoned cars in Colliers Wood and Figges Marsh. Hosted reception for Mitcham and Morden Little League volunteers.

January 2002

Visited St Georges Hospital. Held two tea and coffee mornings in Pollards Hill. Attended launch of Merton's FLAG scheme to help tackle flytipping, abandoned cars and graffiti. Visited Stanford School, Longthornton. Visited Dr Sheikh's new surgery in Middleton Road, Ravensbury.

Procedures of the Houses of Parliament in making laws

1 Government produce a plan for the year's bill to be placed before Parliament.
2 Government produce a green paper for consultation and discussion with a deadline for contributions.
3 It then writes a white paper proposal to be put before the House of Commons. MPs debate the bill and change it if required by voting on changes (amendments). MPs vote for or against any changes. It is sent back to government. They re-write it in the light of the points from the first reading.
4 The government present the bill for the second reading and then it is voted upon. If passed, it is sent to the House of Lords who can suggest changes. It is then sent back to the House of Commons for a third reading.
5 The government present the bill to the House of Commons for the third time for voting. It is then passed again to the House of Lords for them to vote on it. If they vote in favour, the bill becomes law. If they reject it, the government can choose to over-rule and ignore the decision of the Lords by another vote in the Commons. At that point it also becomes law.

MPs and voting

Many votes (divisions) in the House of Commons follow party lines where the political parties choose as a whole to vote for or against a bill or amendment. The political parties ensure that all their party's MPs are clear on the way their leaders would like the vote to go. They also make sure all MPs vote or enough MPs vote to make sure their vote is a success (a simple majority of voting MPs is required to win).

Some issues are considered so important and the opposition is so strong in numbers that the government may get defeated. 'Three line whips' are imposed where the party's MPs must be in the House to vote. They must vote how the government would prefer. Some votes are free votes, such as on fox hunting or age of consent for homosexuals.

Not all MPs vote how their leaders or the government ask them to. Often many MPs defy three line whips because they disagree strongly about an issue. However, since the Labour Party have such a huge majority of MPs in the House of Commons, the government may have had some of their Labour MPs voting against them but they have never been defeated. The largest rebellion of 121 is still far less than the government's overall majority of 179.

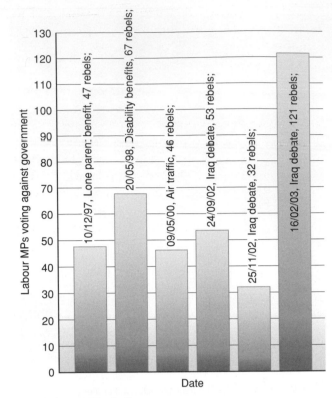

Labour's largest MP rebellions

? 1) How far are MPs free to choose themselves which way to vote in the House of Commons? Consider issues of responsibility to the government and party. Consider also the benefit to the opposition if the government are defeated or embarrassed by a large vote against the government.
2) Assess the benefits to stable government of such large majorities such as the ones held by the current and previous Labour Party governments.

The House of Lords

This body is made up of:

■ 93 unelected hereditary peers
■ 400 or so appointed life peers
■ the chief Law Lords

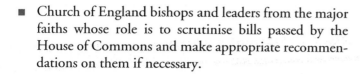

■ Church of England bishops and leaders from the major faiths whose role is to scrutinise bills passed by the House of Commons and make appropriate recommendations on them if necessary.

The main responsibilities of the House of Lords are:

■ deliberation: the provision of a forum for debates on matters of current interest
■ legislation: revision of House of Commons bills. Peers, government and private bodies such as local authorities can introduce bills on non controversial issues to be passed as legislation by the House of Lords
■ scrutiny: select committees scrutinise government policy and administration on, for example, European policy or science and technology
■ Supreme Court of Appeal: following court rulings, it is possible to appeal the decision and secure a review of the case by the House of Lords. The Law Lords rule on the meaning and application of statute law and occasionally become involved in controversial human rights cases such as that of General Pinochet, the former dictator of Chile, on whether he can be tried in another country for crimes he committed in Chile.

Reform of the House of Lords

The vast majority of the Lords are presently white, male, middle or upper class and over 60 years of age. The view of reform groups like Charter 88 is that the Lords need radical reform to meet the needs of a modern advanced multi-cultural society. Most other democracies have directly elected upper and lower chambers, e.g. the House of Representatives and the Senate in the USA. However, counter-arguments suggest that the House of Commons will simply be duplicated if both bodies are elected directly. Election campaigns tend to favour professional politicians rather than those who may have other desirable skills and life experiences.

ACTIVITY

1) Do you think the House of Lords should be directly elected?
2) Using the detail below make a case in favour of a new House of Lords which is fully directly elected.

The Labour government from 1997 have been committed to reform of the House of Lords. They want to make it representative of the population and more responsive to voters. The government launched a commission or enquiry to explore the options, led by Lord Wakeham. The Wakeham Report (20 January 2000) recommended reforms of the House of Lords to make the body more representative and electorally accountable.

The Wakeham Commission's recommendations

Key points for a new second chamber

What should the second chamber do?

Three fundamental tenets guide the report. The second chamber should be 'broadly representative' of Britain in the twenty-first century, provide an 'effective check' on the House of Commons, and give the regions, Scotland, Wales and Northern Ireland, a 'formally constituted voice' at Westminster.

Characteristics

While authoritative, the second chamber should not challenge the democratic authority of the Commons. It should include people who are not professional politicians – some should be able to shed a philosophical, moral or spiritual light on issues, or be experts in a particular field – and who may attend on a part-time basis. There should be no minimum attendance requirement.

No one political party should be able to dominate and the chamber should continue to be 'relatively non-polemical'.

How should they be chosen?

Not principally by election, either direct or indirect; nor by random selection; nor by co-option.

A 'pro-active' independent appointments commission of eight people should be responsible for choosing the new members. A 'significant minority' of them should represent the regions and nations; at least a fifth should not be affiliated to a political party; at least 30% should be

continued

women and at least 30% men. Minority ethnic groups should be represented. 26 should be members of Christian denominations, and five from other faiths.

Members should all have equal rights; there should be no two-tier system of privileges. All should serve for 15 years, except regional members, who should serve for three parliamentary terms. They may be reappointed or expelled, and there should be no minimum age.

What about the existing life peers?

They should be appointed to the new chamber for life, if they wish.

What will the new members and their chamber be called?

They should no longer be peers. Their title, and the name of the chamber, is a question that should be 'left to evolve'.

Scrutinising secondary legislation

The chamber should 'sift' secondary legislation, but any vote against a draft instrument can be overturned by the Commons after three months. Similarly, if the second chamber votes to annul an instrument, the Commons can override the vote after the same period.

Law-making

The Commons should still have the final say in public policy, but the second chamber should be able to force them to reconsider proposed new law.

There should be a new joint committee to help the two chambers agree on bills without excessive delays.

Some private bills should be considered first by the second chamber, rather than the Commons.

The constitution

The second chamber should not be given any extra powers in constitutional or human rights issues. However, there should be two new committees to discuss their interests in, and concern for, these issues.

The chamber should be able to investigate whether government bills comply with decisions of the European Court of Human Rights.

Beyond the southeast

A proportion of the members of the second chamber should represent the regions and nations of the UK. But the chamber should not become a 'federal legislature', and it should not become a forum for liaison between the nations.

No member should be automatically entitled to sit in, or nominate anyone else for, the devolved assemblies.

A new committee on devolution issues should be created, which might sometimes meet outside London.

Holding the government to account

Members of the second chamber can be ministers. Ministers themselves should be able to speak to, and be questioned by, the chamber.

An EU committee should be established to encourage better liaison between the EU and the second chamber.

Justice and the second chamber

The role of the Lords of Appeal should not change. However, they should publish a statement of the principles they mean to observe when they vote in the second chamber and sit on related cases.

Ros Taylor, © *The Guardian,* **20 January 2000**

Vote on Lords reform

MPs reject all options for Lords

MPs voted decisively last night to kick further reform of the House of Lords into the constitutional long grass when they rejected all the options on offer.

In what was a free vote, Mr Blair lost, but it was also a defeat for his opponents.

To the fury of those pro-reform MPs and peers, the crucial Commons votes saw a 390 to 172 defeat for those urging total abolition of the upper house. The 100% election version was narrowly defeated by 289 MPs to 272. An 80% elected house fell narrowly by 284 to 281. Then the pre-vote favourite, a 60% elected and 40% appointed 'hybrid' second chamber, also fell by a more decisive 316 to 253.

The **pressure group** Charter 88 called it 'a bad day for democracy'.

Among last night's surprises was the strength of the vote to abolish a second chamber entirely (172 votes).

Adapted from Michael White and Patrick Wintour, *The Guardian,* **5 February 2003**

ACTIVITY

1) Which option would you consider most democratic?
2) Critics of the elected upper chamber argue that it will undermine the House of Commons. Explain and assess this point of view.
3) To what extent do you agree a second chamber should be abolished all together?
4) What do you think to be appropriate names for the new chamber and its members?
5) What justification can be made for retaining the existing life peers? Following recent reform there has been a reduction in life peers from 800 to 96.
6) To what extent does a 'pro-active independent appointments commission' allow for full accountability to the public for the choice of members? Is this acceptable?

?
1) **What are the key differences between the House of Commons and the House of Lords in terms of powers?**
2) **Summarise the case for and against reform of the House of Lords.**
3) **Summarise the proposals from the Wakeham committee.**

Devolved assemblies and the Scottish Parliament

The intention is to make government more accessible and relevant to people in the nations of the UK. In so doing the hope is that greater interest, involvement and accountability in the decision-making process will develop.

What is the difference between a parliament and an assembly?

- A parliament can raise taxes direct from its citizens, an assembly cannot.
- A parliament can pass laws (primary legislation) that affect its citizens but an assembly cannot.
- An assembly can adapt laws (secondary legislation) from the UK Parliament to better meet the needs of its population.
- A Parliament has more power than an assembly.

Referenda and devolved government

Referenda were held in Northern Ireland, Scotland and Wales separately to decide whether a parliament or assembly should be set up. In all three cases, the referenda had to have above 50% of the voters in agreement. In Scotland, there were two questions: 72% agreed a parliament should be set up, and 64% agreed it should have tax raising powers (hence there were two questions in the Scottish referendum). In Northern Ireland, there were referenda in both Northern and Southern Ireland and a vast majority in both areas supported the setting up of an assembly. In Wales the result was much closer with only 50.3% voting in favour (only 50% turned out whereas the turnout in Northern Ireland and Scotland was much higher, closer to 75%).

? **To what extent do referenda prove conclusive?**

Scottish Parliament

The Scottish Parliament is in Edinburgh at a place called Holyrood. It has 129 members (MSPs). The first elections to the Scottish Parliament were in 1999 – 56 Labour, 36 Scottish Nationalists, 18 Conservative, 17 Liberal Democrats and three 'others'. The Members of the Scottish Parliament are elected by the proportional system called the additional member system where voters have two votes: one for the candidate in the constituency and one for a political party or named member of a political party (see voting systems earlier in this chapter).

The Scottish Parliament's leader is called the First Minister. In 1999 this was Donald Dewar (Labour) but after his sudden death in 2000 he was replaced by Jack McConnell, also Labour. The First Minister appoints a cabinet executive of 11 MSPs and this cabinet is agreed by the whole Scottish Parliament.

The Scottish Parliament after the 1999 and 2003 elections was 'hung' or balanced. Although Labour had most MSPs elected, it did not have more MSPs than all MSPs from other parties added together (no overall control). How would this influence the First Minister's choice of an executive cabinet?

What does the Scottish Parliament do?

The Scottish Parliament has responsibility for:

- health
- education
- local government
- economic development
- transport
- law and police
- the environment
- agriculture
- forestry and fisheries
- sports and the arts.

How does it relate to the UK Parliament?

The UK Parliament in Westminster retains its powers to pass laws which affect all areas of policy but has agreed to avoid the above areas unless exceptional circumstances arise. However, the UK Parliament has MPs from Scotland (about 72) and still passes laws which directly affect Scottish people, for example:

- defence
- foreign policy and Europe

- employment and economic policy
- benefits and pensions
- broadcasting
- constitution.

The taxes raised in Scotland mainly go to the UK Parliament and are then passed (devolved) to Scotland.

The Scottish Parliament can raise or decrease taxes (which makes it a parliament not an assembly) by up to three pence per Scottish resident but most of its funds come from UK Parliament grants. The total budget is roughly £20 billion.

ACTIVITY

1) How might having a parliament of its own allow Scotland to have a more accountable government? Consider the role of the Scottish Parliament and its MSPs.
2) To what extent do you agree with many MSPs that Scotland should have more power, e.g. to raise taxes or decide on its own relationship with Europe?

CASE STUDY: Student loans and top-up fees

Often the devolved assemblies cause difficulties for the government when policy locally conflicts with that of central government.

The UK government and Parliament want a system of paying for higher education fees by a means-tested contribution from the students. The Scottish Parliament decided it wants to stick with student grants and to avoid any fees paid by students. Westminster decided that tuition fees are payable on a means-tested basis by every higher education student in Britain. However, this conflicted with the Scottish Parliament's decision to waive the imposition of a contribution to tuition fees. Since Scotland has responsibility for its own education policy, there now exist separate systems in the UK for student contributions to higher education fees. In Scotland, there are no contributions involved. In England and Wales, there is some form of top-up or graduate tax.

ACTIVITY

To what extent does this difference in policy cause problems for decision-making in Westminster in relation to the newly devolved Scottish Parliament?

The Welsh Assembly

The Welsh Assembly was first elected in 1999. It is located in the city of Cardiff. It has 60 Assembly Members (AMs). The AMs are elected through the additional member system, as is the case with Scotland. In 1999 there were 28 Labour, 17 Plaid Cymru (Welsh Nationalists), nine Conservative and six Liberal Democrats. As with the Scottish Parliament, the Welsh Assembly is a balanced or hung assembly with no one party having overall majority of AMs.

The Assembly has responsibility for the same areas as the Scottish Parliament but it cannot change laws from Westminster. It can only amend them. It has no tax raising powers. The budget for the Welsh Assembly is devolved (given) by the UK Parliament and amounts to about £12 billion.

The Assembly has a First Minister (Alun Michael until he resigned in October 2000, now Rodri Morgan). The First Minister appoints nine AMs to his/her cabinet/executive. The Welsh Assembly cabinet is unique in Europe and European history for having a majority of women (five women, four men).

The Northern Ireland Assembly

After the so-called Good Friday Agreement in April 1998, the Northern Ireland Assembly was set up following a referendum supporting the move. It is similar to the Scottish Parliament in power but remains an assembly because it cannot make laws (primary legislation) on security, policing and the courts, which remain in the control of the UK Parliament.

There are 108 members of the Northern Ireland Assembly (NIAMs). The Assembly is elected by single transferable vote where voters place their preferences in order and a candidate must secure above 50% of the votes to be elected. Often the second and third choices of the voters need to be considered before a candidate secures above 50% of the votes cast.

The Northern Ireland Assembly has a First Minister who appoints ten members to the cabinet/executive. This is agreed by the full assembly.

Politics and differences between political parties are constantly hostile because of the issue of terrorism on both sides. They have great difficulty working together. At midnight on 31 October 2002, the Assembly was suspended and all powers were returned to Westminster. The Assembly could not agree on the powers the executive should have and who should be appointed to the executive. The Stormont castle in Belfast, where the Assembly is housed, now has no powers. The UK Parliament has full control until agreement can be reached between the assembly members.

 To what extent do you agree with the argument that the country of England should have a Parliament?

Regional government

In 1999 (2000 in London), regional development agencies were set up in nine regions of England:

- South West
- West Midlands
- East Midlands
- London
- Yorkshire and Humber
- North West
- North East
- East Anglia
- South East.

The idea is to allow local areas to promote their own economies through investment to support businesses, employment and training, tourism, arts, culture and transport issues. It allows money allocated by central government to be spent on aspects of significance for the regions. In giving more power to regions the idea is that policy will better suit those areas who know the issues rather than Westminster, which some argue can be insensitive to local issues.

The regional assemblies have the right to be consulted on matters affecting their areas. The Secretary of State for Trade and Industry must involve the agencies with decision-making. The members on the assemblies are elected by local businesses, voluntary groups, councils and training providers. The members work for a set fee two days per month.

CASE STUDY: Campaign for English Regions (CFER)

The Campaign for English Regions (CFER) is a pressure group making the case for regional government in England. They argue that a democratically elected regional assembly should be set up in all regions of England in much the same way as those already established in Northern Ireland and Wales. The central argument made by CFER is that distinctive regions exist in Britain and if government is to be effective and decisions are to adequately reflect the interests of local populations then government must be devolved to reach the population more directly. The case is strongly made when as the CFER states, one region of England, Yorkshire and Humber, has more people (5.5 million) than Northern Ireland and Wales together yet the two latter regions of the UK have their own devolved assembly and decision-making bodies.

The CFER has five members:

- the South West
- West Midlands
- North East
- North West
- Yorkshire and the Humber.

They have found support from all parties, a considerable number of local businesses, the media, voluntary and community organisations, local councillors and chief executive officers. A recent government report suggested that regional government was a likely prospect for the future and that strides could be made towards an increased move towards regionalism. It also said that although regional boundaries may not be clear in some areas, this should not stop progress towards regionalism.

Richard Caborne MP, the Minister for the Regions, remains a very strong supporter of regional government and devolution. At a Fabian Society conference in York in November 2000, he put the case for regionalism stating that in Yorkshire and other regions, the local economic base was not established from Whitehall but locally, e.g. the Yorkshire Bank, the Halifax, Yorkshire Electricity. In the eighteenth century, the regions were experienced at governing themselves and making their own economic and social policy. The North–South divide was largely a result of the major decisions affecting the regions over the last 100 years being made in Whitehall rather than the regions. Critics say there will be more bureaucracy and that we already have significant political apathy in the country. An additional tier of government may lead to voter fatigue with even lower turnouts at elections.

?

1) The Conservative Party manifesto in June 2001 said the regional agencies should be abolished because they are undemocratic and costly. To what extent do you agree with this argument and why?
2) What are the five main regions associated with CFER? Why do you think the four other regions have not joined the pressure group?

In June 2003, the government announced it was going to introduce legislation to allow the formation of elected regional assemblies in three areas of England: the North East, North West, and Yorkshire and Humber. Other regions in England had not shown enough interest to justify a move towards regional government. The powers are not yet decided but the local people will vote for or against a regional assembly in a referendum in 2004.

WEB ACTION

Go to *The Guardian Unlimited* website and type in 'regional assemblies for 16 June 2003'. Explore the responses to this move from the Conservative Party and the Liberal Democrats.

European Parliament

The current European Parliament has 626 members (MEPs) elected from 15 member states. The MEPs form groups according to their broad political inclinations. The two largest groups are the Party of European Socialists (including the Labour Party and other left of centre parties) and the European People's Party (Conservatives and Christian Democrats). The European Parliament does most of its work through a committee structure. The Parliament has 20 specialist standing committees each covering a specialist area of European Union activity (e.g. transport, regional policy, environment, agriculture and consumer protection). The committees are also used to cross-examine members of the European Commission and their civil servants as to how they implement EU policy.

The MEPs represent geographical regional constituencies, e.g. Yorkshire and Humber elect seven MEPs by proportional representation from a list of candidates. The European Commission comprises 20 politicians chosen and put forward by national governments and approved by the European Parliament. The Commission presents initial policy proposals to the Parliament and ensures that once passed they are carried out.

Comparison of the European Parliament

The European Parliament represents, in the words of the 1957 Treaty of Rome, 'the peoples of the states brought together in the European Community'. Some 375 million European citizens in 15 countries are now involved in the process of European integration through their 626 representatives (MEPs) in the European Parliament. Elections to the European Parliament occur every five years. In the UK they are elected by the additional vote system, as with Scottish and Welsh Assemblies.

- In Belgium, Greece and Luxemburg voting is compulsory.
- The first direct elections to the European Parliament were held in June 1979, 34 years after the end of World War II.
- In the Chamber, members sit in political groups, not in national groups.
- Parliament currently has seven political groups, plus some 'non-attached' members. These political groups include members from over 100 national political parties.

Political groups

- EPP–ED: the European People's Party and European Democrats
- PES: the Party of European Socialists
- ELDR: the European Liberal Democratic and Reformist Party
- Greens/EFA: the Greens/European Free Alliance
- EUL/NGL: co-federal group of the European United Left/Nordic Green Left
- UEN: the Union for a Europe of Nations
- EDD: Europe of Democracies and Diversities.

The heads of the 15 member states make up the European Council. They meet twice each year to agree a policy framework. The European Commission is made up of one appointed member from each of the 15 states. It proposes discussion documents and papers based upon the council's agreements. Then the Parliament debates the proposals and if approved they become European law. Member states must include the European laws in their own legislative programmes.

Areas of European Parliament power and influence are set out in various treaties and includes among other things:

- the free movement of workers
- the establishment of the internal market
- research and technological development
- the environment
- consumer protection
- education
- culture
- health.

The European Parliament budget

The European Parliament cannot tax. Instead, most of its funds come from member state contributions.

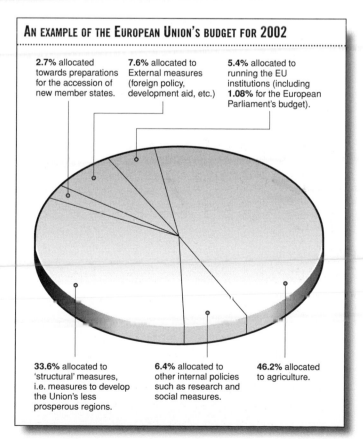

AN EXAMPLE OF THE EUROPEAN UNION'S BUDGET FOR 2002

2.7% allocated towards preparations for the accession of new member states.

7.6% allocated to External measures (foreign policy, development aid, etc.)

5.4% allocated to running the EU institutions (including **1.08%** for the European Parliament's budget).

33.6% allocated to 'structural' measures, i.e. measures to develop the Union's less prosperous regions.

6.4% allocated to other internal policies such as research and social measures.

46.2% allocated to agriculture.

Debate on enlargement of the European Union

The issue of enlargement of the European Union is frequently debated and has key significance for the identity and work of the European Union. At the Nice conference of EU leaders in December 2000, the issue of enlargement of the EU from 15 member states to 21 was addressed. The controversy revolved on how the decision-making structures should be changed as a result of enlargement. For example, should majority voting be the only decision-making basis? Should member states retain their vetoes? If the latter were to happen, then policy may never get passed since, in theory, at least any member of state could veto key decisions where the veto is allowed, e.g. on tax and social security. However, the counter argument asserts that if the veto is lost then a major issue of sovereignty is lost from the member states to the EU: a shift that many are not willing to accept. In this area, as citizens of Britain and the EU, for example, we can recognise our relationship to other member states and their significance to our democratic structures and political identities.

The growing significance on the global political structures of the EU is also noticeable when we consider Europe's relationship with the North Atlantic Treaty Organisation. For example, the moves to advance greater control of military security in Brussels under the EU peace-keeping forces instead of NATO, the dominant security council and force in Europe since World War II. The matter of national security has been an issue not just for individual member states but also for Europe as a whole. The growing importance of the EU as a power base in global economic and national security is an indication perhaps of the future of national security and the role of the EU in global stability.

On 9 October 2002, the European Commission agreed to enlarge the EU from 15 member states to 25. Some will join in 2004 and the rest in 2007.

Exam questions

You must answer Question 1 and either Question 2 or 3.

1) Read **Sources A**, **B**, and **C**, and answer the questions which follow.

Source A

> **Human Rights Act**
>
> **Right to free elections**
>
> Elections for members of the legislative body, e.g. Parliament, must be free and fair and take place by *secret ballot*. Some qualifications may be imposed on those that are eligible to vote, e.g. a minimum age.

Source B

> **Contacting your councillor, MP or MEP**
>
> To be effective, issues should be raised with the appropriate level of government. If your problem is local, contact your local councillor through the council office. MPs or MEPs can best take up problems for which the government or European Union are responsible. Most MPs and some MEPs have local 'surgeries' for which no appointment is necessary. They are often on a Saturday and advertised in the local paper. You can also write to your MEP locally and your MP at the House of Commons.

Source C

> **Who can vote?**
>
> You must be 18 or over on the day of the election and your name must be on the Electoral Register. Whilst some believe that below the age of 18 people lack political maturity, others argue that the voting age should be lowered to 16, as young people of this age already have a wide range of rights and responsibilities as citizens
>
> **Adapted from** *Young Citizen's Passport – Citizenship Foundation*, **Hodder & Stoughton (2000)**

Your answers should refer to the sources as appropriate but you should also include other relevant information.

(a) Outline briefly, using examples, the type of issue a citizen might raise with:

    (i) a councillor,

    (ii) an MP. (**Source B**)   (4 marks)

(b) Outline briefly the differing roles of **two** levels of government identified in **Source B**.   (10 marks)

(c) Examine the case for **and** against lowering the voting age to 16. (**Source C**)   (16 marks)

AQA, 15 January 2002

2) (a) Identify and examine the range of opportunities provided by political parties for citizens to become more involved in the political process.   (10 marks)

(b) Is there still a role for central government when more power is being devolved? Discuss the role of central government in the light of this question.   (20 marks)

AQA, 7 June 2001

3) (a) Briefly examine the case in favour of changing the 'first past the post' system for electing Members of Parliament to a system based on proportional representation.   (10 marks)

(b) Examine and assess some of the reasons for the decline in voter turnout in recent elections.   (20 marks)

AQA, 3 June 2003

1 Types of political action

This section explores the type of activity associated with political processes and looks at:

- legitimacy and motivation for political action
- types of political action
- citizenship and the future of campaigning.

Political activities may involve direct or indirect action. Activity may be local and is most likely to involve media and information technology. The range of activities available for citizen participation in the political system and the community is vast. It can include:

- standing for office
- joining a pressure group
- setting up a consumer group
- voting at elections.

There is a variety of motivations and reasons, many media driven, for political action or for voluntary and community activity.

 Where and with whom would you seek to raise the following issues?
(a) relaxing of school regulations on uniform
(b) stopping a road being built through a green field site
(c) challenging anti-social behaviour in a town centre
(d) lowering the legal age to vote in general elections from 18 to 16
(e) reducing the fares for bus and train travel
(f) challenging famine in less developed societies
(g) stopping wars.

Legitimacy and motivation for political action

What is the strategy and where do you draw the line?

Legitimacy

The perceived legitimacy of an action depends upon the individual's or group's strength of feeling about the issue in question. What may be legal may not necessarily be seen as effective. What campaigners may feel to be morally legitimate and effective may not actually be legal. The releasing of large numbers of captive mink or destroying genetically modified (GM) crops, for example, may be directly associated with a cause. They are not legitimate motives from the point of view of the mink farmer or the

GM crop farmer. Another example of the legitimacy dilemma may be shown by some trade unions who have decided that strike action is a legitimate way of ensuring their case is heard by management. Some unions have agreed a framework to review conditions of employment. One condition for the existence of this framework is that no strike action is taken. Since governments are keen to avoid disruption to public security, the police have agreed never to use strike action.

Motivation

Ideological values and opinions shape individual and group views on specific issues. Such ideological stances are important basic differences between individuals and groups. They often form the basis of differences in policy and action. A person's moral stance on abortion will shape views on whether women have the right to choose to continue a pregnancy or not. Citizens supporting the conservative and religious values of the **pro-life** movement will be more likely to campaign against abortion than supporters of the largely feminist and liberal **pro-choice** movement. Some may choose a direct and confrontational approach. For example, some sections of the American pro-life movement picketed and even bombed abortion clinics (extraparliamentary action). Others may choose to campaign through more peaceful means. For example, lobbying politicians to introduce reform legislation in the House of Commons (parliamentary action).

Strategies

Along with the question of legitimacy is the question of what strategy to adopt when making a case. The organisation must identify what it intends to achieve through its campaigning and the best way of achieving it.

Some initial questions need to be asked and answered:

- how can the media be used to best effect?
- what human resources and skills are available?
- how should they be used?
- should campaigners be employed using telephone canvassing techniques or door-to-door interviewing?
- should a march or demonstration, a conference or a petition be organised?

 1) Identify and describe three types of political action.
2) Explain the circumstances in which the three identified types of action may be used.

Types of political action

Political activity can involve action through councillors or Parliament. It can also involve contacting MPs or by employing professional lobby groups who are able to access MPs and seek to influence them before major votes. There have been measures introduced to restrict the power of lobby groups. In the 1990s, scandals were exposed that involved so-called 'cash for questions', which was almost bribing MPs. However, campaigning groups do attempt to contact MPs directly. Other types of action attempting to influence MPs are mass letter and email campaigns often advertised in the national press.

Alternatively, action can be taken which seeks to influence the public as well as MPs and representatives. This is referred to as extra-parliamentary action. It could include demonstrations where citizens take to the streets or consumers calling for boycotts on the purchase of products.

1) From the different actions described below, identify which are parliamentary actions and which are extra-parliamentary actions.
2) Identify which are likely to be used by involved citizens as a) consumers, b) employees, e.g. trade unionists, and c) employers.

Voting

The most familiar political activity in democratic countries is voting. Our current voting system has traditionally been first past the post. This remains so for local council elections and Westminster Parliamentary elections. However, the systems used for other representative bodies are becoming more diverse. The elections for European Parliament and the Scottish, Welsh and Northern Irish assemblies use a system of proportional representation. Voting, or lack of it, is central to any efforts directed towards democratic renewal and a key component of the current government's agenda. The perceived lack of faith in our political structures and systems of accountability has been blamed in part for the low turnouts at local elections and the falling turnouts at general elections.

Demonstrating

Demonstrating can take the form of mass people gatherings to raise the profile of an issue, e.g. anti-capitalism demonstrations.

Letter to the press (local and national)

This involves stating the case through the media to ask for support or simply to raise an issue. Reading the letter pages in your local newspaper each week can help to identify some local issues raised by individuals.

Letters to MPs, MEPs, MSPs, AMs and councillors

This can be a general letter to a group of MPs or all MPs/representatives. It could be a single letter to your own MP/representative asking him or her to take up your case with the government or relevant authority.

134 May day anti-capitalist protesters, May 2001. 6000 police on foot, on horses and in vans stop demonstrators marching down Oxford Street in London

In groups of four or more, agree an issue that you would like to know more about and what the government is doing in this area. Write a letter asking for the information to your local MP. You can find the name of your local MP through advertisements in the local press or through www.parliament.uk. The address for the House of Commons is: House of Commons, London, SW1A 0AA.

Jenny Hollingworth from Nottingham with her guide dog, Henna, deliver a petition to 10 Downing Street calling for the law to be made tougher on the use and sale of fireworks, February 2002

Contacting pressure groups

You may wish to join a pressure group because you feel strongly about an issue the group are campaigning for and would like to offer support. You could be asking a pressure group to support your case. Pressure groups are able to lobby representatives and use the media to raise an issue. They are structured organisations often with the skills to campaign effectively.

Petitioning

Petitioning is often associated with mass demonstrations and marches, e.g. a march to the local council offices to protest at the closure of a school. At the end of a march, march-leaders or representatives usually present a petition of signatures to a statement, giving the council a measure of the strength of feeling on an issue. This will hopefully influence their decisions. Many people present petitions to Downing Street as an attempt to influence government directly.

Refusing to take part (boycott)

Many people in Liverpool refuse to buy *The Sun* newspaper. This was because during the 1980s *The Sun* had a front page depicting football supporters at a match where a tragic crush killed nearly 90 people, mainly Liverpool supporters. The people of Liverpool were insulted by the image and have since boycotted the newspaper. As a consequence, the newspaper sells far fewer copies in Liverpool than any other city.

Seeking election

The MP for Wyre Forrest Dr Richard Taylor felt so strongly about the restructuring of the health service in his community that he decided to stand for election to the House of Commons in the general election of May 2001. He won by a large majority and was mandated to campaign for a better system of health service provision in his **constituency**.

In small groups, try to identify other examples of boycotts that have taken place.

Dr. Richard Taylor, MP, after winning the Wyre Forrest constituency in Worcestershire, June 2001

?

1) Identify nine types of political action.
2) Using examples, explain the difference between parliamentary action and extra-parliamentary action.
3) Explain what is meant by the following types of action:
   (a) mass demonstrations
   (b) petitioning
   (c) boycotts
   (d) strikes.
4) Choosing any issue of importance to you, select which of the above campaigning strategies may be most effective and explain why. It is highly likely that you will choose more than one.

Strikes

Trade unions organise a range of campaigns to promote the interests of their members. One such strategy is to call on all their members to refuse to go into work and to demonstrate/protest by withdrawing labour. Such moves have been happening for centuries and still happen today. The strike is intended to send a very clear message to managers and government that the workers are not willing to accept the conditions of work. Strikes have been called for various reasons. They are not always about pay.

Burning issue to firefighters' pay

Standing on a picket line in Coventry on a January morning was never going to be much fun. It's cold and blustery, and it keeps trying to rain as firefighters from Canley fire station's Red Watch warm themselves around a burning brazier.

The strike has already cost each of them between £700 and £800 in wages. Not for the first time, the men on the picket line vent their feelings of frustration. But for once, they aren't talking about the stubborn stance of Deputy Prime Minister John Prescott, the 4000 job cuts proposed by the Bain Report, or the poor support they've had from the national press.

Right now, it's the actions of an unknown soldier which have got the firefighters scratching their heads in disbelief.

The men on Red Watch waved to the crew of a military Green Goddess fire engine as it drove past their picket line. But they say that instead of a wave in return, one soldier greeted them with a one-fingered salute which won't be found in any army training manual.

'I just don't understand it,' says 46-year-old station officer Derek McAteer from Willenhall, who was a soldier manning Green Goddesses when the last fire strike took place in 1977. 'We have always supported the army. They are just doing their job. We don't have any gripe with them and they shouldn't have any with us. We are standing up for something we believe in and they should respect that.'

A single obscene gesture from a disgruntled squaddie doesn't mean much in the scheme of things. But it perhaps reflects what a battle the firefighters are having to keep the public on their side.

The firemen say that not only has the government refused to give an inch in the dispute, but it has done its best to portray the firefighters as a greedy bunch being led astray by crackpot union leaders.

And the strikers say they are annoyed, but not too surprised, that most of the national press appears to be dancing to the government's tune.

But they take heart from the support they get when they are out on the street. Canley's firefighters reckon that four out of ten passing drivers toot their horns in support of their cause. They've had pensioners dropping £1 coins into collection buckets, wood for their braziers dropped off by city firms, and food delivered by the local fish and chip shop.

One thing which has helped keep the public's support has been the firefighters' instinct to leave the picket lines when people's lives have been at stake.

'When it comes to public opinion, a lot depends on how things are presented to the public,' says Mr McAteer. 'One paper asked people whether firefighters should earn £30,000 a year, and people said yes. But when they were asked whether firefighters should get a 40% pay rise, which would be the same thing, people said no.'

The firemen say the government's pay offer, widely reported as being 11%, is actually less than that because it is 4% one year, then 7% the next. And that pay rise would only be given if the firefighters agreed to 'modernisation' of the service, as laid out in the government-appointed review conducted by Sir George Bain.

The Bain Report, published just before Christmas, has changed the focus of the firefighters' campaign. It proposes that 3500 firefighters should have their jobs cut, and that firefighters should share call rooms with police and ambulance services to save money. It even suggests the fire service should charge to attend road accidents and give safety advice.

They fear that the Bain Report could lead to the closure of 11 of the 41 fire stations in the West Midlands, and they have heard rumours that Coventry might have just four fire engines each night instead of the current seven.

Paul Barry, 22 January 2003, *Coventry Evening Telegraph*

1) Why were the firefighters striking?
2) In your view, how effective was the strategy of strike action in this case?
3) How important are the views and support of the public to the success of the campaign?
4) What is the firefighters' impression of most media coverage?
5) What was the government's view on the demands from the firefighters?

What are the two reasons for the train drivers' strikes? In your view, do both issues justify strike action and such disruption? Explain your answer.

Citizenship and the future of campaigning

A thorough exploration of citizenship must consider what the future holds for active participation, access to civil

CASE STUDY: Train drivers' strike

Train drivers threaten new Arriva row

Northern stations were empty during the two-day strike

Trains run by the Arriva Trains Company were halted for two days in January over a pay dispute resulting in a strike by the guards on the trains. The strike resulted in most of the 1600 Arriva trains services across the north of England being cancelled for two days. A further strike will go ahead in February 2003 for two days following the unsuccessful conclusion of talks between the Arriva management and the train guards' union RMT (Rail, Maritime and Transport Union).

Members of the RMT union are demanding a more equal pay structure for guards and drivers.

Adapted from BBC News, 31 January 2002

rights and future issues for promoting social inclusion. In September 2000, over 3 million people voted to decide who should win *Big Brother*, the Channel 4 reality TV game show. The same happened the following year. The votes were cast and counted with a result announced all within two hours. There are implications here for the way we vote as a process that has obvious potential for the future of electing leaders and identifying public opinion. Although voting is only one aspect of citizen participation, the case indicates some dramatic changes for the future. New technology can speed up the communication processes within a **democracy** but might not lead to a more reasoned and intelligent discussion of issues, values and actions.

New movements

In the book *Storming the Millennium*, the authors focus on rave groups, bisexual groups, anti-roads protesters, disabled people and anti-racist movements as new movements campaigning through various means for social change. The book also explores the newly emerging 'cyberpolitics', a new arena for social and political influence. The issues may appear as single issues, indicating perhaps the end of a collective political movement. However, the editor makes the point that each of us is affected by the campaigning groups. We all have direct interest in the issues involved.

New political movements may all be single-issue movements, usually taken to mean relevant only to a minority, but they all address universal issues.

Jordan and Lent (1999), *Storming the Millennium: The New Politics of Change,* **Lawrence & Wishart, p10**

Use of the Internet

It seems that active citizenship, in terms of political activity and influence, has undergone considerable systematic changes due to the influence of the Internet and the new emerging issues of priority. All political activity is and will increasingly be structured around the use of electronic communication.

[Cyberspace] is a place we are when we communicate with each other but are physically separated. Under this definition, cyberspace has existed for a long time (e.g. telephones). However, with the marriage in the last 30 years of computer and communications technology, whole communities have erupted there ... Computer-mediated communication allows

the creation of virtual communities that have several characteristics which are different to non-virtual communities: global many-to-many communication [is] anti-hierarchical, [is] identity fluid and [emphasises] the importance of information [in today's multi-media society].

Jordan and Lent, *Storming the Millennium: The New Politics of Change,* **p80**

Jordan is arguing that a new space for political influence, campaigning and debate is emerging.

Information on the Internet

Politicians are available for scrutiny on the Internet. Information on government policy is readily available and affordable so communities of debate emerge where sharing information and ideas informs the political debate. The issues of censorship and control of information remain as yet unresolved. Access to the Internet is expanding as public libraries are being refashioned into community learning resources. Voluntary groups see an Internet presence as an essential aspect of their communication work. Campaigning groups organise email protests as they once (and still do) organised street demonstrations. Large corporations such as BT present the new information and communication technologies as forces for social inclusion rather than exclusion. Whether the virtual environment can fully replicate the beneficial and productive experience of face-to-face community engagement has yet to be seen.

ACTIVITY

1) Explain how developments in technology are influencing the nature of political and campaigning action.
2) Identify some of the single-issue campaigns that have emerged recently.

2 Types of political organisation

This section explores political organisations and their activities. It looks at:

- pressure groups
- examples of pressure groups
- trade unions
- political parties and their membership.

Pressure groups

There are thousands of pressure groups in Britain, far more than political parties. Pressure groups vary in size. Some have as many as 150,000 members, e.g. the Confederation for British Industry. Others may have fewer than 100 and tend to be more local, e.g. a resident's action group. Pressure groups vary in type. Some are international environmental campaigning groups such as Greenpeace or the Make Trade Fair group. Others focus on specific themes such as operation black vote. Pressure groups also vary in their activities. Some campaigns use direct measures such as demonstrations and boycotts, others follow indirect routes such as lobbying MPs and publicity campaigns. For this reason, some prefer to be called lobby groups rather than pressure groups. Many use a combination of both direct and indirect campaigning (pressure).

Although pressure groups are very diverse and numerous none of them select and put up candidates for election. They may argue that voters should vote for a particular candidate but if they put up candidates, they then become more like a trade union or a **political party**. Pressure groups tend to avoid the complexities of running in elections because they want to influence whoever is in power. They want to keep out of being a political party themselves where policies would have to be formed in areas the pressure group do not wish to get involved in.

Many consider it vital to the health of democracy that a system of pressure groups exists aside from party politics and trade union activity.

Adapted from www.historylearningsite.co.uk

Membership of pressure groups

The table below suggests people are more willing to join pressure groups in recent years and less willing to join political parties. Bear in mind, however, that membership of political parties remains higher than membership of the pressure groups listed. One organisation that could be described as a pressure group is the Royal Society for the Protection of Birds (RSPB), which has over 1 million more members than all political parties in the UK added together.

ACTIVITY

1) Describe the patterns of membership for political parties and for pressure groups over the period 1996–2002.
2) Explain why the Green Party might be the only party to have increased its membership over that period.

Examples of pressure groups

WEB ACTION

Using a search engine such as Yahoo, explore the websites of the pressure groups below.
- What are their aims?
- What strategies do they use to campaign?

MEMBERSHIP OF POLITICAL PARTIES AND PRESSURE GROUPS

	1996	2000	2001	2002
Political parties				
Conservative	350,000	318,000	320,000	330,000
Liberal Democrat	98,611	71,641	74,176	76,023
Labour	400,465	311,000	300,000	280,000
Greens	3500	3700	4000	5000
Pressure groups				
Amnesty International	125,362	136,348	154,611	160,000
Greenpeace	194,309	176,000	193,500	194,000
Friends of the Earth	94,528	105,185	110,248	111,000

Adapted from John Williams (2002), *Sociology Review*

ent and win, e.g. Martin Bell elected MP for Tatton in 1997 and Dr Richard Taylor MP for Wyre Forrest elected in 2001, it is far less likely although more frequent in local elections than national elections.

There are a number of realistic frustrations and difficulties which emerge as a result of being a member of a political organisation. It has to be said that local party organisations vary in efficiency, size of membership and level of activity. Some areas have strong traditions in voting for one particular political party and so the party/s which are not strong in an area tend to have fewer members and be less active. Being a member of a political party in an area where they are not strong, constantly losing elections, is very frustrating and so the benefits of party membership do vary.

Author interview with an active member of a political party

In his autobiography published in 1991, the late Eric Heffer said that in his younger days he worked as a dockworker and found himself moving from town to town. At the time, he was a member of the Communist Party, which he later left to join the Labour Party. On his movements around the country, the first thing he did was to find a place to live. The second was to find the local branch of the Communist Party and get in touch with fellow members.

Political parties have student branches and local parties exist in most districts allowing for quick inclusion into at least parts of a community. The party organisations are always keen to see new members and will probably be seeking ways of finding out your skills and interests quickly so as to encourage you to commit time towards specific tasks.

Political affiliations

Political parties usually have foreign affiliations, e.g. the Christian Democrats in Germany and the Republican Party in the USA are associated with the British Conservative Party. The Australian Labour Party and the Democratic Party in the USA are associated with the Labour Party. As a result, there are opportunities to make connections abroad.

Party conferences

The conference of any political party in theory is to finalise or agree policy. Most conferences are an annual gathering of party members and workers to share practice as well as agree policy. In doing so, ordinary party members have the opportunity to meet, often informally, with key or leading figures in the party to discuss policy which otherwise rarely

happens. As well as the spectacle of key speeches at conferences such as the leader's speech, which are clearly delivered to a wider audience than those at conference, much of the activity involves social gatherings and informal discussions at fringe events. These are often organised by the associated 'think-tanks' and organisations/pressure groups. Also attending the conferences are the overseas delegations from affiliate political parties worldwide, which broadens the scope of a normal party activist.

> 1) What are the main differences between pressure groups and political parties?
> 2) What is a trade union and what do trade unions do?
> 3) What political parties have dominated British government and elections over the last century?
> 4) Explain what political parties do.
> 5) Identify some of the reasons why people join political parties.

3 Voting behaviour and what influences voting/non-voting

This section explores the extent to which patterns of voting emerge in relation to class groups, age groups, ethnic groups, religion and region. It looks at:

- models of voting behaviour
- tactical voting
- voter turnout
- turnout and minority ethnic groups
- participation in elections
- turnout and attempts to improve it
- voting and region.

As well as exploring the relationship between social group and voting behaviour, equal emphasis must be given to those not voting.

Models of voting behaviour

Theories explaining voting behaviour can be broken into three main areas: class position, party identification and rational choice.

Class position

This relates to patterns of voting behaviour associated with social class, gender, religion, ethnicity and region. The social group you are associated with has a direct influence on the way you vote. This theory is less fashionable now because many consider the class groupings to be less influential on behaviour in general as well as voting preference.

The difficulty with this approach is that the strength of support for one political party has reduced. Experiences and influences through family background and tradition in your area of work have less impact on your voting intentions. The table below illustrates the point well.

Social class has arguably declined as an influence on social behaviour and it has become more complex to define the issue. However, social class still matters and has a significant influence on the way people vote.

CHANGES IN CLASS VOTING (CONSERVATIVE % LEAD OVER LABOUR)					
	1974 (Oct)	1983	1992	1997	2001
A B C1	+37	+39	+32	+5	+4
C2	−23	+8	−1	−23	−20
D E	−35	−8	−18	−38	−31

A B refers to professional and often highly paid
C1 refers to higher professions, e.g teachers and solicitors
C2 refers to skilled non-manual workers, e.g. office workers
D E refers to skilled and semi-skilled manual workers from street cleaners to electricians
Notice that class position is associated with occupation in this case.

MORI, Butler, D and Kavanagh, D (2002) *The British General Election of 2001*, **Palgrave, p257**

Although some disagree, many argue that the working class are a minority in terms of numbers when compared to the middle and upper classes. However, if the working class are shrinking then the Labour Party can only get elected by appeal to the middle class. The table above indicates that the appeal of the Labour Party has grown among the middle classes, which delivered their election landslides of 1997 and 2001. The 2001 general election showed that middle class and working class voting preference was now more similar than ever before. The difference was reduced not by changes on both 'sides' but by a dramatic drop in middle class support for Conservatives. The support for Labour fell only 4% from 1974–2001, which contrasts

with a drop of Conservative support by the middle classes of 33%. Class still matters because the core working class vote has not changed. There is no evidence to suggest that the middle classes who changed from Conservative to Labour so dramatically will not do the same at the next general election but in the opposite direction.

1) Tony Blair and the Labour Party tried (successfully) to attract the middle classes to vote for them. Based upon the evidence above, to what extent do you think they were right to do so?
2) Some argue that the Labour Party are neglecting their 'core' vote and will be punished at the next election for doing so. To what extent do you think the working class could have as much impact as the middle class on the overall result of the next general election?
3) Many in the Conservative Party argue their policies should be designed to win back the support of the middle classes. To what extent do you think this would be a wise move as a means of winning the next general election?

Party identification

The idea with this model is that you prefer a party that your profession and family or life experience closely associates with. For example, if you were brought up in a household with a strong political opinion and preference, you are most likely to carry this on. If you are employed in a profession strongly associated with trade union activity, this will influence your choice of party.

The table below illustrates the weakening of the strength of ties voters feel to a political party.

ACTIVITY

1) Explain why family background may influence the strength of association for one political party.
2) Which occupations are strongly associated with Labour and which Conservative? Try to give some reasons for your views.

Rational choice

This theory suggests that no strong tradition or association with one political party exists to many people. The issues

TRENDS IN STRENGTH OF PARTY IDENTIFICATION 1987–2000

	1987	1993	1996	1998	2000
Very strong	11	9	9	8	6
Fairly strong	35	33	28	28	26
Not very strong	40	44	47	48	49
No party identification	8	10	10	11	13

There has been a gradual and persistent decline in attachment to political parties over the last few decades. Whereas in 1987, 46% said they felt 'very' or 'fairly' strongly attached to the party they supported, [in 2000] only 32% feel that way.

British Social Attitudes 2001–02, **National Centre for Social Research, (Sage)**

Issue	%
Unemployment	30
Asylum seekers/immigration	27
Europe	26
Protecting the environment	26

MORI, Butler and Kavanagh, *The British General Election of 2001*, **p237**

ACTIVITY

1) Imagine you are responsible for publicity and research to support your political party. On the basis of the evidence above, which issues would you focus upon and why?

2) Using the same question and the same issues, carry out a survey of your classmates. Compare your findings to those above.

of the day influence your preference for a political party. These issues may change but reflect individual priorities and will be the defining influence on the way you vote. For example, if you are an individual who sees the health service as the most important issue of the day, you will pick the party you feel more strongly supports your perception of best policies on healthcare.

More recent thinking argues that the first two models are least favoured in trying to explain people's reasons for voting and that the third, the rational choice, is increasingly influential. The idea is based upon the argument that class, tradition and family background has less influence on the way you vote than the issue/s you consider important. In short, voting behaviour is less predictable and patterns of voting predictability are less fixed and reliable.

Important issues

'At this general election (2001), which, if any, of these issues do you think will be very important to you in helping you decide which party to vote for?'

Issue	%
Healthcare	73
Education	62
Law and order	50
Pensions	40
Taxation	37
Managing the economy	31
Public transport	31

?

1) **The Labour Party are traditionally associated as the party most likely to be best on health, education, pensions, public transport and unemployment. Given this point, why do you think Tony Blair as leader of the Labour Party was so keen to change the Labour Party's image among the voters as being soft on crime, the party of high taxation and poor management of the economy?**

2) **Assess the view that the three models of voting behaviour no longer remain relevant following the 1997 and 2001 general elections.**

Tactical voting

Tactical voting is an increasingly important factor in voting behaviour. The idea is based upon voting for the party that is most likely to beat the party you would least wish to win an election. In many constituencies, a voter's preferred party may have no chance of beating the more dominant party. An individual may decide it is better to vote for the Liberal Democrat candidate, for example, than their preferred party as the Liberal Democrats stand a better chance of winning. Such tactical voting was highly influential in the 1997 general election and was, many argue, a contributory factor in the Conservative Party's huge loss of seats. Tactical voting is a well-established motivation in local elections. Many argue that voters are getting more sophisticated in their voting behaviour. The electorate is seen as less inclined to stick to one party or candidate than in previous times.

Example

Do you vote to avoid a least favoured result and accept 'second best' or do you stick to your beliefs?

Kettering 2001 general election result
- Turnout 67.4%
- Conservative 43.5%
- Labour 44.7%
- Liberal Democrats 10.2%
- Other 1.6%

Imagine you are a Liberal Democrat supporter and you were voting in Kettering in the next general election. You believe from the figures of the last election in 2001 that the Liberal Democrats are not likely to have any chance of winning. You would prefer a Conservative MP to a Labour MP. You have decided to vote tactically as an attempt to avoid the Labour candidate winning the seat. Who do you vote for?

Hereford 2001 general election result
- Turnout 63.5%
- Conservative 38.7%
- Labour 15.1%
- Liberal Democrat 40.9%
- Green 2.6%
- Other 2.4%

You are a Labour supporter but would prefer a Conservative MP to a Liberal Democrat. Who do you vote for?

Norfolk North West 2001 general election result
- Turnout 66.2%
- Conservative 48.5%
- Labour 41.7%
- Liberal Democrat 8.4%
- Other 1.4%

You are a Liberal Democrat supporter and would prefer a Labour MP to a Conservative MP. Who do you vote for?

Using the examples above it is clear that a small number of people have to challenge their conscience to continue to vote for one party as usual or consider keeping their least favoured candidate out by voting for the next largest party. Most tactics are either by Liberal Democrats or by Labour. The Conservative Party seem to attract fewer tactically cast votes. The motivations/influences for the way people vote in elections are very complex. A good example of the com-plexities in voting behaviour comes from the way the housemates and the public voted in the reality TV show 'Big Brother'.

> **?** 1) Most tactical voting is either from Liberal Democrat to Labour or Labour to Liberal Democrat. The Conservatives seem to benefit little directly from tactical votes. Identify and explain one reason why this might be the case.
>
> 2) Allegedly, voters are more willing to vote tactically in local elections than general elections. Explain why this might be the case.

Voter turnout

Much has been made of the continued reduction in voter turnout over the last 50 years and becoming most pro-nounced at the 2001 general election. Turnout in local and European elections has not only been falling but has always been lower than at general elections.

VOTER TURNOUT (2001) BY AGE, SEX AND SOCIAL CLASS (%)	
Men	61
Women	58
A B	68
C1	60
C2	56
D E	53
18–24	39
25–34	46
35–44	59
45–54	65
55–64	69
65+	70
All GB voters	59

A B refers to professional and often highly paid
C1 refers to higher professions, e.g teachers and solici-tors
C2 refers to skilled non-manual workers, e.g. office workers
D E refers to skilled and semi-skilled manual workers from street cleaners to electricians

Butler and Kavanagh, *The British General Election of 2001,* **p257**

1) Re-write the voter turnout list in order of percentage turnout with the highest first. Which groups had the highest and which groups had the lowest turnouts?
2) Cross-reference the turnout trends with the party preference for each group (see table above). If there was a uniform turnout what might be the impact on the overall general election result?

Some suggested reasons for the low turnout in 2001 general election include the following.

- Many saw the result as a foregone conclusion. Labour was ahead of the polls over the last five years by some considerable margin and few commentators believed the Conservative Party had a chance.

- Some argue that the election was not made exciting and the media had little controversy to highlight and attract public interest.

- It is possible to say that fewer party workers were active during the campaign and that less leaflets were posted through doors. Consequently, fewer people were engaged with the issues and many may have even forgotten or not noticed 7 June was polling day.

- The result was less important than other elections. In 1992, 86% felt the result was 'very' or 'fairly' important, in 1997, 79%, and in 2001, 66%. Of those 'unlikely to vote', 77% did not mind who won (MORI).

- Many argue that there was little difference between the political parties especially given that Labour had allegedly taken a poll lead in the areas traditionally considered Conservative strengths, such as law and order.

- Reduced attachment to political parties.

- June (2001) is closer to the holiday season than May (1997).

Butler and Kavanagh, *The British General Election of 2001*, **p259**

Turnout and minority ethnic groups

In the UK turnout has been shown to vary by area, age, gender, ethnicity, social class and education. The people least likely to vote in the UK are from communities of black Caribbean and black African heritage. People from black African heritage have one of the lowest levels of registration to vote. Reasons for not registering to vote include fears of harassment, language barriers, alienation from the political system and having recently moved.

Black minority ethnic groups are affected by having a younger age profile, experiencing higher levels of social and economic disadvantage and higher likelihood of living in urban areas. All these features are associated with low turnouts but are features particularly relevant to black and minority ethnic groups. However, people of Indian origin are more likely to vote than any other minority ethnic group and Bangladeshi and Pakistani are less likely to vote.

Adapted from the Electoral Commission, www.electoralcommission.org.uk

1) Try to identify some reasons for the low turnout among ethnic minority groups. Consider issues of social class, region in which a high proportion of minority ethnic groups live, and image of the main political parties.
2) Explain and assess this statement: 'The socially excluded are the ones most in need of a say/influence on the political agenda. They are the people who most need to vote yet are the groups with the lowest turnout.'

Participation in elections

Seven categories of participation in elections

David Denver researched voting behaviour in detail and explored the relationship between political participation and voting. He set out categories of voter involvement in the political process (elections) and correlated this with voting at elections.

1 Apathetics: no interest or involvement in politics or elections; do not follow election on TV.
2 Minimalists: some passing interest but do not follow the election campaign closely.
3 Spectators: follow the campaign mainly through the media (hence spectators).
4 Talkers: follow the campaign in the media and discuss the issues with others.
5 Proselytisers: talk with others about the campaign; hold strong views and will seek to persuade others to accept their view.
6 Helpers: follow and discuss the campaign and seek to persuade others, but are also willing to contribute either financially or with time to the election campaigns of one political party.
7 Gladiators: very aware, active and committed workers contributing considerably to the campaign.

Based on data from the British Election Survey 2001 (BES), the percentage of the electorate for each group was as follows (general election turnouts in brackets):

- Apathetics 12% (29%)
- Minimalists 8% (54%)
- Spectators 37% (62%)
- Talkers 27% (68%)
- Proselytisers 7% (71%)
- Helpers 8% (73%)
- Gladiators 2% (91%).

Notice the relationship between activity/interest in the campaign and turnout.

A major influence on voter turnout and participation in elections is the **socialisation** of the voters. This is the influence of background environment from family and friends on the way voters think about an election. The table below relates attitudes to the campaign among the apathetics and the participating categories in response to the statements:

'Most of my family and friends think that voting is a waste of time.'

	Apathetics	Participants	Turnout
Agree	24%	11%	42%
Disagree	8%	16%	65%

'It is every citizen's duty to vote in an election.'

Agree	12%	12%	56%
Disagree	36%	6%	20%

Denver, D *Sociology Review*, **November 2002**

ACTIVITY

What conclusions can you draw from the data above about beliefs of family and friends and individual attitudes to the election and in terms of turnout?

Turnout and attempts to improve it

Compared to other European countries, the turnout in the UK general election of 59.4% placed it 24th out of 25 countries in terms of turnout. The trend throughout Europe, however, is of declining turnout in all countries. The picture is more severe still when local election turnouts are explored.

WEB ACTION

In European elections turnout in 1999 was only 24%. You will be able to explore through the Electoral Commission website for the results and turnouts in the forthcoming 2004 European elections.
Using a search engine. type in 'electoral commission' and explore the latest research they have done on measures to tackle low turnouts at elections.

Turnout in local elections

Something consistently apparent in local elections is low turnouts. Local election turnouts now regularly fall below 30% and the average turnout is 40%. In metropolitan areas, turnouts are consistently below 30%. Britain is now the country with the lowest turnout in local elections.

Some measures designed to improve voter turnout in local elections include the following.

- Allowing more polling stations, e.g. in supermarkets, DIY stores, university campuses and post offices.
- Making postal voting easier and more available to all voters without having to give a reason (e.g. disability). New Zealand tried this in the 1960s and doubled their turnout from 30% to 60% very quickly.
- Compulsory voting where voters are fined for not voting.
- Making voting stations open earlier and stay open perhaps for two days not one.
- Electronic voting via the Internet at home.

In May 2000, the government identified 30 pilot areas to try out some of these ideas. The scheme was a mixed success. The lengthening of voting time and electronic voting did not increase turnout much but postal voting made a big impact (average of 14%). The pilots continued at the 2001 general election and the May 2002 local elections. They are considered useful moves with some success but they have not dramatically improved voter turnout.

Wilson and Game, *Local Government in the UK*, **pp224–5**

Compulsory voting

Compulsory voting as a response to low turnout is more common than is often realised – Argentina, Australia,

Austria, Belgium, Brazil, Chile, Costa Rica, Ecuador, Greece, Mexico, Turkey, Uruguay, and Venezuela.

Compulsion does not apply equally in all cases and to all elections. In Austria, compulsion only applies in some Länder [regions]. In Brazil, voters over the age of 70 are excluded from the obligation to vote, as are 16–17 year olds and illiterates. In Greece, compulsion applies up to the age of 70, but only if the voter is living within 200 miles of the constituency. In Italy, voting is compulsory, but the only penalty for non-voting is for the voter to have his or her name posted outside the town hall, and to have a certificate of good conduct (now largely fallen into dis-use) stamped with 'Did Not Vote' for five years. The voter is, in effect, named and shamed, an act believed to have harmful consequences in employment.

Adapted from Fabian Society, 2 January 2003,
www.fabian-society.org.uk

Voting and region

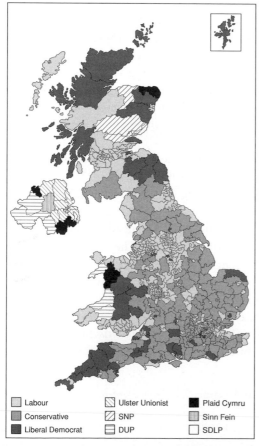

Labour	Ulster Unionist	Plaid Cymru
Conservative	SNP	Sinn Fein
Liberal Democrat	DUP	SDLP

Constituency map of UK shaded according to political party holding the seat, www.bbc.co.uk

ACTIVITY

1) Evaluate the likely effect of each of the measures above in terms of their effect upon voter turnout.
2) Try to identify any additional strategies that may have an effect.
3) Identify points for and against making voting compulsory in local, UK/national and European elections.

WEB ACTION

Explore through the website **www.parliament.uk** for details of the general election results for five rural and five urban seats.

ACTIVITY

1) With reference to the map (left), describe the pattern of Labour, Liberal Democrat and Conservative seats in relation to urban and rural areas.
2) Identify some possible reasons for the pattern of party preference in rural and urban areas.
3) Turnout is lowest in inner city areas (see Sunderland result). Explain why this might be the case.

1) For all five categories of class group, age group, ethnic group, religion and region, summarise the main trends in party preference.
2) For each of the five groups, identify three reasons for the general pattern.
3) Under each of the three main parties, make a list of the groups most likely to vote for them.
4) What do you think is a typical Conservative, Labour and Liberal Democrat voter?
5) Why might religious belief influence voter preference?

4 The mass media and the political process

This section explores the role and influence of the mass media on the political process, with particular reference to elections and electioneering. It looks at:

- models of media involvement in the political process
- the power of the mass media to influence the political process.

Models of media involvement in the political process

Consensus model

This model suggests that the media offer a narrow range of opinion on political themes and the issues and tone of coverage reflects the establishment concerns. The model bases its argument on the assumption that the media are dominated by middle aged, middle class southern males. Consequently, a narrow in-built bias exists which influences the content and style of the media content. A kind of union exists between policy makers and policy reporters: a 'cosy' union between an establishment elite of journalists and reporters and policy-makers. The media reflect the dominant group's views and interests when it comes to politics.

The media are a central tool of government and a close working relationship exists between policy-makers and the press. There is also a close union between the Prime Minister and the press barons such as Murdoch. Blair has gone to great lengths to court the media and secure favourable relations.

ACTIVITY

1) What does this say about power in the political process?
2) Are the newspapers more powerful than Blair?

Rupert Murdoch, the media tycoon who owns News International

Pluralist model

This refers to a plurality (multi-range) of contents. It believes a balance in reporting of events exists in the media. A varied range of views on a diverse array of issues exists in the main media outlets and within them. Political issues are reported with bias by most newspapers but the fact that most newspapers differ in their views allows a balance overall. Television and radio news programmes must offer a balance of views especially at election times. The Internet allows access to any range of opinions on any issue.

The press and journalists are increasingly aware that in order to survive they must appeal to their consumers and 'give them what they want'. In a market economy, if a newspaper fails to sell to enough people, their profits will fall. A range of views and issues are addressed but are constructed with the views and interests of the consumers in mind. It is the consumers of media outlets that produce the bias not the other way around. In the case of the BBC, the Press Complaints Commission and Broadcasting Standards Council serve to ensure a balance of views are presented in as impartial a way as possible to maintain a service to the public.

?

1) The BBC gets most of its funding from the government. Why do you think this is the case? To what extent is this justifiable given other independent media outlets have to run as a business?
2) 'Bias exists in most media content because total impartiality is impossible.' Assess this view in the light of the models above and evidence from your own experience.

The media and the general election 8 June 2001

Given the importance of the Internet in modern mass media communications, you would expect the traditional sources of information on campaigns in newspapers, on television and radio to decline. Although the Internet did prove influential, the impact on voters and the campaign was not quite so significant as first expected.

The 1959 campaign 42 years earlier [than 2001], had been described as the first 'television election'; many spurred on by political activity on the Internet during the 2000 elections in the USA, expected 2001 to be the first British 'Internet election'.

Butler and Kavanagh, *The British General Election of 2001*, **p224**

In fact, the Internet did not play a major role in the election but the party websites were more detailed than ever before. They were mainly used to support candidates via passwords and to encourage party workers to maintain up-to-date information on where key figures were visiting and what the latest developments were. The Internet was also important in briefing journalists on policy, but as for a mass influence, this was less than expected. 'Of those voters with Internet access, only 18% used it to find political information during the campaign.

Butler and Kavanagh, *The British General Election of 2001*, **p226**

THE PERSUASIVENESS OF MASS MEDIA IN THE ELECTION CAMPAIGN (%)

'Please tell me how much influence, if any, each of the following had on your decision about what you would do on the day of the general election.'

	Great deal	Fair amount	Not very much	None at all	Don't know
Election coverage on TV	13	36	20	30	1
Election coverage in the papers	8	30	22	39	1
Parties' leaflets or letters	4	22	25	49	1
Party election broadcasts on TV	6	16	20	57	1
Radio coverage of the election	5	17	18	58	3
Views of friends and family	6	14	20	60	1
Opinion polls	2	11	21	65	1
Billboard advertising	2	8	17	72	1
Personal calls from parties	2	6	9	80	3
Election coverage on the Internet	1	3	5	87	4

MORI/Electoral Commission, 9–18 June 2001, Butler and Kavanagh, p215

ACTIVITY

1) From the table above, which form of campaign technique had least influence on the electorate and which had the most?
2) Given that a large percentage of respondents said 'none at all', evaluate the importance of campaigning on decisions at election times.

?

1) Evaluate the extent to which newspaper readers changed their minds over the dates of the last two general elections.
2) Which paper had a divided readership and which papers were mainly read by supporters of one party or another?
3) Assess the extent to which the evidence above suggests newspapers change the views of their readers or do they confirm already existing preferences/prejudices?
4) Using the materials above and evidence from your own experience, make a case for and against one of the media models (consensus or pluralist).

PARTY SUPPORTED BY DAILY NEWSPAPER READERS (%)

Newspaper	Conservative	Labour	Liberal Democrat
Daily Telegraph			
2001	65	16	14
1997	57	20	17
Daily Mail			
2001	55	24	17
1997	49	29	14
Financial Times			
2001	48	30	21
1997	48	29	19
Daily Express			
2001	43	33	19
1997	49	29	16
The Times			
2001	40	28	26
1997	42	28	25
The Sun			
2001	29	52	11
1997	30	52	12
Daily Star			
2001	21	56	17
1997	17	66	12
The Independent			
2001	12	38	44
1997	16	47	30
The Mirror			
2001	11	71	13
1997	14	72	11
The Guardian			
2001	6	52	34
1997	8	67	22

MORI, Butler and Kavanagh, p180

The power of the mass media to influence the political process

The Sun newspaper declares what it considers to be its decisive role in two recent general elections

What does the first headline 'The Sun what won it' suggest about the belief the newspaper had about its power to influence the political process?

Below is an illustration of the impact the mass media may have on the political process. The media are attributed considerable power to set the agenda of public concern and debate. The case study of the naming and shaming of paedophiles offers a good illustration.

CASE STUDY: Sarah's Law, _News Of the World_ campaign

Tabloid sets vigilante terror on innocent man
Unwitting victim of 'name and shame' campaign

A man told yesterday of his terror at being mistaken by vigilantes for one of the alleged paedophiles named and pictured by _The News of the World_, as Labour and Conservative frontbenchers joined in condemning the paper.

Ian Armstrong was last night still afraid for his life and of leaving his Manchester home, as teenagers continued to gather outside to torment him and his children.

On Sunday, the day the list was published, a 300-strong mob had surrounded his house, and later a window of a neighbouring house belonging to his ex-wife was smashed with a brick.

The case underscored criticism of the Sunday newspaper's decision to name and print pictures of 49 men that it alleged were paedophiles.

The Home Secretary, Jack Straw, and the Tory home affairs spokeswoman, Ann Widdecombe, united in condemning the tabloid. But it won support from the mother of the murdered schoolgirl Sarah Payne, eight, whose death the paper said had motivated its decision to 'name and shame' child sex offenders.

It is thought that the fact that Mr Armstrong wears a neck brace led to him being mistaken for a man alleged to be a sex offender, Peter Smith, 60, from Warrington, in Lancashire, who was pictured by the paper wearing a neck brace.

Mr Armstrong, 49, said that people had abused his children, screaming 'paedophile's kid, rapist's kid' at them. 'It's just a nightmare, I wish I could wake up from it. There are 14 kids outside the house now. They're saying "we're going to get our dads on you".

'Three or four times today they've backed a six-year-old child halfway down the path to my door shouting, "Do you want this one?" Yesterday the mob were shouting "paedophile, rapist, beast, pervert".

'I'm scared of what will happen at nightfall.'

Greater Manchester police, who have fitted a panic alarm to Mr Armstrong's home, blamed an 'irresponsible reaction to emotive stories in a national newspaper'.

The News of the World's actions, condemned by senior police officers, presented a dilemma for the government. A leaked memo written by Tony Blair revealed Labour to be fearful of being outflanked by the Tories on the populist issue of law and order.

In the Commons, Mr Straw rebuked the paper: 'In our judgment the press in these matters ought to act on the advice of the police, above all, who have the concern of public safety there before them.'

Ms Widdecombe said: 'This incident shows that _The News of the World_, whatever their intentions may have been, are inciting a lynch mob mentality. They should now think about campaigning in a different way on an issue we are all worried about.'

The editor, Rebekah Wade, stood by her pledge to name 110,000 child sex offenders. She said that the paper did not advocate vigilante action, but asserted that placing convicted men on the sex offenders register did not give children sufficient protection.

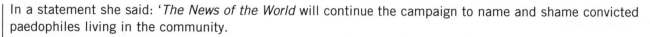

In a statement she said: '*The News of the World* will continue the campaign to name and shame convicted paedophiles living in the community.

'Since publication of Sunday's paper our phone lines have been inundated with overwhelming support from our millions of readers, confirming our belief that every parent has an absolute right to know if they have a convicted child sex offender living in their neighbourhood.'

Since Sunday, the paper has been condemned by the Association of Chief Police Officers, penal policy groups, and child welfare organisations.

The parents of Sarah Payne, whose naked body was discovered last week, backed its campaign. They said: 'I don't condone in any way any vigilante attacks, but parents have the right to protect their children and children have the right to protect themselves. There's no way a child should come forward and say someone has hurt them only to find that ten years down the line that person is back on their street again.

'Paedophiles can't help themselves. We need to help them stop, by looking after our children.'

Yesterday a spokesman for the National Society for the Prevention of Cruelty to Children said that, when contacted by *The News of the World* on Thursday, it had declined to give its support to the campaign: 'We felt at the time that it would be a populist campaign, and not something that we would want to be associated with.'

Vikram Dodd, © *The Guardian*, **25 July 2000**

ACTIVITY

1) To what extent do you believe *The News of the World* behaved irresponsibly in its naming and shaming campaign?

2) Should every parent have the right to know the conviction histories of all their neighbours?

3) What alternative methods to 'naming and shaming' could the newspaper adopt to campaign in this area?

Exam questions

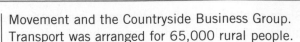

You must answer Question 1 and either Question 2 or 3.

1) Read **Sources A**, **B** and **C** and answer the questions which follow.

Source A

> **Saving the pound**
>
> Conservative leader William Hague has recently launched an 'Internet poll' regarding 'saving the pound'.
>
> Members of the public can log on to the Conservative Party website and register their support as part of the Conservative campaign to save the pound.
>
> **Adapted from a TV broadcast, ITV, April 2000**

Source B

> **A modern House of Lords**
>
> The House of Lords must be reformed. The right of hereditary peers to sit and vote in the House of Lords will be ended. This will be the first stage in a process of reform to make the House of Lords more democratic and representative. The present legislative powers of the House of Lords will be unaltered.
>
> The system of appointment of life peers to the House of Lords will be reviewed to ensure that over time life peers more accurately reflect the proportion of votes for parties cast at the previous election. We are committed to maintaining some independent life peers. No one party should seek a majority in the House of Lords.
>
> **Adapted from the *Labour Party Manifesto*, 1997**

Source C

> **The Country Sports Rally**
>
> A march in London in favour of country sports such as fox hunting was jointly organised by the British Field Sports Society, the Countryside Movement and the Countryside Business Group. Transport was arranged for 65,000 rural people.
>
> Janet George, of the British Field Sports Society, warned Labour that: 'People in the countryside are very angry at what they see as a 20-year campaign by extremists against them … If Labour try and push the countryside away, I think the countryside will push back.'
>
> **Press Association, March 1997**

Your answers to Question 1 should refer to the source materials as appropriate but you should also include other relevant information.

(a) **Source A** indicates one way in which the Internet can increase the citizen's role in the political process. Identify **two** other ways in which the Internet can assist political participation. (4 marks)

(b) **Source C** gives an example of one form of protest by a pressure group. Why are some forms of protest more successful than others? (10 marks)

(c) Explain and assess the advantages and disadvantages of people becoming more 'active citizens'. (16 marks)

AQA, 7 June 2001

2) (a) Identify and explain how citizens' lives are affected by their local councils. (10 marks)

(b) 'The main form of political participation for citizens is increasingly in pressure groups rather than in political parties.' To what extent is this view supported by the evidence? (20 marks)

AQA, 17 January 2001

3) (a) Referring to a campaign known to you, briefly explain its aims and the degree of its success. (10 marks)

(b) 'The mass media are far too powerful in influencing political decision making.' Discuss and evaluate this view. (20 marks)

AQA, 15 January 2002

CHAPTER

6

Political Ideology and Political Action

In this chapter you will explore political ideology and political action including:

- the changing nature of the ideologies of **conservatism**, **liberalism**, **socialism** and **feminism** and more recent ideologies – **New Right**, Third Way
- the relationship between changing ideology and **political party** policy through differences between some political parties' general election **manifestos**
- case studies of national, international and local campaigning which will explore the nature and effectiveness of campaigning.

The chapter is broken into four sections

1 Outline of traditional ideologies (pp 130–131)
2 Recent ideologies and the impact on political parties (pp 131–133)
3 Ideology and manifestos of the main political parties (pp 133–136)
4 Case studies of campaigning on local, national and international levels (pp 136–141)

Key terms

Campaigning – strategies used to influence a government, organisation or public opinion on an issue

Ideology – a set of ideas some of which have been called: liberalism, conservatism, socialism, feminism, New Right, Third Way/ **communitarianism**

1 Outline of traditional ideologies

This section explores the traditional political ideologies and looks at:

- Liberalism
- Conservatism
- Socialism
- Feminism

Ideology has been defined as an organised set of ideas. Ideas about the social, political and economic systems can be clustered together into groups. Philosophers, economists, sociologists, political scientists and psychologists have written extensively about ideology. Coxall and Robins (1998) define ideology as 'any system of interrelated ideas offering a comprehensive world view and able to mobilise large numbers of people for or against political change'.

A number of major ideologies have dominated western European societies at some time or other, e.g. liberalism, conservatism, socialism, feminism, **ecoism**. Some of these ideological groupings have helped determine the basis for political parties. Some ideologies, which have dominated in the past, have been adapted to form new ideologies. However, most ideologies overlap to an extent in today's society so that they are not entirely separate.

Liberalism

Liberalism developed following the demands for reform throughout Europe most significantly during the French Revolution in the 1750s.

The key concern for liberals is individual freedom. Liberalism's thrust is the protection of individual rights against interference by state and other bodies. To this effect, liberals prefer a minimal role for government but believe state intervention is necessary to offset the worst social effects of the free market economy, e.g. poverty. Liberalism strongly recommends political power being devolved into more local regions to enhance democratic accountability and reduce government centralisation.

Liberalism believes in a tolerant and pluralist society where everyone has a contribution to make and an equal chance to make their voice heard. By pluralism, liberals mean a celebration of diversity and equality of opportunity and influence from all sections of society. Liberals believe that there is an essential goodness, rationality and humanity in individuals and that no individual has a justification for restricting the rights of others.

Conservatism

Conservatism developed as a reaction to the tide of reform demanded by the revolutionary movements inspired by the French revolutionaries.

Conservatism combines:

- pessimism about human nature
- a preference for gradual change
- support for leadership by experienced elites
- assertive nationalism
- a strong commitment to the preservation of law and order.

Private property is seen as the basis of freedom and its security is in everyone's interest. Conservatism places considerable emphasis upon the need for powerful law-enforcement agencies to protect private property, to preserve public order and respect for the rule of law.

Many features of conservative ideology have influenced other ideologies.

Socialism

Socialism gained momentum during the industrial revolution in the 1800s. It was a move to establish greater representation for workers employed in factories and in industry generally.

Socialism, like liberalism, is optimistic about human nature. Its leading beliefs are that societies should be based upon an equal distribution of wealth, income and power. If this is achieved, co-operation will be more humane, civilised and productive than societies based upon hierarchy, inequality and competition. **Democratic socialism** focuses upon gradual reform based upon electoral consent and parliamentary accountability and the monitoring and regulation of the worst excesses of market forces. Radical forms of socialism favour political change through revolutionary action to replace capitalism (a system of economics based upon private property and profits).

Feminism

The feminist movement has a long history but gained momentum during the early 1900s. Its demands were made for equal treatment under the law and in representations in Parliament along with men.

For feminists there has been a long tradition of male domination in society. Feminists see their primary aim as challenging this male domination (**patriarchy**). For some feminists (radical) this means direct opposition and challenge through direct confrontation and action. Other feminists (liberal) argue for continuation of more gradual reforms.

This ideological perspective has gone through a number of changes as developments towards greater gender equality have been achieved. For feminists, gender is the primary source of social division. For further development of gender, male domination and patriarchy see Chapter 7.

2 Recent ideologies and the impact on political parties

This section explores more recent ideologies and looks at:

■ the New Right
■ the Third Way
■ the impact on political parties of ideological change.

When considering recent ideologies it is important to recognise that ideologies often undergo transformation and adaptation, reflecting a changing society. The following recent ideological trends are forged from new ideas blended with traditional ideological approaches.

The New Right

This ideological perspective evolved from some parts of nineteenth century liberalism (economic policies) and some parts of twentieth-century conservatism.

It revolves around the policies during the 1980s of Ronald Reagan in the USA and Mrs Thatcher in Britain. In some ways it is being renewed by current Conservative leaders like Michael Howard and George W Bush. Their main ideas centre on introducing free market policies, lowering taxation and reducing state intervention in areas of welfare and economic management. There is a strong support for

national identity and an advocacy of a 'strong state', e.g. strengthened powers for the police and law enforcement agencies. The approach is peculiar for conservatism, since it attempts radical not gradual reforms.

The Third Way and Communitarianism

There has been heated debate about the 'Third Way' and what it means ideologically. The debate in Britain took off in the mid 1990s and in particular after the election of a Labour government (New Labour) in May 1997. The Third Way is an adaptation of the socialist, liberal and some components of the New Right ideologies. Some prefer to refer to the term 'a new social **democracy**' rather than 'the Third Way'. Academics, such as Professor Anthony Giddens in Britain and Amitai Etzioni in the USA, have identified considerable economic, social and political changes in society to the extent that a new ideology is needed. The new ideology should match the growing complexities of a modern advanced society in the new millennium.

In _The Third Way to a Good Society_, Etzioni recognises that the ideology is not yet fully defined.

It should be acknowledged at the outset that the Third Way is indeed fuzzy at the edges, not fully etched. … But this is one of the main virtues of this approach: it points to the directions that we ought to follow, but is neither doctrine nor a rigid ideological system.

Etzioni, A (2000) _The Third Way to a Good Society_, **Demos, p13**

Etzioni argues that capitalism is the economic basis upon which most societies are ordered. It is the source of much personal fulfilment and satisfaction. However, he points out that individual fulfilment is not based solely on material wealth. There are moral, spiritual and communitarian components to individual and societal fulfilment. Etzioni argues that we must extend our involvement in these wider aspects of fulfilment as well as with material wealth if social inclusion is to be extended and citizen's rights are to be accessed by all individuals. He believes that only when we cultivate a belonging and responsibility to others, will we establish personal fulfilment as individuals. Only then will society's gross inequalities be successfully challenged.

Ever-increasing levels of material goods are not a reliable source of human well-being and contentment … the pursuit of well-being through ever higher levels of consumption is sisyphian [unattainable and hopeless]. This is not an argument in favour of poverty and self-denial. However, extensive data shows that, once basic material needs are well-sated [established] and securely provided, additional income does not add to happiness. The evidence shows that contentment is found in nourishing relationships, in bonding, in community building and public service, and in cultural and spiritual pursuits.

Etzioni, *The Third Way to a Good Society*, **p57**

Etzioni argues that an inclusive society, 'the good society' as he calls it, requires a fundamental shift from self-interest and selfish pursuit of material wealth to a greater awareness and participation in the community.

The Labour Prime Minister Tony Blair has been heavily influenced by communitarian thinkers like Etzioni and Third Way ideas. For Blair, the Third Way comprises the following components:

The Third Way is to my mind the best label for the new politics which the progressive centre-left is forging in Britain and beyond … It is founded on the values which have guided the progressive politics for more than a century – democracy, liberty, justice, mutual obligation and internationalism … The Third Way is not an attempt to split the difference between right and left. It is about traditional values in a changed world. And it draws vitality from uniting … democratic socialism and liberalism … Liberals asserted the primacy of individual liberty in the market economy; social democrats promoted social justice with the state as its main agent … Our mission is to promote and reconcile the four values which are essential to a just society which maximises the freedom and potential of all our people – equal worth, opportunity for all, responsibility and community.

Tony Blair in Fabian Society pamphlet 588, September 1998

1) Define 'ideology'.
2) Identify three ideological groups and briefly outline their main differences.
3) Explain what happens to some ideologies over time.
4) Identify the properties of the older ideologies that feature in the more recent types.

The impact on political parties of ideological change

Ideas behind political parties are written in their constitutions and policies. The Labour Party reworded one impor-

tant aspect of its constitution in 1996. There was much discussion about it because the emphasis of the Labour Party policy would be affected once the constitution was changed. The Labour Party dropped the concept of communal ownership of the means of production. Instead they adopted a mission statement that emphasised community cohesion, rights and responsibilities over actual deliberate government intervention to redistribute wealth and ownership.

The new Clause IV 1996

The Labour Party is a democratic socialist party. It believes that by the strength of our common endeavour we achieve more than we achieve alone, to create for each of us the means to realise our true potential and for all of us a community in which power, wealth and opportunity are in the hands of the many and not the few. A community where the rights we enjoy reflect the duties we owe, and where we live together freely, in a spirit of solidarity, tolerance and respect.

www.labour.org.uk

'Old' Clause IV 1918

To secure for producers by hand or by brain the full fruits of their industry, and the most equitable distribution thereof that may be possible, upon the basis of common ownership of the means of production and the best obtainable system of popular administration and control of each industry and service.

Laybourn, K (Sutton, 2000) pxii, www.labour.org.uk

ACTIVITY

Explain how the two clauses of the Labour Party constitution differ.

'Old' and 'New' Labour

The difference between the 'Old' Labour and 'New' Labour ideologies can be illustrated by an overview of their contrasting approaches to government and party policy.

Old Labour up to the 1990s

- Appeal to the working classes
- Importance of public ownership
- Redistribution of wealth from middle classes to working classes through taxation and spending

- Central role for trade unions in party policy and economic management
- Party leadership subjected to party decisions
- Campaigning through party activists
- Little interest in constitutional reform, e.g. devolution.

New Labour since the mid 1990s

- Appeal to all voters
- More emphasis on free market for economic growth
- Redistribution as and when the economy grows, lower taxation
- Good relations with business are vital, fewer privileges to trade unions
- Leadership has more power
- Campaign through modern media communications from 'central office'
- Constitutional reform central to policy.

Jones, B *et al* **(2001)** *Politics UK,* **Longman, p248**

Discuss the differences between the two policy summaries of Old and New Labour.

3 Ideology and manifestos of the main political parties

This section explores the relationship between ideology and political parties linking ideas with manifesto/policy structures of political parties. It looks at:

- the Conservative and Labour manifestos for the 1983 UK general election
- the 2001 general election manifestos
- policy and ideology: a comparison between the major political parties.

The Conservative and Labour manifestos for the 1983 UK general election

Conservative manifesto 1983 (extract)

We have reversed the decline of Britain. It is now once more a force to be reckoned with. We have stopped the defeatism that was in the air in 1979, its over-manned, over-taxed, over-regulated and uncompetitive economy. The national recovery has begun but there is still a long way to go. Unemployment can only be reduced by patiently rebuilding the economy. Our opponents believe that unemployment can be solved by more borrowing. This is a cruel deceit and will only create another economic crisis and more unemployment.

Labour manifesto 1983 (extract)

Our priority will be to create jobs and give a new urgency to the struggle for peace.

We will:

- introduce a crash programme of employment and training, with new job subsidies and allowances
- repeal Tory legislation on industrial relations and make provision for introducing industrial democracy
- begin the return to public ownership of those public industries sold off by the Tories
- spend more on education, including on essential books and equipment; end the assisted places scheme, and stop selection in secondary schools
- encourage and assist local authorities to begin a massive programme of house-building and improvement, through an immediate 50% increase in their housing investment programmes. Priority will go to the urgent repair and replacement of run-down estates. We will freeze all rents for the first full year
- give more help to public transport, with funds to improve services, keep down fares, and increase investment.

www.psr.keele.ac.uk/area/uk/man.htm

1) Using the summary extracts of the manifestos of Labour and Conservative parties in 1983, describe briefly how they differ.
2) Using examples, explore how the manifestos for 1983 and 2001 differ for both the main parties.

WEB ACTION

Using the Internet, find **www.psr.keele.ac.uk/area/uk/man.htm** and explore the Liberal-SDP manifesto. How does it differ from the two main parties' manifestos of the same election in 1983?

The 2001 general election manifestos

Conservative Party (extract)

We present here the most ambitious conservative programme for a generation.

We will free entrepreneurs to build businesses and to create prosperity, free those who use public services to choose what is best for them and free those who work in our schools and hospitals and police service from endless political interference.

We want to set people free so that they have greater power over their own lives. ... This meddling and interfering government is eroding our freedoms as well as weakening the institutions that give us a sense of common purpose.

At this election, Britain has a choice between a Labour Party that trusts government instead of people and a Conservative Party that trusts people instead of government.

Labour Party (extract)

First, we will sustain economic stability and build deeper prosperity that reaches every region of the country. Skills, infrastructure, the technological revolution – all are vital to raise British living standards faster. We will put as much energy into helping the 7 million adults without basic skills as we did when tackling long-term unemployment through the New Deal.

Second, we seek to achieve a renaissance of status and quality for public services and their staff. We will build on our success in primary schools to overhaul secondary schools. We will invest in new resources and empower doctors and nurses to transform health services and we will seek to extend the very best in culture and sport for all.

Third, we seek to modernise the **welfare state**. The benefits system will be restructured around work; support for children and families through the tax and benefits system will be transformed; cash and services for pensioners will be radically improved.

Fourth, we will strengthen our communities. We will reform the criminal justice system at every level so that criminals are caught, punished and rehabilitated. And because we know that without tackling the causes of crime we will never tackle crime. We will empower local communities by combining resources and responsibility.

Fifth, we will turn our inner confidence to strength abroad, in Europe and beyond, to tackle global problems – above all, environmental degradation and the shame of global poverty. We will engage fully in Europe, help enlarge the European Union and make it more effective, and insist that British people have the final say on any proposal to join the euro.

Liberal Democrat Party (extract)

Three simple words: freedom, justice, honesty. These sum up what the Liberal Democrats stand for.

Freedom – because everybody should have the opportunity to make the most of their life. Justice – because freedom depends on fairness. Honesty – because where fairness has a cost, like investing in schools, hospitals and pensions, we explain how it will be paid for.

This manifesto sets out our priorities: investing in schools and hospitals to cut class sizes and waiting times; extra police to prevent crime and catch criminals; increasing the basic state pension; and providing free personal care.

All our policies have a green dimension. So there is an environmental section in every chapter, a green thread binding together all our thinking. Without steps to preserve our planet for future generations, none of our policies would have much purpose.

Green Party (extract)

The Green Party is reaching for the future. We are working to create a caring and secure society in Britain, at peace with itself and the world. A multi-cultural society, in harmony with nature, where justice underpins every aspect of national life.

There might be more material wealth in our society than ever before, but it is bought at a heavy price. It is spread increasingly unfairly between rich and poor. It is not used, as it should be, to provide decent public services and quality of life for all. As a result, our health service is failing and our railways are crumbling. Stress, depression and juvenile delinquency stand at record levels.

This manifesto presents the policies to cure these ills and make our vision real – policies that will provide for our needs without denying those of future generations; share wealth fairly at home and abroad; gain control of the spiralling global economy; and give everyone a stake in how it is run.

We are reaching for a future that is sustainable and just.

ACTIVITY

> To what extent do the manifesto statements show differences in the ideological thinking between the political parties?

Policy and ideology: a comparison between the major political parties

Below, four manifesto themes are focused upon to expose policy and ideological differences between the main political parties – Europe, family, regional government and electoral reform.

Europe

Conservative

Conservatives seek to curb the power of EU to influence national parliaments. They reject the idea of the euro and wish to reform EU decision making structures but are enthusiastic about enlargement. Conservatives see a need for European co-operation but put the national parliaments first; they should be more powerful than the European parliament.

Green

Hostile to the undemocratic power of the EU, the Greens believe economic policy should be made at more local levels. Efforts to extend the economic and monetary union across Europe should be stopped and Britain should not join the euro currency.

Labour

Labour will do all it can to allow more European countries to join the EU. It believes in the single market and a **referendum** on the single currency. Labour says some areas of the EU power need to be redefined and clearly spelt out.

Liberal Democrat

Liberal Democrats are firm supporters of the European Union but do not have blind faith in it and suggest areas of its activity need reform. They are strong supporters of the single currency but will put it to referendum. Liberal Democrats believe the EU should be enlarged as soon as possible to include more European countries.

Family

Conservative

Conservatives want to cut taxes for married couples to promote marriage as the basis for family life. They promote more choice as to which schools parents should send their children to.

Green

Greens say little on family but called for an increase in child benefit, pensions and raising income support, and introducing a basic wage for volunteers and carers. Encourage more council housing to allow more choices in where to live and to abolish homelessness and families forced into temporary accommodation.

Labour

Tax cuts for parents of newborn children. Introduce a new child trust fund for every newborn child, nursery places for all three year olds, extend paid maternity leave and introduce paid paternity leave, and raise child benefit. They believe marriage is the best foundation for families but focus policy on children in families not the parents. Introduce a national children's champion who will speak up for children's rights.

Liberal Democrat

Challenge child poverty by extra payments to all families with children on income support. Abolish Child Support Agency and replace it with a family court system. Fund early years education support system, increase funding on nurseries, extra money for schools.

Regional government

Conservative

Abolish regional development agencies and abandon the idea of regional government.

Green

Regional elected assemblies, given more power, in the long term have power to raise taxes.

Labour

Increase funding for regional development agencies. Referenda on whether local people want regional government.

Liberal Democrat

Give regions in England more democratic power, referenda on local regional assemblies, promote regional development agencies.

Electoral reform

Conservative

No change to the voting system.

Green

Introduce proportional representation for election to Parliament either additional member system (AMS) or single transferable vote (STV). Reduce voting age to 16. Fixed dates for elections to Parliament, limits to election spending.

Labour

Change to the voting system will be considered by review of the Jenkins proposal but any change will be subject to a referendum.

Liberal Democrat

Reform voting system for Parliament. Prefer the single transferable voting system but subject to a referendum. STV introduced immediately for local and European elections. Reduce voting age to 16. Introduce new methods of voting, e.g. electronically.

ACTIVITY

1) How do policies differ between the main political parties?
2) To what extent do the policy differences reflect differing ideological viewpoints?

4 Case studies of campaigning on local, national and international levels

This section explores the techniques and strategies used by various campaigning groups to make their case and impact upon political agenda. It looks at:

- the Countryside Alliance
- opposition to war with Iraq. Stop the War coalition
- anti-globalisation protests.

CASE STUDY: The Countryside Alliance

The Countryside Alliance promotes the interests of rural people, including all field sports, sensible wildlife management, and wider countryside concerns such as jobs, landscapes and freedoms. They campaign and educate through the media, in Parliament, in schools and throughout the UK. For more information and detail go to www.countryside-alliance.org

407,791 voices cry freedom

The so-called 'Liberty and Livelihood' march, organised by the Countryside Alliance, September 2002

On 22 September 2002, Whitehall was swamped by 400,000 countryside marchers, which, up to that point, was the largest mass demonstration ever held in the UK. However, the 'Stop the War' march in February 2003 had between 750,000 and 2 million demonstrators depending on the figures you accept.

The placards, swaying in the sunshine, conveyed an attitude of defiance. 'We will not be culturally cleansed', read one; 'Future Criminal' read another carried by an eight year old; 'Revolting Peasant' another, carried by an adult, dressed in the Sloane Ranger's weekend uniform of plum-coloured corduroys.

Then, at precisely 10 a.m., with whistles, horns and bagpipes blaring, the Liberty march began to roll from the eastern corner of Hyde Park and into Piccadilly.

Kate Hoey, the Labour MP and darling for many of the marchers for her brave and lonely stance within her party, stood at the front, alongside Richard Burge, the Alliance's chief executive.

There were no speeches, no rally, no concert to raise the spirits before the long journey home. Once they had passed the counting station, the marchers were asked simply to disperse to allow those behind to complete the route.

Some 400,000 people came to London from all over the country to tramp along the streets and simply be counted.

To be on the streets yesterday was to feel you were part of something much larger even than the important issues that had drawn the masses to the capital.

For every marcher talking about hunting, there was another telling you about the local bus service, the closing post office, the price of lamb, and the greed of the supermarkets.

The Telegraph,
23 September 2002,
www.telegraph.co.uk/news
(© Telegraph Group
Limited 2003)

CASE STUDY: Opposition to war with Iraq. Stop the war coalition

There were a number of campaigning themes associated with opposition to the war with Iraq.

Action happened on an international level. The French and Germans were opposed to war with Iraq unless there was an international agreement (**mandate**) to go to war. The French and Germans decided they were going to vote against any move towards war. They did not think the weapons inspectors had been given enough time to investigate whether Iraq had any weapons of mass destruction.

Action happened on a national level. Although the House of Commons voted in favour of the government's policy of going to war with Iraq, 139 Labour MPs voted against the government. Robin Cook the cabinet minister resigned over the issue and was given a standing ovation in the House of Commons after his resignation speech – a very rare thing to happen at Westminster. Many church leaders, such as the Muslim Council of Britain and the Archbishop of Canterbury, voiced their opposition to war.

Action happened in the national press. The Asian paper *Eastern Eye* opposed the war; *The Daily Mirror* opposed the war, as did *The Guardian* and *The Independent* newspapers. The Prime Minister met voters and held televised debates on the policy of war with Iraq.

Action happened on a local level. Manchester students called a one-day strike on 19 March 2003. School pupils and students walked out and rallied in Manchester city centre. Many student unions organised demonstrations throughout the country to voice and demonstrate opposition to the war.

Action happened through small groups such as a 'die-in' outside the Houses of Parliament. A small group of demonstrators left for Baghdad to act as a 'human shield' against any military conflict and bombing.

The most significant action was through the campaign group set up to oppose the war, the 'stop the war coalition'. The organisation campaigned in the national press, in mass demonstrations, and called for mass email and letter pressure to MPs.

UK National Demonstration: Iraq: Stop the War!
Stop the Slaughter! End the Occupation!

Anti war with Iraq demonstration, organised by the Stop the War coalition, April 2003

On 12 April 2003, over 200,000 people demonstrated in Central London to call for an end to the occupation of Iraq. This was one of the many campaigns on or around this date in different countries throughout the world.

A massive crowd in Hyde Park heard a range of speakers, including Pakistani cricketer Imran Khan, denounce Tony Blair and George Bush and their lies about 'liberating' the Iraqi people while bombing and shooting them, and their claims that Iraq had 'weapons of mass destruction'. Britain and the US have nuclear, chemical and biological weapons.

People brought flowers, cards and wreaths to lay outside 10 Downing Street as we walked past. We also stopped both demonstrations as they arrived at Parliament and held a minute's silence in memory of all those who have died so far in Iraq.

www.stopwar.org.uk

WEB ACTION

CASE STUDY: Anti-globalisation protests

The anti-globalisation movement is not an organisation in itself. Finding information on it and its activities requires searching news websites.

There have been numerous protests, often violent, designed to disrupt global economic summits organised by international organisations, such as the World Trade Organisation, the European Union, and the United Nations. Some groups of radicals argue that global capitalism is out of control and no longer benefits society or all the people within it. The anti-globalisation movement seeks to challenge the authority of the most powerful countries and corporations in the capitalist world and expose the exploitation they impose on weaker nations and the mass of the population.

Some of the issues the demonstrators seek to raise at international economic summits are:

- climate change
- exploitation of less developed nations
- vast profit control and ownership inequality
- unemployment
- unequal distribution of power and wealth in society.

Given the diverse nature of the issues, the demonstrations are organised from a variety of groups and attract a wide range of campaigners. Many groups join anti-capitalist and anti-globalisation campaigns who are seeking to change the capitalist system but prefer to use less violent means of protest. However, the violent activities of some anarchist groups tend to steal the headlines.

It has been estimated that by the mid 1990s, nearly 40,000 multi-national companies accounted for one fifth of the total global economy.

Consider the following points.

- Firstly, the changing nature of campaigning illustrated by the anti-globalisation movement of international significance and at times a more violent approach by some.
- Secondly, compared to the other two groups above, the effectiveness of a campaign when there is no clear organisation associated along the lines of a formal **pressure group**.

The anti-globalisation movement is growing and has secured considerable publicity and academic interest in recent years. It is seen as a new form of issue and protest style.

http://news.bbc.co.uk/hi/english/static/in_depth/uk_politics/2001/open_politics/foreign_policy/globalisation.stm

The battle of Seattle: anti-globalisation protestors disrupting a World Trade Organisation summit in November 1999. Police used tear gas to control the demonstrators

Anti-capitalist riots in Genoa, July 2001

ACTIVITY

1) Explore all three of the campaigning organisations and identify the aims of the campaigns and the strategies of the campaigning groups.
2) Having identified the main aims of the campaign groups, discuss the extent to which they were achieved.
3) Assess the effectiveness and justifications for each of the campaigning group's strategies.
4) For each of the campaigns, identify the features that have a national, local and international element.
5) For each campaign, explore and describe their techniques in using the media as a campaigning tool, in particular the Internet.
6) Using the websites identified for each group, explore the activities of the campaigning groups and assess the type and nature of their campaigning literature.

Exam questions

You must answer Question 1 and either Question 2 or 3.

1) Read **Source A** and answer parts (a)–(c) which follow.

Source A

> Over recent years, there seems to have been an increase in '**direct action**' campaigning, both in terms of the number of campaigns and in the number of people involved. Examples in Britain include the campaign to save fox hunting and the 'country way of life', and the so-called 'fuel protests'. On a wider scale, in Europe and North America, there have been the May Day 'anti-capitalism' demonstrations.
>
> Some direct action campaigning has resulted in violence, with people on both sides being injured as well as property being damaged. It is, however, sometimes difficult to judge the impact of such campaigns. While the May Day 'anti-capitalism' demonstrations now receive a lot of publicity, and the scenes of protest are shown worldwide on the television, some argue that other forms of protest can be more effective. For example, consumer boycotts, such as large numbers of consumers refusing to buy genetically modified foods, strike directly at the profits of the producers and the large supermarkets. It can be claimed that this form of direct action has a far more significant effect on capitalism than mass demonstrations.

Your answers should refer to the source materials as appropriate but you should also include other relevant information.

(a) According to **Source A**, what kind of direct action can have a greater impact than mass demonstration, and why? (4 marks)

(b) Using **Source A** and your own knowledge, discuss the arguments for **and** against the use of mass protests and demonstrations as a form of direct action. (10 marks)

(c) With reference to any campaign known to you, examine the reasons for the apparent increase in direct action campaigning. (16 marks)

AQA, 3 June 2003

2) (a) Explain how any **two** of the following influence voting behaviour: age, ethnicity, geographical region, social class. (10 marks)

(b) Explain and assess how any campaign known to you has used the media to influence political decision-making. (20 marks)

AQA, 28 May 2002

3) (a) Identify and explain the main ideas currently associated with any **one** of the following ideologies:

(i) Conservatism

(ii) Socialism

(iii) Liberalism. (10 marks)

(b) Briefly outline a particular local, national or international pressure group campaign with which you are familiar, and assess the extent to which it has been successful or unsuccessful in achieving its aims. (20 marks)

AQA, 17 January 2001

CHAPTER 7

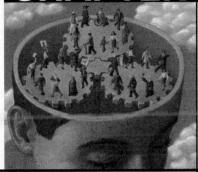

The Citizen and Social Identity

In this chapter you will explore society, socialisation and community identity including:

- the process of **socialisation** and how it influences social differences and identities
- the ways differences in identity influence a citizen's power in society
- the role and influence of social class, gender, sexuality, ethnicity, age and **nationality** on a citizen's social identity
- the role of the **mass media** in local, national and global contexts in the creation of social identity
- debates about the influence of the mass media examined in the context of competing models, including the processes of agenda setting, bias, labelling and stereotyping.

The chapter is broken into five sections

Key terms

Culture – shared identities among a group or society; involves broad identity associated with shared or recognised norms and values

Identity – individuals' characteristics that may reflect the culture/society they belong closest to

Mass media – organisations communicating with a large (mass) number of people at any one time but may be experienced through a third party

Norms – behaviour expected of you from the society you live in (normal)

Socialisation – process of learning the culturally/socially accepted rules of behaviour, norms and values upon which they are based

Values – aspects of social life considered important or priorities, often of a moral basis

1 Social integration

This section explores the socialisation process where individuals connect with the wider society and form social identities. It looks at:

- socialisation and identity
- norms and values: the basis of social identity
- socialisation.

Socialisation and identity

Participation and belonging in society are affected by our individual identities. Equally important to the way we perceive ourselves is the way others relate to and understand us and our culture. As individuals, we have our own unique identity. But our culture and identity are mainly learned.

Types of identities form patterns in some areas of society, e.g. Cornish culture or Londoner/Mancunian/Glaswegian, but there are aspects of identity that unify individuals across society even in global terms. These shared aspects of identity are called **universal institutions**. Some argue these shared components of identity are becoming more numerous and recognisable. It may be possible to map an identity that is increasingly universal, 'a global identity in a global village'.

 ? Explain why a global mass media, world travel and mass population migration might be leading to an increasingly shared global identity.

Learning cultural identity

How do we learn our cultural identity? Sociologists refer to the process of learning of social values and culture as socialisation. Families socialise in the first instance through parents and adults teaching the young ways to behave in a social situation. This stage is referred to as **primary socialisation** because it is the first stage in which an individual is introduced to social behaviour. It tends to be distinct to the certain families and households because some households have rules that others do not.

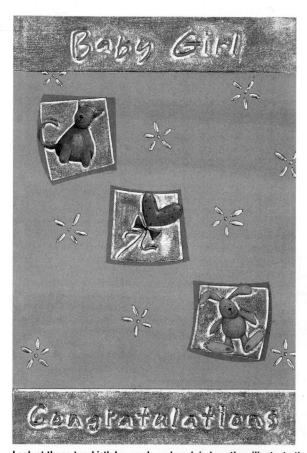

Look at these two birthday cards and explain how they illustrate the contrasting experiences of socialisation of boys and girls

5 week-old triplets. Can you tell whether they are boys or girls? Gender identity is learnt from social interaction (socialisation) whereas sex is biologically determined

In small groups, carry out a survey of your classmates and explore the rules/code of conduct for the evening meal. Compare your findings and identify any similarities or differences that may emerge.

The second stage of the socialisation process is referred to as **secondary socialisation**. This is carried out mainly by institutions such as the education system (mainly school), religious teachings and mass media images. During this process, the individual is exposed to wider sets of social rules, which may differ from those teachings experienced in the primary stage. In the secondary stage, the individual is developing a sense of belonging to a more public sphere than the relatively private world of the family/household.

Socialisation is the process whereby the helpless infant gradually becomes a self-aware, knowledgeable person, skilled in the ways of the culture into which she or he is born.

Giddens, A (1997) *Sociology*, **Polity Press, p25**

Norms and values: the basis of social identity

Through the process of socialisation, individuals adopt a sense of belonging to a wider social identity and awareness. They gain a connection to a social world, an individual identity in a group situation. During this process the rules of social behaviour and the lifestyle priorities associated with a particular culture or society are established. These are called norms and values.

It is important to remember that the learning of social rules and patterns of behaviour (self and group identity) continue throughout life. There is no doubt that the early years of learning form the basis of identity and are considered the most significant stages.

Socialisation

The process of identity formation is not a one-way process from, for example, parent to child. The learner of social messages (e.g. table manners) is not a passive individual but an active player or participant in the process.

Individuals adapt messages to their own interpretations and filter their experiences through an ever-changing social world. Those individuals conveying messages are not fixed social beings but themselves are ever changing and re-moulding their values and behaviour. Rules of behaviour at the table vary over time and are sometimes even ignored or disobeyed.

The individuals, organisations and social institutions involved in the process of socialisation include the following.

- Households and families of various types: extended – grandparents, uncles, aunts, cousins, close family friends – and nuclear – brothers, sisters, half-brothers, half-sisters, step parents, etc.
- The mass media is of increasing importance to the study of identity in developing and/or re-enforcing our views, establishing models of behaviour, lifestyle or fashion. There is also a significant agenda setting capacity whereby the dominant values of our society get continuous and extensive coverage.
- Teachers and the education system, including peer and group association.
- Religious **practice** has an influence upon identity and places of worship and religious teachings within churches, synagogues, temples and mosques, are vital to the socialisation process. They promote belief systems, spirituality and moral norms and values.

2 Culture and difference

This section explores differences according to culture and the themes of diversity in societies and looks at:

- culture and contrasting cultures
- citizen identity in a global/universal context
- multi-cultural Britain: a racial and ethnic profile
- socialisation institutions
- a global identity.

Culture and contrasting cultures

The term 'culture' involves a wide range of aspects including:

- gender
- age
- sexuality
- ethnicity
- nationality
- religion
- race
- language.

Culture can be referred to as collectively shared identities, a collection of common features associated with specific social groups. All societies have a wide variety of cultural groups and are increasingly complex. For example, it is difficult to define British identity, but we often refer to the British culture as different to French culture. We often refer to English culture and distinguish it from Scottish or Welsh (note the theme of nationality in the cultural identities). It is also important to remember that a shared identity may exist within a small sub-section of society referred to as a **sub-culture**, e.g. youth culture groups such as punk, grunge, rave, etc.

'Normal behaviour' (i.e. acceptable, appropriate) in any one society or culture is recognisable to those within. It may well be strange, perhaps insulting or offensive, to others. The basis of the normal behaviour is a value system that underpins and motivates behaviour. For example, the importance of private property in western European societies. This informs the legal and socially accepted defence of private property, which is the basis of many laws and rules of state. Culture has at its heart a set of norms and values unique (to an extent) to a particular society.

Every culture has its own unique patterns of behaviour, which seem alien to people from other cultural backgrounds.

Giddens, A (1997) *Sociology*, **Polity Press**

British culture in contrast to other cultures

For breakfast you may eat toast, breakfast cereal or bacon and eggs. It is unlikely that you would eat sago or ants for breakfast, though these might be appealing if you were a member of the Manus tribe in New Guinea or an Australian Aborigine. You would probably converse over your breakfast in English, though you might equally speak in Welsh, Gujerati or Italian.

The clothes you dress in will probably be those which are defined as appropriate for your age, sex and social status by British culture. In other cultures norms of dress might differ widely – Australian Aboriginal Bushmen go virtually naked, while women in many Islamic cultures are expected to cover up their faces and bodies entirely when in public.

The fact that you sleep in a bed in a special room called a bedroom is the norm in British society but a Chinese peasant in Xinkiang would probably sleep on a *kang* or raised platform with their family members in the room that is also used for eating and other everyday activities.

Adapted from Taylor, P (1997) *Investigating Culture and Identity,* **Collins, pp2–3**

ACTIVITY

1) Identify patterns of behaviour associated with your own culture, which may contrast with another culture. Consider aspects such as table manners, family structure, religious practice and greeting etiquette.
2) What aspects of behaviour (norms) vary according to gender groups within societies?
3) What do you think is significant for British Muslim culture as the increasingly westernised younger generation bridge the two contrasting cultures?
4) To what extent do religious orientations and beliefs influence cultures?
5) Can you identify the features of English identity which unify it and make it distinct to other cultures such as Scottish?
6) 'Ethnicity and culture are wholly learned and race is biologically determined.' Explain this statement.

?

1) Define 'socialisation'.
2) Define 'norm', 'value' and 'culture'.
3) Identify some of the key agencies of primary and secondary socialisation.

Citizen identity in a global/universal context

Many argue that as a population we are becoming increasingly international in our identity. In a world where intercontinental travel is much cheaper, quicker and safer than any previous period, we mix as cultures and groups more than any other period of history. We are increasingly aware of lifestyles, experiences and identities of other countries and cultures than ever before. This is partly due to the efficient and immediate global communications networks such as satellite television.

A formal system of education exists in almost every society. A form of family exists in almost all societies. Most advanced societies have some form of mass communication (mass media) system involving communication to large audiences simultaneously through newspapers, posters, television, etc. Religious institutions exist in most societies. Some sociologists suggest that in western European societies and North American societies these aspects of social activity are becoming less significant in the traditional sense. Sport exists in all societies and many argue that sport is a dimension of social life that is essential and inevitable. Sport also establishes a sense of identity that has unified cultures for centuries, e.g. the Olympics. It is possible to explore universal similarities in terms of:

■ language
■ literature
■ architecture
■ film
■ youth culture
■ patterns of work.

There may be similarities between societies around these universal institutions but these do vary according to the specific society in which they operate. Despite the similarities, differences exist between societies because they have their own values and priorities that shape them. As well as being aware of differences between societies in terms of the way the universal institutions work, it is also equally important to be aware of social changes in cultures over time.

Multi-cultural Britain: a racial and ethnic profile

One change resulting from global population migration is ethnic and racial diversity, an aspect of societies. **Racial mixing** is part of the modern society and cultures are adapting accordingly.

ACTIVITY

What does the following data tell us about Britain's racial identity in terms of the age profile and the future age profile of white, Black, Indian, Pakistani/Bangladeshi and others?

Socialisation institutions

Education

Over 100 countries in the world follow what is broadly called a high school diploma or the international baccalaureate. England, Northern Ireland and Wales follow an AS

POPULATION BY ETHNIC GROUP AND AGE IN GREAT BRITAIN 1998–9 (%)					
	Under 16	16–34	35–64	65+	All (millions)
All ethnic groups	20	26	39	15	57.1
White	20	25	39	16	53.0
Black					
Caribbean	23	27	40	10	0.5
African	33	35	30	2	0.4
Other	52	29	17	...	0.3
Total	34	30	31	5	1.3
Indian	23	31	38	7	1.0
Pakistani/Bangladeshi					
Pakistani	36	36	24	4	0.7
Bangladeshi	39	36	21	4	0.3
Total	37	36	23	4	0.9
Other groups					
Chinese	19	38	38	4	0.1
None of the above	32	33	32	3	0.7
Total other groups	30	34	33	3	0.8

The vast majority of the members of ethnic minorities of the younger age groups were born in Britain. In 2000–01, about one person in 14 in Great Britain was from a minority ethnic group. In general, the minority ethnic group have a younger age structure than the white group and the Bangladeshi group have the youngest age group of all ethnic groups.

Adapted from *Social Trends*, **2002**

and A2 system with less 'breadth'. The French system of education follows a different set of priorities than the English system. For example, the French have had citizenship education as part of their education system for over 100 years. In contrast, the English have had some form of citizenship education but have only made it formalised and compulsory since September 2002. Similarities exist but distinctions between societies do also.

Family and household structure

Families and their structures vary from society to society. For example, families in South Asia tend to be extended whereas in western Europe, families and households tend to be smaller with fewer children. Some form of marriage exists in most societies. However, the Mormons of North America have a system of **polygamy**. Many Muslim and Hindu families have arranged marriages and more strict procedures to follow before marriage between two adults of differing sex takes place. Some families in liberal 'western societies' are same sex (and sometimes married). These

are not allowed by, for example, Catholic Christians or Muslim religions.

Explain how the images below illustrate racial mixing around universal institutions such as marriage and family.

Mass media and communication

Some societies, e.g. the USA, have a powerful television network. Other societies, e.g. China, have fewer televisions. Many argue that the mass media are dominated by the western and North American media industry such as Hollywood, Microsoft and satellite television.

Our ability to communicate across the globe immediately, to travel quickly and more frequently, and to expe-

A couple with mixed racial backgrounds unite in the universal institution of marriage

rience events from the remotest parts of the globe through satellite mass media communication technology are all aspects of very recent technological advance. They have transformed individual identity in terms of national and cultural identity and our sense of community. Of particular significance is the domination of global media outlets by a small group of big corporations. Many argue that this is leading to western cultural values dominating cultures across the globe. American images and icons from 'blockbuster' movies like *Titanic* saturate cinemas, video stores and cable TV companies throughout the world.

Religion and faith

Religious activity exists in some form in all societies. However, in UK society religion is less influential to cultural lifestyles and values than previously. The **secularisation** process refers to religion losing its influence in society. We have science to explain natural phenomena, such as death and disaster, and we have more demands on time. Christians seem less keen to attend church and

other activities replace the church, which once operated as the centre of communities. This trend is happening in many advanced industrial societies. In UK society there is also evidence to show that certain religions remain strong and are growing. Cultural identity in multi-cultural societies is characterised by diversity. The table below illustrates contrasting trends in church membership.

ACTIVITY

1) Following the trends from 1990, complete the columns for 2000 and 2005
2) Briefly describe the pattern of church membership from the figures below.
3) Evaluate the extent to which church membership is in decline.
4) How might figures for church attendance over the same periods differ from the church membership figures?

CHURCH MEMBERSHIP IN UK (MILLIONS)						
	1970	1980	1990	1992	1994	1995
Roman Catholic	2.7	2.4	2.2	2.1	2.0	1.9
Anglican	2.6	2.2	1.7	1.8	1.8	1.8
Methodist	0.7	0.5	0.4	0.4	0.4	0.4
Mormon	0.1	0.1	0.2	0.2	0.2	0.2
Jehovah's Witnesses	0.1	0.1	0.1	0.1	0.1	0.1
Muslim	0.1	0.3	0.5	0.5	0.6	0.6
Sikh	0.1	0.2	0.2	0.3	0.3	0.4
Hindu	0.1	0.1	0.1	0.1	0.1	0.1
Jews	0.1	0.1	0.1	0.1	0.1	0.1

Adapted from *Social Trends*, **2000**

ACTIVITY

Describe how the images in the photographs below and opposite illustrate the changing nature of religious activity in a global society.

A global identity

Some theories argue that we can still generalise about distinct cultural identities, e.g. 'British', despite the variety of different individual and group identities within any one society. Others argue that we can no longer refer to any distinct culture anymore because of cultural mixing.

Social activity in advanced industrial societies is far more difficult to predict and explain. The increasing unpredictability of social behaviour, e.g. breaking up of the class system, gender, racial, sexual and global identity, makes the social world more difficult to generalise about.

A Hindu priest on the bank of the Ganges river in India, at the largest gathering of humans ever recorded at the Hindu festival of Kumbh Mela, 2001

A company run by a family of Asian origin, selling carpets from an old Christian church

'Lord of the Rings'. John Lynch, aged 69, has about 300 body piercings and for some symbolises a cult of body transformations

Postmodernist approach

Postmodernists take the fracturing of predictability in society to the extreme and dismiss any concept of generalised patterns of behaviour. The value systems influencing action (norms) are so unpredictable and diverse that motivations for action are very difficult if not impossible to generalise about. Postmodernists see little direct and necessary connection between the past and the present. Predictability is no longer possible in a world changing out of recognition in so many ways. To this end, Jameson (1991) argues that postmodern culture may comprise the following features.

1 Superficiality, detached depth or emotion. Television advertisements often comprise images and stories that bear little resemblance to the product itself. This was the case with the Guinness advertisements of surfers on a big wave or an old Olympic swimmer. Both give images of lifestyle not the product itself.

2 It is **ahistorical** and immediate. The mixing DJ Fatboy Slim uses music from all genres and times to construct sounds. It produces a complex web of sound of no distinct period or type.

3 It is timeless. Often popular music or films bear no resemblance to current affairs and often no reference to the priorities of a time and place. The film *Gladiator* produced images of the period of Roman dominance but no accurate reflection of any events.

4 New technology allows us to engage in events without needing to be aware of the background. We all use computers but very few of us know how to build a computer and nor do we need to.

Our awareness of events is on a superficial level, as they happen not on how they happen.

Adapted from Taylor, *Investigating Culture and Identity*, **pp228–9**

> **?**
> 1) Define 'postmodernism'.
> 2) Explain how postmodernists see culture changing.
> 3) Define 'globalisation'.
> 4) Describe global identity with reference to at least two of the areas discussed above.
> 5) Explain how religion is changing in the context of a global identity.

Despite the complexity of modern society, many sociologists still refer to a common structure which influences identity. We still have patterns of behaviour associated with men and not women, e.g. household chores are still done mainly by women; most people live in or aspire towards a typical nuclear family structure; many more black Afro-Caribbean people are stopped and searched than white people.

Global identity – case study (sport)

Sporting activities are an aspect of all societies. It could be argued that a common global cultural identity and unity around sport is emerging.

Sport typifies many social differences in UK society. To what extent are class differences evident in the two illustrations below?

Cricket supporters watch England play India in the Fourth NPower test match, September 2002

Nottingham Forrest supporters taunt Derby County supporters in their Nationwide League Division One football match, September 2003

CASE STUDY: Sport and global common identity?

In his book, *Global Sport: Identities, Society, Civilisations* (1999), Joseph Maguire argues that a global identity is forming around international sports and sporting competitions, such as the world cups in soccer, Rugby Union and League, and cricket in both women's and men's forms of the games. There is no better example of a universally familiar game than soccer and its world cup competition. The World Cup is a massive business with a huge following globally and potential revenue on massive scales for the hosts. Large Premier League clubs such as Manchester United have massive followings in other countries and continents such as Japan and most commonwealth countries. The global expansion of sport in most part owes a debt to satellite and international broadcasting.

Despite this apparent universality around sport there is clear evidence, argues Maguire, that the game and other sports are adapted to suit other cultures. As a result, it is not universally distinct but is adapted in many ways to suit different cultures. For example, the soccer J-League in Japan has no drawn games. They play an extra-time period with a golden goal. Perhaps the Japanese are adapting the game with the audience in mind more so than in other parts of the world.

Cricket

Cricket had experienced something of a revolution in the advent of one-day international cricket in the 1970s by Australia. The one-day game is now a central part of cricket across the world. The first one-day world cup for cricket was in 1975. It was played in England, a country with many critics of this form of the game. In the 2003 cricket season, England developed a shorter version of the one-day game. Changes happen in local areas

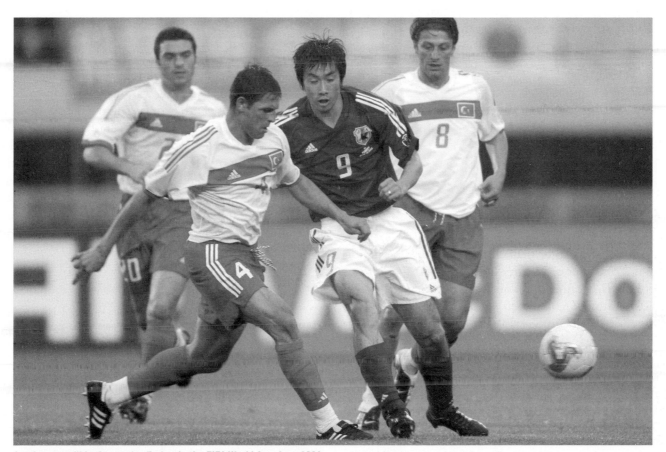

Continents collide. Japan play Turkey in the FIFA World Cup, June 2002

of the world, whilst some are incorporated, and others are distinct to that region. A **monoculture** universally associated with sport cannot be fully identified.

It is true to say that sports once unique to specific societies are being exported across the globe and have been for centuries. The difference now is that the exporting is happening at a much faster rate. For example, Kebbaddddi, the Indian wrestling game, was screened on Channel 4; Sumo wrestling, the Japanese wrestling game, is also shown on Channel 4. Soccer gave rise to American football, which is a huge sport in the USA. But the game has been exported back to England to the extent that England now has a thriving American football league. Examples like these illustrate cultural mixing but it is not yet possible to identify a single cultural identity across the globe associated with sport.

3 Social groups, identity and participation

This section explores the impact that different identities may have on life-chances and participation in society. It looks at:

- social class and identity
- age and identity
- race, ethnicity and identity
- gender, sexuality and identity.

Identity is a complex term and has caused much debate. For our purposes, the issue of identity can be explored by considering influences upon it from the following social dimensions:

- age
- social class
- ethnicity
- gender
- religion
- sexuality.

Social class and identity

Some sociologists argue that social class is now less significant as a character or identity issue than perhaps 20 years ago. This is because traditional social structures, which allowed distinctions between social classes, have broken down or disintegrated.

Employment

Aspects such as employment status are key determinants of one's social class. There is no doubt that work is a central theme to many people's lives and identities, but the type of work and the norms and values stemming from it have radically changed. For example, what do we mean by the term 'manual labour'? Is it applicable to a modern technologi-cally advanced society? What do we mean by 'work', i.e. what distinguishes work from leisure? Where do we work and with whom? How much do we earn?

Given an ever-complex world of work, our identities associated with it are changing. To be working class means a very different thing now than 20 years ago. Exploring the debates about the class system illustrates the difficulties in defining identity. It also exposes the hazards of making generalisations in social research.

Categories of class

In the 1960s, two sociologists, Goldthorpe and Lockwood, offered a categorisation of class that allowed clear distinctions to be made between the various levels. However, in the affluent 1960s, both writers felt that class was itself changing. Many affluent workers were beginning to buy consumer goods and adopt lifestyles that were limited to middle class groups. However, owning a washing machine or going on a foreign holiday did not make someone middle class. The possession of material goods may make one feel better and increase self-esteem or even status in a material society but it does not necessarily alter class position.

The changing class classification (groups) system

1   The Registrar General's scheme, renamed by government in 1990 as 'Social class based on occupation', is:

I	Professional occupations
II	Managerial and technical occupations
IIIN	Skilled non-manual occupations
IIIM	Skilled manual occupations
IV	Partly skilled occupations
V	Unskilled occupations
VI	Armed forces

This scheme was reviewed and has now been adapted (see NS-SEC below).

2 Advertisers and market researchers use a similar scheme, known as the 'ABC1' scale.

Group A
Professional workers (lawyers, doctors, etc.), scientists, managers of large-scale organisations.

Group B
Shopkeepers, farmers, teachers, white-collar workers.

Group C
1 Skilled manual (i.e. hand) workers – high grade, e.g. master builders, carpenters, shop assistants, nurses.
2 Skilled manual – low grade, e.g. electricians, plumbers.

Group D
Semi-skilled manual, e.g. bus drivers, lorry drivers, fitters.

Group E
Unskilled manual, e.g. general labourers, barmen, porters.

3 The National Statistics Socio-Economic Classifications (NS-SEC)

This is the new occupational scale to replace the Registrar General's scale.

1 Higher managerial and professional occupations
1.1 Employers and managers in larger organisations (e.g. company directors, senior company managers, senior civil servants, senior officers in police and armed forces)
1.2 Higher professionals (e.g. doctors, lawyers, clergy, teachers and social workers)
2 Lower managerial and professional occupations (e.g. nurses and midwives, journalists, actors, musicians, prison officers, lower ranks of police and armed forces)
3 Intermediate occupations (e.g. clerks, secretaries, driving instructors, fitters)
4 Small employers and own account workers (e.g. publicans, farmers, taxi drivers, window cleaners, painters and decorators)
5 Lower supervisory, craft and related occupations (e.g. printers, plumbers, television engineers, train drivers, butchers)
6 Semi-routine occupations (e.g. shop assistants, hairdressers, bus drivers, cooks)

7 Routine occupations (e.g. couriers, labourers, waiters and refuse collectors)
8 Never had paid work and the long-term unemployed.

http://www.hewett.norfolk.sch.uk/curric/soc/class/reg.htm

ACTIVITY

1) In which category would you place David and Victoria Beckham?
2) What features of someone's character other than wealth would you need to be aware of before you classified a person who had just won a multi-million pound lottery jackpot?
3) How much difficulty would you have in categorising a person with a degree in English and history working in a supermarket on the checkout tills?
4) To what extent is the fact that someone is born into a hereditary peer lineage an automatic inclusion into the higher social groups?
5) Where would you place a person whose primary role is caring for their children?
6) Is this categorisation still useful? If not, why not?
7) Given the information above, explain what is meant by the following statement.

Different schemes (of class classification) have been used in a wide variety of social science and other contexts – for example, research on social policy, market research, research on voting behaviour and social mobility. The range of different theoretical and practical applications for which different class schemes are utilised suggests that it is not possible to identify particular schemes which are 'right' or 'wrong'; rather, different schemes are more or less appropriate for particular tasks.

Crompton, R (1998) *Class and Stratification: An Introduction to Current Debates*, **Polity Press, p76**

Harriet Bradley adds further points that illustrate the complexity and changing nature of class. She suggests that we also need to incorporate aspects of gender and race in order to gain a thorough understanding of social class.

Race and gender make the analysis of class much more complicated … The experience of working class and black women is obviously different from that of white middle class women. Segregation is more marked in manual jobs and low-paid service work than in the professions. Family relations differ between class and ethnic groups. Black and working class women suffer from the racist and patriarchal policies fostered by the state, while middle class women may well be administering these policies to them.

Bradley, H (1992) in Bockock, R and Thompson, K (eds) *Social and Cultural Forms of Modernity*, **Polity Press, pp52–3**

Contradictions of class and status between societies

It is important to recognise that symbols of social status are often contradictory between societies. For example, the Nike and Nescafé corporations have been accused of exploiting cheap wage labour in less developed countries such as the Philippines or parts of India. In those societies, working for Nike or Nescafé will mean low income and exploitative conditions, if the charges are accurate, about their treatment of the workforce. In contrast, in western societies, to possess Nike trainers and to consume Nescafé coffee is seen as a status symbol of affluence and style.

Social class and citizen participation

Not only are aspects of working class identity changing, so is the identity of middle-class groups. Will Hutton (1995 and 1997) has documented the creeping threat of insecurity of income and threats of unemployment through the increased casualness of jobs and the labour force. As a result, being middle class no longer necessarily involves security at work, home or income. This undermines many perceptions that middle class identity is stable and secure.

On citizen participation, Hutton makes the point that with increasing numbers of individuals facing insecurity and the threat of unemployment and low income, those from the insecure 60% of the population participate less and less. For example, the trade unions are less powerful now, have fewer members and less money to influence society and represent the interest of working class groups. The secure 40% are more active and dominant in decisions about social legal and political changes in society or communities.

The motives of the affluent 40% may well be honourable and may genuinely attempt to include all members of society in their decisions. In fact, the majority of low income and insecure groups are less included. Citizen participation does rely in part upon financial and employment security because we are then more able to take part and give time to areas of the community which are not our immediate family concern. Traditionally the community was served by social and political activity through the factory social club, e.g. Rolls Royce. But with factory closure, participation is

restricted to areas and industries of shrinking numbers who have security at work and stability in employment.

Trade unions

The main reason for falling membership and power of trade unions is the increased insecurity of work and the reduction in employed people in the coal, docks and steel industries. In the more secure areas of employment such as teaching (non-agency), the unions have relatively greater power given their stability of membership made possible by a relatively stable and secure job. Reform and influences upon legal and social change are increasingly representative of the secure workers, which includes some middle class jobs but fewer of them, as insecurity spreads. Recently even the teaching unions have faced casualness through the use of agency staff and threats of performance-related pay.

Today's young men and women have drifted away from the institutions, which used to foster class identities (trade unions, community associations, churches, schools, etc.). Willis argues their interests lie in commercialised culture which promotes individualised consumer identities rather than a sense of class membership.

Willis (1990) in Bradley, H, Bocock, R and Thompson, K (eds) *Social and Cultural Forms of Modernity,* **p54**

Social class and education

An individual's identity will in part reflect the school they attended. What are the values and lessons taught at private fee-paying schools so that the vast majority of Oxford and Cambridge graduates originate from them and go on to dominate the majority of leading public figures in government, church and the judiciary? Attending public school is considered a privilege and works as an opportunity to establish one's self in an 'old school tie' network. Many commentators argue (e.g. Paxman, 1991) that there are styles of speech, manners of dress and extents of confidence that are particular to a public school background, distinguishing one's identity from that of a state-educated person.

The article below outlines the debate about the selection processes for entry into Oxbridge. Gordon Brown, the Chancellor of the Exchequer, in May 2000, asserts that the ancient higher education institutions are elitist and biased in favour of the privileged few that attend public school. The argument indicates the remaining significance of class as an issue for education identity and citizenship participation even in the twenty-first century.

Brown scorns Oxford elitism

The chancellor yesterday launched an outspoken attack on 'old school tie' elitism at Oxford and Cambridge, which he claimed rewarded privilege instead of potential.

To the dismay of academic leaders at Britain's two most prestigious universities, Gordon Brown used a speech to a TUC audience in London to berate Oxbridge in the wake of the much-publicised case of Laura Spence, the Tyneside comprehensive sixth former rejected by Magdalene College, Oxford.

Denouncing the decision as 'an absolute scandal', Mr Brown said the teenager with ten A-starred GCSEs and the ambition to be a doctor – who later won a £65,000 medical scholarship to Harvard – had been the victim of 'an interview system that is more reminiscent of the old boy network and the old school tie than genuine justice in our society'.

The chancellor told the TUC: 'It is about time we had an end to that old Britain when what matters to some people is the privileges you were born with rather than the potential you actually have.

'I say it is now time that these old universities open their doors to women and to people from all backgrounds. And we are determined that in the next ten years the majority of young people will be able to get higher education.'

Ms Spence welcomed the chancellor's attack: 'I think it's wonderful that Gordon Brown has decided to stick up for people all around Britain who are under-represented in places like Oxford. It's not quite so important to me because I have my place in a university abroad now. But I think it's very important for all of the other youngsters in the country, particularly those who aren't from typical Oxford backgrounds.'

Oxford's vice-chancellor, Colin Lucas, called the remarks 'deeply disappointing', and insisted that while Oxford had 'opened its doors' the university was not complacent and continued to redouble its efforts to widen access.

'I am dismayed that claims of this kind are made without knowledge of the real facts behind the headlines,' he said. 'Oxford University is constantly seeking out the most able students to come and study with us – whatever school they have been to, whatever their background, whatever their accent.'

Oxford has this year made 53% of offers to UK students from the state sector, with a near exact gender balance. That compares with an average of 48% over the past ten years.

However, while the proportion of state-educated students at Oxford has finally been hauled over the halfway mark, the share of state school pupils accepted is substantially below the proportion who apply, while the proportion of undergraduates from private schools – currently 49% – is dramatically higher than the 8% of the nation's children who go to independent schools.

Private lessons

In 1999, 48% of people who won places at Oxford were from private schools, as were 42% of applicants. For Cambridge, the figures were 43% and 36%.

18% of students at all British universities and higher education institutions are from private schools.

7% of school pupils and 18% of A level students are at private schools.

Lucy Ward and Michael White, © *The Guardian,* **26 May 2000**

Referring to the article above:
1) Define 'old school tie elitism'.
2) Explain what a typical Oxford applicant appears to be and discuss why this stereotype may be apparent.
3) Discuss the extent to which elitism exists in our university system and explain why this may impact on the life-chances of UK citizens.
4) Is elitism wrong? Explain your answer.

?
1) Define 'social class'.
2) How does social class identity develop?
3) How does a citizen's social class identity influence social, political and economic participation?
4) Why is it difficult for all to agree on a list of social class categories?

Age and identity

Definitions of common terms such a 'young' and 'old' are increasingly difficult to agree upon. However, the power of the elderly to influence political processes is increasing through, among other things, their skills and experiences as well as increasing numbers. The so-called 'grey vote' is changing the political agenda, establishing greater recognition of the rights of the elderly and the needs of an ageing population.

The 'old'

Some of our perceptions of what it means to be 'old' are changing as many choose early retirement or are made redundant before state pensionable age. Furthermore, most people can expect to live until the age of 80, 15–20 years beyond retirement age, which both extends the potential for economically active phases and the influence in the socialisation processes, contributing to the family and care services and, for example, child support. Work and its changing nature have importance in terms of age as our traditional perception that 'work' is the preserve of the young is no longer appropriate as more employment opportunities are in service sector, non-manual areas of the economy.

The 'young'

Following legislative restrictions on children working, compulsory schooling and legal protection from abuse, over the last century the political agenda has also shifted to incorporate the rights of young people, in particular children. The identity of individuals according to age has become an important and changing aspect of citizenship.

> **?** 1) Do you agree that the retirement age should be raised to 70 for men and women, men alone, or neither? Explain your answer.
> 2) Some people have suggested a reduction of the voting age from 18 to 16. Make a case for and against this proposal.
> 3) Define 'old age'.
> 4) Explain how the role of the elderly in society is changing.

Race, ethnicity and identity

Antony Giddens defines the terms 'race' and 'ethnicity' as follows:

- Race (in terms of racial differences) 'should be understood as physical variations singled out by the members of a community or society as socially significant.'
- Ethnicity 'refers to the cultural practices and outlooks of a given community of people that set them apart from others. Members of ethnic groups see themselves as culturally distinct from other groups in society, and are seen by those other groups to be so in return.'

Giddens, *Sociology*, pp210 and 212

There are overlaps between race and religious and cultural backgrounds which lead many to conclude that race no longer remains a useful term of distinction between individuals or groups. In recognition of the complex diversity of most societies, the term 'multi-cultural' is now frequently used as a reference to ethnically diverse societies such as the UK.

Most societies, certainly advanced industrial societies, comprise huge varieties of racial and cultural backgrounds. The aspects of ethnicity and race are crucial to identity of individuals and groups. Social exclusion has often been the product of racial prejudice and discrimination. However, the issue of race is not the only area of exclusion in relation to ethnicity. Religious and cultural isolation are also aspects of social exclusion. Irish immigrants into England in the eighteenth century faced significant discrimination by the native population. The Catholics in Northern Ireland claim discrimination and social exclusion by Protestant groups who possess the same racial background. There is no doubt that race and cultural ethnicity have a significant impact upon one's identity. The way one is treated by others has a substantial impact upon identity and a person's self-confidence.

> **?** 1) Define 'multi-cultural' and 'monoculture'.
> 2) Distinguish, with examples, between race and ethnicity.

Gender, sexuality and identity

The social roles performed by the different sexes (gender roles) still allow for some generalisations. Women still do more household chores than men. However, the traditional gender patterns are being eroded. 'Boys like football and girls like shopping' are stereotypes and generalisations that are no longer true in modern society. Over the last 20 years, norms in behaviour of men and women have transformed. There is a range of reasons for this including:

- reduced childbirth rates
- increasing economic independence of females
- changing employment conditions for men and women
- greater freedoms to express and explore sexuality for men and women
- increasing diversity in types of relationship between and within the sexes, e.g. cohabitation before marriage is the norm in Christian societies.

Our identity is heavily based upon our sexuality but sexuality is increasingly far more fluid or far less defined legally and socially than in previous generations. It was only 30 years ago that homosexuality was actually illegal and that a sexually tolerant society was to some unimaginable. In the new millennium, it seems any social stigma attached to sexuality is less apparent. MPs are far less anxious to avoid their homosexuality being made public knowledge. It is important to note that many individuals (men and women, famous or not) do still face discrimination and social isolation as a result of their sexuality. Anthony Giddens (1992) outlines what he considers to be an establishing 'plasticity' in sexuality, which typifies modern culture. A sexuality which is moulded and adapted to fit individual needs, no longer based solely or at all upon the basic purpose of reproduction.

In gay relationships, male as well as female, sexuality can be witnessed in its complete separation from reproduction. The sexuality of the gay woman is organised of necessity almost wholly with regard to the perceived implications of the pure relationship. That is to say, the plasticity of sexual response is channelled above all by a recognition of the tastes of the partners and their view about what is or is not enjoyable and tolerable.

Giddens, A (1992), *The Transformation of Intimacy*, **Polity Press, p143**

Jeffery Weeks makes the point that over the last 100–200 years the issue of sexuality has become centrally significant, to western European culture in particular, and fundamental to our character.

Our present-day common sense takes for granted that these terms demarcate a real division between people: there are 'heterosexuals' and there are 'homosexuals', with another term for those who do not fit into this neat divide, 'bisexuals'. But the real world is never as tidy as this, and recent historical work has demonstrated that, not only do other cultures not have this way of seeing human sexuality, neither did western cultures until relatively recently.

Weeks, J in Bocock, R and Thompson, K (eds) *Social and Cultural Forms of Modernity* **(1992) p241**

The issue for sexuality is what is acceptable or normal sexuality. How far do prejudices remain in society about sexuality? Sexual prejudice in society influences social inclusion and access to citizenship rights, e.g. freedom of expression.

The debate over the repeal of Section 28 concerns the guidance given to teachers on their advice to pupils on sexual identity. Some argue that a denial of information and guidance from teachers is a denial of the sexual identities of young people and their rights to guidance and support on request. Others suggest that the issue of homosexuality is not an area for teachers to expose young people to.

?

1) Should young people be guided on homosexuality by their teachers or should they be left to explore for themselves? Explain your view.
2) Research the archives of broadsheet newspapers using the term 'Section 28'. Describe what it is and how it relates to teaching of sexuality in schools. It has been abolished in Scotland. Should English and Welsh schools also abolish it?
3) Distinguish between sex, sexuality and gender.
4) How might one's sexuality be a basis for prejudice?

4 Identity and the mass media

This section explores the role mass media plays in influencing our identities and looks at:

- what are the mass media?
- models of ownership and control of the mass media
- models of media influence.

What are the mass media?

The mass media are forms of communication intended to reach a large number of the population simultaneously. Mass media refers to any source of communication to a mass audience that is delivered through a third party. If we heard a speech at a political gathering, this would be first-hand communication. If we later watched television coverage of it or read about it in newspapers, this would be a third party, mediating the message before delivering to a mass audience. Forms of mass communication include:

- TV
- newspapers
- journals
- books
- radio
- magazines
- posters
- the Internet.

Messages in the mass media arrive second hand and are screened (mediated) by a third party before we are exposed to them. Even reality TV is edited, as illustrated by the *Big Brother* coverage cutting to the chicken coop as soon as something interesting happens. There is a team of media employees and employers working on messages before we experience them – editors, journalists, feature writers and advertising teams, etc.

Third parties

The third party working behind the scenes is subject to cultural identity just as any of us are and so their values are going to influence decisions on what to write, publish or broadcast. This indicates that messages are rarely neutral. In some small or large way, the content of the media is filtered through a set of cultural values or prejudices. One possible exception to the rule is the Internet. Although some restrictions have been introduced, the Internet is undermining the role of the third party mediator. It is not effectively monitored and people are free to publish and consume what they wish through the Internet, acting as message deliverer and editor at the same time.

Although some argue the media's influence is over-estimated, the importance to today's society cannot be questioned. The invention of the clockwork radio has revolutionised the communications process. Sources of education, current and world affairs and emergency support is now available to remote areas of the world without electricity and power needed to access TV and the Internet. Most of us have mobile phones and advertising companies are exploring more and more strategies to contact us through text messaging. Most of us in the UK have two or three televisions and videos per household; many have DVD players, play-stations, Internet access, etc. We are a society communicating all together but most of the messages are mediated.

> 1) Define 'mass media'.
> 2) List five types of mass media outlet.
> 3) Explain why the content of the mass media cannot be entirely impartial.

Models of ownership and control of the mass media

The extent of influence the mass media has is much debated. Two themes emerge. First, how far does ownership influence content (ownership and control)? Second, how far does exposure to messages influence behaviour of individuals or groups (effects)?

It is possible to identify three models of media ownership.

Model 1 Traditional Marxist model

This model suggests that the media are owned and controlled by the dominant group in society – the wealthy power elite, as the traditional **Marxist** approach calls them. It argues that the likes of Rupert Murdoch are able to own and control vast sections of the media and squeeze out smaller media

outlets. A small number of owners are able to dictate the content of the media and ensure that favourable headlines and stories are printed and broadcast. This encourages an acceptance of the social system and all its inequality.

The media owners are so powerful they can influence and dictate the activities of the government of the day. For example, Tony Blair is much criticised for his careful courting of Rupert Murdoch to ensure favourable headlines and newspaper support for the Labour Party, especially at election times.

CASE STUDY: Record company control

Robbie Williams after signing an £80 million deal with the record company EMI, October 2002

Despite signing his record deal, Robbie Williams believes we should be allowed to copy (burn) music from the Internet because there is no way of stopping it. The record companies want people burning copyright music to be prosecuted. However, record companies have recently allowed people to burn up to ten CDs from the Internet before copyright is breached.

1) Describe the power and control possessed by the media industry, in this case the music production companies.
2) To what extent are the media industry justified in their protection of profit? In your response, consider the artist in the process as well as the consumer and the employees of the music publishing companies.

always dependent on audience size and profitability through advertising.

1) Identify some media outlets that have been 'axed' and explain why.
2) Why are the BBC allowed to impose a licence fee on all households with a TV?
3) Construct a data content analysis sheet and record the identities of the newsreaders on all five terrestrial channels over one evening.
   - How many are men?
   - How many are middle aged?
   - How many are white?
   - How many speak with an accent?
   Apply these findings to the hegemonic model. Do your findings support or reject the theory?

Model 2 Hegemonic model

The media are dominated not just by a small minority of owners with enormous power but also by the fact that the majority of the individuals working in the media are white, male, middle class, middle aged southerners. Given the rather mono-cultural background of people working in the media industry, the content of the message is likely to be biased in favour of the relatively small range of dominant ideas and values in the media industry.

Numerous attempts have been made to broaden the range of identities seen in the media, e.g. Gita Guru-Murphy, the Channel 4 newsreader and current affairs commentator, has long campaigned to increase the number of minority ethnic groups in media, news and current affairs programmes.

Model 3 The pluralist model

The facts about a tiny minority owning the vast majority of the media outlets and that a narrow cross-section of society is seen in the media is not disputed by this model. However, they do point to considerable changes over the last ten years. The point of clear difference this model has with the other two is that the pluralists believe the audience dictate the content of the media, not the owners. The public gets what it wants. It simply would not buy newspapers, magazines and watch television programmes if they did not like them. Circulation and viewing figures are all important in keeping a media outlet cost effective and profitable. If the public turn its back on a message, the message will disappear. The market force of supply meets demand applies here: no demand, no supply.

The BBC is a not-for-profit organisation which seeks to fund programmes that would not be commercially viable. The reason this is considered important is that vital information and investigation would be lost if we left content strictly to the pressure of the marketplace. Content is not

WEB ACTION

Search the Internet using Yahoo and type in 'Rupert Murdoch'. Browse through and explore the latest headlines relating to Murdoch. Then look for links to News Corporation Ltd. Browse through their main website for detail on Murdoch's corporation. Comment on its global scale, range of interests, number of people employed and apply these findings to the Marxist model.

Models of media influence

Effect models

The media affect individuals in different ways and the mass media has an influence on us all but not necessarily in the same way. The images of the bombings of Baghdad are memorable to many but to others it was just another war film. Quite how much as a society we have become desensitised to tragedy and horror is difficult if not impossible to measure. However, it is reasonable to assume that the television as a mass media source influenced events in the war with Iraq more than radio because of the visual and spoken images.

Explain which types of mass media have most influence and why. Consider:

- size of audience

Television image showing the bombing of Baghdad, March 2003

- style of message (formal, informal, advertisement or information presentation)
- techniques of communication (visual, written, spoken)
- permanence of message (written or a quick hit on a website?)
- time of exposure.

Effect models are numerous but three approaches are identified that offer distinct contribution to the debate on the effects of the media messages.

Hypodermic syringe model

This model suggests there is a direct impact on behaviour caused by exposure to media images. There is a one-way flow of influence from media message to behaviour, e.g. violence on TV causes violence in society. Proving a link between message and effect on behaviour is almost impossible to any reliable extent. Few doubt that the messages do have an effect because media advertising is big business and

millions would not be spent on it without the certainty of it having some effect. This model is a good starting point but it over-generalises the complex processes of influence of the mass media upon identity.

Multi-stage, multi-use model

- We do not believe all we see, hear and read in the media. Many people may associate with characters in soap operas but not many believe them to be real. Or do they?
- We are exposed via a third party to messages in the media but the third party adds their own opinions. For example, a person could describe a story on the news and their interpretation of what was reported will be imposed on their account to us (multi-stage).
- We ignore some parts of the media and pay more attention to others. Discrimination in uses of the media means we are affected by it on different levels. For example, is the radio just background noise but not

something we concentrate on? Do we ever read every story in a newspaper? Which soap opera do we prefer? Do we watch documentaries and the news? What magazines do we choose to read? All choices by consumers of media messages allow the effects to be widespread and different according to the user (multi-use).

In this model, the effects are more complex and involve separating it from other causes of behaviour. We may be influenced by the media but more in terms of it reinforcing our existing prejudices, which we establish from other sources and areas of society.

Cultural agenda setting model

Identity and culture according to this model are increasingly linked to the mass media, which has ever-increasing involvement in our day-to-day lives. The images to which we are subjected and to which we subject ourselves are recognised by sociologists as highly significant in character and cultural identity formations.

This model suggests that the mass media develop an image in our perceptions of different social groups, which distort reality. We see, read and hear stories that rely on stereotypes and generalisations to catch our attention and to ensure catchy headlines that stand out or shock. The stereotypical images are culturally biased towards middle class language, white and male identity. Images that are sexist and racist are frequently evident in the media. These distorted representations lead to a distorted perception of groups different to our own, whatever they may be.

The mass media are frequently accused of stereotypical imagery painting narrow images of, for example, ethnic minority groups, age, social class and gender groups.

Stephens *et al* (1998) considers representation of age in the mass media by using the work of Alex Thio (1989) who argues ageist stereotypes in the mass media take the following forms:

- older people are usually senile
- older workers are not as productive as younger ones
- most elderly people live in poverty
- most elderly people are lonely
- most elderly people end up in nursing homes and other institutions
- most elderly people have no interest in or capacity for sexual relations

- most elderly people are set in their ways and unable to change
- most elderly people feel miserable.

Thio, A (1989), c. Stephens, P *et al,* **(1998)** *Think Sociology,* **Nelson Thornes**

To what extent do the above stereotypes apply to all mass media representation of older age?

The effect of the constant bombardment of stereotypes is not that we fully believe them, nor that they are ignored. So frequent is our exposure to distorted reality that we begin to form an impression of other groups. That impression then begins to influence our perception of other groups. The stereotypes in the media are particularly influential upon our perceptions of others that we encounter least.

Not only do the messages of the media have an effect but also what is not in the media has an effect. For example, some stories are kept out of the media so that stories are kept quiet. The media set the agenda in terms of stereotypes but also in what we are exposed to. For example, many argue that soap operas are a very good way of keeping the public concerned with artificial worlds and away from the real world.

1) Which of the above 3 models do you consider most convincing and why?
2) To what extent do you believe bias exists in the media and in what ways?

5 The role and impact of the mass media

This section explores, from a variety of angles, the impact the mass media has on society, the political system and individual identities. It looks at:

- asylum seekers
- *Big Brother* and reality TV
- war with Iraq
- the body, gender and the media.

Asylum seekers

A typical media image of asylum seekers

ACTIVITY

1) Describe how this image presents a stereotypical message about asylum seekers.
2) Assess the role the media can play as a campaigning tool for groups wishing to promote the cause of asylum seekers.
3) In your opinion, to what extent does the mass media act responsibly with regard to the issue of asylum, immigration and the rights of asylum seekers?

The right to asylum (protection) is written in Article 14 of the **Universal Declaration of Human Rights**: 'Everyone has the right to seek and to enjoy in other countries asylum from persecution.'

In 2002, the UK had about 100,000 applications for asylum. About 40% of these will be granted and that usually leads to a temporary permit to live and work in the UK. Much of the debate about asylum seekers has been over what to do with the people claiming asylum whilst their claim is being processed rather than the causes of people seeking asylum. Also the mass media coverage tends to focus on illegal asylum rather than emphasising the majority of legitimate asylum seekers. Many people argue that asylum seekers are scapegoats presented to us by the media as the cause of unemployment, high crime, and even terrorism.

Big Brother and reality TV

An unmistakable image for *Big Brother* fans

The phenomena of reality TV exaggerates the extent to which the media influence us. There is no doubt that since the growth (worldwide) of *Big Brother* communication between television and audience has changed irreversibly. The series was watched by millions who voted weekly using electronic systems and who grew intimate with people (not characters) they had never met but felt they knew.

War with Iraq

During the 21 days of war with Iraq, *The Daily Mirror*, *The Sun* and *The Mail* had on average seven pages of news and pictures on the war every day. Most of these were the front and first five to eight pages. The broadsheets were the same. There can be no clearer example of saturation. The television news programmes all had headlines and special features on the war. Many channels had extra programmes, 'updates on the war'. The radio was the same. We were saturated and most of us watched the war in peak time, live in our living rooms. We do not believe all that we read, see and hear, but if we see, hear and read little else, the agenda is limited in terms of what else we consider and discuss.

Among the tabloids, *The Mirror* consistently opposed the war, yet the other tabloids supported it. There was some balance in coverage in terms of view, at least. However, the issue dominated the media, the agenda was set where the vast majority of outlets were in favour of the war.

Iraqis carry an injured employee after the Al-Salhiya telecommunications centre was hit by a missile during the war with Iraq. The missile landed as journalists were being escorted on a guided tour by the Baghdad information ministry. It indicates the central role played by the media during the war. March 2003

The body, gender and the media

What does the front cover of this popular women's magazine suggest the priorities of the women readers are?

Recent debate (covered in the media) has focused on representations of female (and male) bodies and the extent to which they perpetuate and create stereotypical representations. Also debated is the question of how far the mass media can and should be encouraged to be more realistic and responsible in their representations of body image.

ACTIVITY

According to the article below, how does the mass media influence female gender identity?

Skinny models 'send unhealthy message'

Eating disorder warning as BMA urges media 'realism'

British doctors yesterday called on the media to use female models with more realistically proportioned bodies instead of 'abnormally thin' women who contributed to the rise in the numbers of people suffering from eating disorders.

A report by the British Medical Association (BMA) claimed that the promotion of rake-thin models such as Kate Moss and Jodie Kidd was creating a distorted body image, which young women tried to imitate. It suggested that the media could trigger and perpetuate the disease.

'Female models are becoming thinner at a time when women are becoming heavier, and the gap between the ideal body shape and reality is wider than ever,' said the report. 'There is a need for a more realistic body shape to be shown on television and in fashion magazines.'

The report, which says young women look at thin models and see themselves as fat in comparison, calls on broadcasters and magazine publishers to use a more realistic range of body images. It also suggests society should put more emphasis on better eating and health to increase awareness about the impact of poor nutrition and dieting on young women.

At a conference to launch 'Eating disorders, body image and the media', Vivienne Nathanson of the BMA said: 'Let's see many different sizes and shapes reflected in the images of women we see in the different types of media. Let's play up the fact that it is not shape that matters. It is health that matters.'

The report is published just weeks before Britain hosts a 'thin summit' on 21 June to tackle the issue of the media and body image. An estimated 7 million women and 1 million men in Britain suffer from eating disorders. Anorexia affects up to 2% of British women aged between 15–30, and between six and ten of every 100 patients die as a result of their illness.

The report concludes: 'The media can boost self-esteem where it is providing examples of a variety of body shapes, roles and routes of achievement for young men and women. However, it often tends to portray a limited number of body shapes and messages linking external appearance with success.'

After compiling two years' research, the BMA found that young women are now dieting at an increasingly earlier age and that this is an important precipitant factor in the development of eating disorders. The report points out that eating disorders are a mostly western phenomenon and that fewer Asian and black women apparently suffer from them. It says that in young men, perceived body image is 'a crucial factor in the onset of the illness'.

The report adds: 'Advertising, in particular, may influence young people's perception of fashion and beauty and attitudes towards food. Young women may compare themselves to extremely thin models, working in the fashion industry or advertising products, and perceive themselves as fat in comparison, rather than healthy and attractive.'

In 1998, a survey by the Bread for Life campaign, cited by the Eating Disorders Association, showed that 89% of women between 18–24 wanted more 'average sized' models used in magazines.

Yesterday, however, the London-based Premier agency, which represents Naomi Campbell and Claudia Schiffer, said women who bought fashion magazines featuring thin models were as much to blame as their editors and the advertisers who used them. Agencies, advertisers and magazines were only responding to consumer demand.

'Advertisers, magazines and agencies supply the image that consumers want to see,' said a spokesman. 'Statistics have repeatedly shown that if you stick a beautiful skinny girl on the cover of a magazine, you sell more copies.

'Agencies would say that we supply the women the advertisers, our clients, want. The clients would say that they are selling a product and responding to consumer demand. At the end of the day, it is a business and the fact is that these models sell the products.'

Audrey Gillan, © *The Guardian*, **31 May 2000**

---

1) Outline the three models of media ownership.
2) Outline the three models of media effects.
3) With reference to examples, define and explain stereotyping in the media.
4) How does ownership and control of the media affect its content, if at all? Explain your answer.
5) Define and explain 'pluralism' in a media context.

Exam questions

You must answer Question 1 and either Question 2 or 3.

1) Read **Sources A, B, C** and **D** and answer the questions which follow.

Source A

Westridingshire County Council is a Local Education Authority with the legal responsibility for providing state education for all 15–16-year-old children in its area. Westridingshire is largely rural although the southeast of the county is urbanised. Half of the population of Westridingshire is concentrated in this urban area with the rest much more thinly scattered across the rural part of the county. The urban section has a declining industrial base which has resulted in greater poverty and unemployment than elsewhere in the county.

As part of its periodic review of education provision, the County Council has identified three primary/junior schools in rural areas that have very few pupils and which are not cost-effective to keep open. Council officials have suggested that there is a case for the closure of these three schools.

In response to this possibility, parents, school governors and others have formed the 'Save our Rural Schools Campaign Group' with the aim of keeping these three schools open.

Source B

Survey of pupil costs by type of school in Westridingshire County Council

School type	Number of pupils	Cost per pupil
All primary/junior	215 (average)	£1800
Urban area primary/junior	320 (average)	£1500
Threatened rural primary/junior	17 (average)	£8000

Source C

Councillor says 'No choice but to close rural schools'

County Councillor Smith, who represents one of the urban communities in Westridingshire, has said that there is no choice but to close three tiny rural schools. He commented that 'My ward has high unemployment, few job opportunities and a high level of material deprivation. Education is vital to the future of areas like this.

'We have nothing against the rural communities but the money currently being spent on schools "out in the sticks" providing education for a very few pupils could be spent on schools in deprived areas like ours. At present, pupils and families in these rural schools are receiving virtually private-school type education at our expense.'

Source D

The National Council for the Support of Rural Communities

This organisation has been campaigning for government to accept its policies for small rural communities. The main points include:

- an acceptance that providing small communities with a similar level of public services involves greater cost
- a recognition that many essential services in rural areas – including transport, banks, post offices – are not provided at the same level as in urban areas
- an understanding that the needs of rural communities are different from, but just as important as, the needs of other areas
- central and local government should recognise that when a specific service is withdrawn, this has a further effect on the whole community, often leading to the withdrawal or reduction of other services
- ways should be found to integrate service provision, for example, through using school premises for the delivery of other public services such as welfare, social services, day-care, and so on.

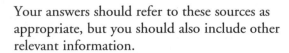

Your answers should refer to these sources as appropriate, but you should also include other relevant information.

(a) Identify **two** reasons which could be given in favour of keeping open the threatened primary/junior schools in Westridingshire.
(4 marks)

(b) Discuss and evaluate the ways in which the 'Save our Rural Schools Campaign Group' (**Source A**) could create positive media attention for its aims. (10 marks)

(c) Identify the possible outcomes to the issue identified in the sources and evaluate how far it might be possible to reach a solution that is satisfactory to all concerned. (16 marks)

AQA, 25 January 2001

2) (a) Examine the role of socialisation in the creation of a person's identity. (10 marks)

(b) Assess to what extent the attitudes and behaviour of citizens are determined by the mass media. (20 marks)

AQA, 11 June 2002

3) (a) Examine the ways in which the mass media may stereotype and label some groups of people. (10 marks)

(b) Assess **two** different models of the influence of the mass media over the attitudes of citizens. (20 marks)

AQA, 18 June 2001

CHAPTER 8

Citizen Inequality, Life-chances, Social Exclusion and the Underclass

In this chapter you will explore life-chances and inequality including:

- issues of health, education and employment associated with social class, ethnicity and gender inequalities
- the impact of some anti-discrimination policies designed to tackle social inequality
- the causes and consequences of poverty in relation to its impact on individuals, families and society
- the debate about the nature and existence of an underclass in modern UK society.

This chapter is broken into seven sections

Key terms

Discrimination – deliberate or unintentional unequal treatment of an individual as a consequence of their racial, ethnic, social, physical, economic or national identity

Equal opportunities – making sure the chance to take a full and active part in social, legal, political and economic aspects of society is dispersed evenly

Poverty – involves relative and absolute definitions. Relative reflects a lack of resources to enjoy a normal standard of living – that which is expected as normal by the society you live in. Absolute – a lack of resources to clothe, feed, provide shelter and basic healthcare

Social exclusion – being isolated and unable to take a full part in normal social, economic and political life as a consequence of discrimination, inability or ignorance

Underclass – a group in society consistently isolated for a variety of reasons from taking an active part in social, legal, political and economic processes in society to the extent a unique culture (often hostile) exists among this group distinct from mainstream society

1 Citizenship, life-chances and inequality

This section explores how life-chances are affected by social status and looks at:

- what is social exclusion?
- what is wrong with social inequality? Should we care?
- social inequality: a general picture
- employment trends, wealth inequality and social exclusion
- low pay and insecure employment.

What is social exclusion?

The government research body, the Social Exclusion Unit, uses the following definition for social exclusion:

Social exclusion is a shorthand label for what can happen when individuals or areas suffer from a combination of linked problems, such as unemployment, poor skills, low incomes, poor housing, high crime environments, bad health and family breakdown.

Exploring the area of social exclusion involves considering aspects of:

- health
- poverty
- education
- employment trends
- geographical location
- age
- gender
- social class
- ethnic group
- societal discrimination in these social groups.

Leon Dash as a reporter on the *Washington Post* in the USA carried out a long-term study into the life of a black American called Rosa Lee and her friends and family. Dash gives a detailed account of life and its anguishes for Rosa, graphically describing the horrors and hardships of life on a low income. He argues a case for an identifiable if complex group, which can be called an underclass.

Although his study directly refers to American society, Dash sees clear relevance to the UK. In his Pulitzer prize-winning book, *Rosa Lee*, he gives an account of the difficulties faced by policy makers in tackling social exclusion and the difficulties of Rosa Lee and her family and friends.

Viable solutions to poverty will never be simple. As Rosa Lee's story shows, immense difficulties await any effort to bring an end to poverty, illiteracy, drug abuse, and criminal activity. In the poorest neighbourhoods, these problems are woven together so tightly that there's no way to separate the individual threads, especially in those communities overwhelmed by drug abuse. Reforming welfare doesn't stop drug trafficking; better policing doesn't end illiteracy; providing job training doesn't prevent a young man or woman stealing. But complex does not mean intractable.

Dash, L (1999) *Rosa Lee*, **Profile Books, p254**

Dash ends on a more positive point. The approaches to social exclusion are complex and involve all areas of society from government to individuals, businesses to **charities**. There must be ways to address the unacceptable levels of social exclusion. However, Dash makes the point that measures to tackle social exclusion have too often ignored the importance of the viewpoints of the individuals and communities they are designed to address.

What is wrong with social inequality? Should we care?

Will Hutton (2000), by asking the question 'should we care?', explores the problem of neglecting to tackle persistent income inequality on the whole of society.

Even after five years of economic growth averaging at about 3% and a fall in unemployment to 1.3 million, some 2.5 million people over 50 (but still of working age) in Britain sit idle or are economically inactive. A fifth of British households have nobody at work; in the river valleys of the old industrial conurbations like Strathclyde, Merseyside and Tyneside, this proportion rises to 30% … Inequality not only divides our cities and undermines our neighbourhoods, it … pollutes our minds and sensibilities with an inability to empathise with the circumstances and conditions of our poorer neighbours.

Hutton, W in Carpenter, A *et al* (2000) *What If …? Fifteen Visions for Change for Britain's Inner Cities*, **Community Links**

Once the gap grows too large between the rich and poor, there is no basis for social cohesion and community with groups outside our own income and lifestyle. Society then becomes ever more fragmented and divisive and we all suffer. Hutton believes we are close to that stage now.

ACTIVITY

1) How do you account for the fact identified by Hutton that 2.5 million people over 50 are economically inactive when the overall unemployment rate is 1.3 million?

2) What was likely to be the main employment type in the 'river valleys of the old industrial conurbations'?

3) Attempt to summarise in your own words what Hutton means in his last sentence of the quotation above.

WEB ACTION

Go to **www.jrf.org.uk/knowledge/findings/ socialpolicy/930.asp**. Click on the 'here' and you will access a summary of the survey details and the various **indicators** they use to measure poverty and social exclusion.

ACTIVITY

1) The JRF research uses a variety of indicators to test social exclusion. These indicators are called 'socially perceived necessities'. How far do you agree that all of these 'necessities' are vital or essential? (See below for some of the necessities.)

2) What is your assessment of the extent and scale of poverty in Britain given the data on the web pages?

Social inequality: a general picture

The Joseph Rowntree Foundation have, for over 100 years, been researching the extent and impact of poverty. They have recently begun analysis of the wider aspect of social exclusion. Recent research explores familiar themes of poverty and low income such as:

- inadequate housing, e.g. inadequate heating and over-crowding
- mortgage arrears
- lack of household insurance
- participation in civic activities, e.g. using libraries, buses and public services
- participation in activities considered normal to the majority of society, e.g. choice of clothing, holidays, having a bank account.

A recent report by the Joseph Rowntree Foundation suggests poverty rates are highest among:

- women
- children
- adults living in one-person households including pensioners
- large families
- families with a child under 11
- young people, those who left school at age 16 or under
- households with no paid worker
- separated divorced households
- lone parent households
- local authority and housing association tenants
- households dependent on income support.

Poverty and Social Exclusion in Britain, **Joseph Rowntree Foundation (2000), p69**

Employment trends, wealth inequality and social exclusion

Many economists and social scientists have referred to the drift towards low pay and temporary part-time employment conditions for an increasing proportion of the workforce (e.g. Hutton (1997), Field (1995)). Such trends have particularly affected women and people from minority ethnic groups and people working in the older heavy manufacturing industries. The conditions of employment are inevitably crucial to the ability of individuals to take a full part in social life for a number of reasons.

Employment and social activities

In industrialised societies, work is a key aspect of social integration. Many social activities revolve around the workplace and have developed as a result of working life – trade unions, workers societies and social clubs. Employers have long recognised the benefits to a workforce of encouraging a social dimension to the company or factory. Fitness clubs and social outings are examples of more recent times. The Fiat car manufacturer in Italy or Rolls Royce in Britain encourage a workforce to socialise outside working hours by providing sporting and social facilities for the workers. These practices stretch back to the early days of motor manufacture but are still evident in many organisations. Many of the older employers or industries, such as coal mining and mill working, saw whole communities established as a response to employment in the relevant field. A strong sense of identity and community belonging stems from employment.

Economic power and resources

There is a direct relationship between economic power/ resources and the ability to engage fully in a community and to influence it and make choices within it. Participation is not just an issue of being able to afford to buy your own home, for example, or luxury items. Being fully engaged in the social community requires economic power to influence decision-makers and to effectively communicate with others. If an individual is able to afford to buy their own computer and to connect to the Internet, then the potential for social engagement and influence is greatly enhanced. However, there are other dimensions to power such as educational and cultural capital – the knowledge to use the computer or the ability to write copy that newspaper editors will read and publish.

Given the central and fundamental relationship between work, social life and integration, the dramatic transformation in patterns of employment since the 1980s and 1990s onwards have a huge influence upon the degree of social participation.

Low pay and insecure employment

- Nearly 2 million people were paid at an hourly rate of less than £3.65 (half male average earnings) in spring 1998. 10% of all employees are paid less than this amount, three-quarters of them being women.
- The sector with by far the greatest proportion of low-paid workers is hotels, catering and distribution, with 22% paid less than £3.65 an hour in 1998. Other services have the highest proportion, at 11%.
- Part-timers are particularly vulnerable to low pay: 29% of part-timers are in low paid work, compared to 5% of full-time workers.
- Low pay is very unevenly distributed across different ethnic groups. Over 25% of Bangladeshis and Pakistanis who have paid work are low paid, 15% of Indians, 11% of blacks and 10% of whites.

- Vulnerability to low pay also varies between regions of the UK. The north of England has the lowest rates of pay, with almost 20% in parts of Yorkshire and Humberside having hourly wages below half the national average male rate. The areas with the lowest proportions of low-paid workers are Strathclyde and Central Clyde side, London and the South East.
- Workers in small firms are considerably more likely to be low paid than workers in establishments of 50 or more workers: 22% of workers aged 25 and above in establishments of ten or fewer employees are low paid, compared with just 5% in the largest organisations.
- Temporary employment has grown significantly in the last five years, up 0.5 million from 1.2 million in 1992 to 1.7 million in 1997. In the summer of 1997, temporary employment made up 7% of all employment for men, and 9% of all employment for women.
- 75% of the jobs that unemployed people get after leaving the claimant count (the total number of people claiming benefit) are temporary, part-time, self-employed, or much less skilled than the jobs they have previously held.

Adapted from *Monitoring Poverty and Social Exclusion,* **Joseph Rowntree Foundation (1998)**

Low pay, below minimum wage (£3.65 per hour in 1998).

The over 25 age group are the more mature earners and the group most likely to have higher demands on household incomes, e.g. mortgages and dependent children.

80% of over 25s on low income are women.

The area of the economy with the highest rates of low pay is the catering, hotel and distribution area. It is this sector where most temporary and insecure employment exists. It is also this area where women make up the highest proportion of workers.

Adapted from *Monitoring Poverty and Social Exclusion,* **Joseph Rowntree Foundation (1998)**

1) Explain how the information above makes women more vulnerable than men from low paid and insecure work among the over 25s.
2) 'Low pay at an age when there are high demands on household income (among over 25s) can be described as a double-edged sword.' Explain this statement in relation to low pay and the risk of poverty.

1) How might employers encourage social activity outside the workplace?
2) Explain what is meant by insecure employment.
3) How might economic power enhance or restrict a citizen's ability to participate in society?
4) Why should we care about social inequality?

2 Poverty and social exclusion

This section explores poverty and how it causes social exclusion and looks at:

- effects of poverty
- the problem of defining and measuring poverty.

The term 'poverty' is used in everyday language but not always fully understood. Much dispute exists between definitions of poverty, its measurement, causes, effects and what should be done about it.

The United Nations defines poverty as:

a condition characterised by severe deprivation of basic human needs, including food, safe drinking water, sanitation facilities, health, shelter, education and information. It depends not only on income but access to services.

The Copenhagen UN Summit on Social Development (1995), p57

Effects of poverty

No one individual or group is affected by poverty in the same way. Exploring the effects of poverty often involves examining specific experiences of individuals and families affected by it. However, there are general consequences of the problem that apply to broad social groups.

The Child Poverty Action Group gives some insight into the impact poverty can have on children. Children from households in lower socio-economic groups (e.g. unskilled) have double the death rates of those in higher socio-economic groups (e.g. professionals). Children from parents of unskilled background are more likely to die from accidents and consult their GPs about serious injuries than those from professional backgrounds. Growing up in poverty leads to:

- poorer attendance records at school due to illness and truancy
- a lower literacy and numeracy record
- poorer attendance in education after 16
- greater likelihood of lower wages in later life
- higher rates of unemployment
- greater likelihood of experiencing prison
- greater likelihood of lone parenthood.

Adapted from the Child Poverty Action Group, www.cpag.org.uk

ACTIVITY

1) Using the material above, explore some of the causes and consequences of poverty.
2) What explanations can you give for the consequences of poverty?

WEB ACTION

Find **www.cpag.org.uk** and explore their latest research issues and campaigning literature.

A specific illustration of the effects of poverty comes from Rebecca Dittman's account of her experiences during a Radio 4 broadcast exploring poverty (3 August 2002). The case study below gives insight into the problems caused by poverty and introduces the problem of how poverty is to be measured.

CASE STUDY: Rebecca Dittman

The £53.00 that I was receiving, did not cover all of my costs for housing benefit and for council tax benefit. Having said that, I was then faced with having to pay all of my utility bills, electricity, gas, telephone, etc., from that, and then after those bills had been paid, you then were left with a very small amount to be able to buy food and whatever was left had to go towards all those essentials that we need to keep spirit and body together.

Rebecca Dittman was a single person claiming benefit because she was unemployed. Her benefit was £53.95 per week.

ACTIVITY

1) Using the list of essential outgoings below, estimate the cost of each and try to balance the weekly budget of £53.95 that Rebecca received.

Essential outgoings, weekly	Estimated cost (£) weekly
Electricity	
Gas	
Telephone (landline, not mobile)	
Food (give specifics)	
Clothing (give specifics)	
Hygiene (give specifics)	
Travel/transport (public not private)	
Total costs	

2) Explain what Rebecca means by '... those essentials that we need to keep spirit and body together'. Such 'essentials' will depend on your definition of 'essential'. Draw up a list of what you consider to be additional essentials to the ones on the list above and cost each as you did above.

3) Add the costs of the two lists together and explain to what extent you agree or disagree that the income Rebecca received was enough to live on.

The problem of defining and measuring poverty

In the activity above you have been exploring the effects of poverty caused by low income. It is easy to argue that individuals on low incomes are excluded from taking a full part in society. However, the problem exposed by the activities above relates to the definition and measurement of poverty. What definition should we use when measuring poverty?

Social commentators have referred to two broad types of poverty: absolute and relative.

Absolute poverty

This is when an individual lacks the basic resources to maintain an adequate diet, accommodation and clothing, which leads to a deterioration in their health. For example, an individual sleeping on the streets will be cold and exposed to illness of many kinds. An individual with fewer than 2000–2500 calories per day may suffer from loss of weight and perhaps malnutrition. An individual without adequate clothing may be exposed to illnesses associated with cold, e.g. pneumonia.

Relative poverty

This is a type of poverty where an individual will possess the basics and so not necessarily have health risks. They would not have the means to take a full part in society through lack of resources, e.g. to fund travel or purchase of books and newspapers, etc.

Remind yourself of the 'added essential' you identified in the activity above. Here you were defining what is essential in a society such as Britain (affluent and industrially advanced). Items such as TV may be considered vital in order to play a full and active part in society. What else would you add? A computer?

The types of things considered essential to avoid poverty will vary from individual to individual. The problem lies with definition. This leads to problems when trying to measure how many people are considered to be in a state of poverty. The wider your list of essentials, the wider your definition of poverty and so your total number of people measured as 'in poverty' will be higher. The larger your group, the bigger the social problem.

Below is an example of two types of measuring technique. One uses half average income and the other uses a 'basket of goods' deemed essential.

Budget standards

Budget standards are baskets of goods and services which consist of:

- food items
- clothing items
- consumption of fuel
- leisure goods and services.

This basket of goods is priced and the total cost of the basket of goods then becomes a 'standard'.

The government uses this method to calculate the basic rate of benefits. This method was devised by Seebohm Rowntree at the turn of the century in his investigation into poverty in York. It was used by William Beveridge in 1948 as the **welfare state** developed. It is still used today by the government.

Half average earnings

Here the average earnings are measured and the benefit rate is measured according to half of this rate.

Households below average income 1998–9

There is no 'official' poverty line. Instead, a widely used definition of poverty is based on 50% of average income after housing costs, found in the report *Households Below Average Income: 1994–5–1998–9* (DSS (2000) Government Statistical Service, CDS, http//www.dwp.gov.uk/publications/dss/2000/hbai/index.htm). For other definitions of poverty the publication *Poverty: The Facts* by C Oppenheim and L Harker (Child Poverty Action Group, 1996) is a good starting point.

These are the latest official figures available and were published in July 2000.

- One in four (14.3 million) people in the UK were living in poverty in 1998–9 compared with under one in ten in 1979.
- Children are even more likely than any other group to be living in poverty – more than one in three (4.5 million) were living in poverty in 1998–9 compared with one in ten in 1979.

Different family types face different risks of falling into poverty.

- Over half of lone parents (62%) live in poverty.
- Couples with children account for the largest number of people in poverty (4.9 million).
- 25% of all family types in the UK live in poverty.

Income inequality is increasing.

- Average income increased by 12% between 1994–5 and 1998–9.
- The highest proportion of children living in poverty (35%) is in Wales.
- Of all of the regions, London has the greatest income inequality.
- 30% of children live in families without a full-time worker.
- Women and children are more likely than men to experience persistent low incomes.

Note: These figures exclude homeless people and those living in institutions, such as hospitals, nursing homes, residential care homes and prisons. It can be argued that two-thirds, rather than half, the average income is a truer measure of poverty.

The Child Poverty Action Group

In the tables below is data recorded by the Child Poverty Action Group using the half average income measure. Notice the differences in the weekly income (£) compared to the rate received by Rebecca in the activity on p 176 (£53.95).

THE POVERTY LINE UK (50% MEAN INCOME) FEB 2000 PRICES AFTER HOUSING COSTS	
	1999–2000
Single adult	£83
Couple with no children	£151
Couple with three children (aged 3, 8 and 11)	£252
All family types	£151

NUMBER OF PEOPLE AND CHILDREN LIVING IN POVERTY IN THE UK (INCLUDING SELF-EMPLOYED)

	People			Children		
	Total population (millions)	Number in poverty (millions)	% of total population	Total population (millions)	Number in poverty (millions)	% of total population
1979	54.0	5.0	9	13.8	1.4	10
1994–5	55.8	13.3	24	12.7	4.0	31
1999–2000	56.6	14.3	25	12.8	4.5	35

Note: the figures for people include children

THE RISK AND NUMBERS IN POVERTY BY FAMILY TYPE (INCLUDING SELF-EMPLOYED)

	% of group in poverty*			No in poverty			% of total**
	1979	1994–5	1999–2000	1979	1994–5	1999–2000	
Pensioner couples	21	23	25	1020	1219	1350	9
Single pensioners	12	32	37	520	1376	1554	11
Couples with children	8	23	24	2220	4784	4872	34
Couples without children	5	12	12	490	1380	1464	10
Single with children	10	55	62	460	2310	2914	20
Single without children	7	23	22	530	2231	2718	15

* the proportion of each group on poverty, e.g. 24% of couples with children living in poverty 1998–9

**groups as a proportion of a total population living in poverty, e.g. couples with children account for 34% of the total population living in poverty

Department of Social Security, Households below average income 1994–2000, Corporate document services, 2001

In response to accusations that the benefit level is set too low, Malcolm Wicks, the Government Minister, offers the following argument on a Radio 4 programme.

Mr Wicks explained the government had to work within the budget available to them: 'Almost 30% of what we spend on everything publicly has to take its priority alongside our need to build up the health service and schools.'

He stressed the importance of maintaining an incentive to work: 'We have to set benefit rates which are reasonable but do not become a disincentive to work. We are in the business not just of making work possible but making work pay.'

Radio 4's *Inside Money* **broadcast on 3 August 2002**

ACTIVITY

1) Which formula do you consider the most accurate as a measure of poverty: the basket of goods or half average income?
2) Explain what Malcolm Wicks means by 'making work pay'.
3) 'There is no official poverty line.' Why do you think this is the case?
4) From the tables above, summarise the trends in poverty.

1) Define 'absolute' and 'relative' poverty.
2) Describe some of the effects of poverty.
3) Explain two ways of measuring the extent of poverty in society.

3 Theoretical approaches to the causes of poverty

This section explores the theories associated with poverty and its causes and looks at:

- individual and cultural explanations – the **New Right**
- structural explanations – social democratic approach
- the underclass.

Individual and cultural explanations – the New Right

The main theory associated with this approach to poverty comes from the New Right. The New Right prefer the term 'low income' to poverty. They feel the term 'poverty' no longer applies to anyone in the absolute sense in a modern advanced UK society.

Lifestyle causes

The causes of poverty from this perspective focus upon a series of largely behavioural aspects. The New Right emphasise individual lifestyles as a possible cause, even a major cause of poverty. For example, no individual on a low income is forced to smoke. The fact that a larger proportion of individuals on a low income smoke and have worse health as a consequence is no excuse for an expensive habit causing limited resources to be spent inappropriately. Poverty and low income can in part be explained by individual behaviour. Therein lies the solution to poverty – spending limited resources more carefully, e.g. not buying cigarettes.

Welfare dependency and the dependency culture – the 'nanny state'

Other New Right theories exploring the causes of poverty focus attention on the welfare state. The system of benefits allows individuals to neglect their own responsibility to seek employment, health and general welfare, and instead allow a 'nanny state' to support and provide for them. The result of this 'nanny state' is a lack of enterprise and motivation to solve problems of low income. There are hints at this New Right perspective from the comments of Malcolm Wicks above. He suggests that welfare benefits should not be at a level which encourages people to stay away from work or, on the other hand, makes the attraction of seeking paid employment even if it is low paid seem less worthwhile.

The New Right argue that the welfare state over the years has caused a series of cultural changes leading to poverty/low income. One such cultural change is the loss of family support and responsibility in a number of matters including support for low income and economic hardship. The New Right argue that the welfare state is seen as the first port of call for financial support when it should be families who take primary responsibility to support those in need of financial support. This does not prove to be possible for all in society since not everyone has family members to call upon. However, the majority do and should call upon family members first. The New Right argue that the welfare state provision should take into consideration all available support before deeming someone worthy of receiving state benefit support.

Loss of morality

The fabric of society and its basis of family stability support has been undermined by the welfare state. The state allows, even encourages, divorce and family separation when we should be emphasising the moral responsibility of marriage and avoiding the negative impact of family breakdown. The result of this trend in family breakdown has been to undermine the family and generate a culture of dependence, not on the family as it should be, but on the welfare state. As a result, more poverty is caused by the welfare system. For example, a large proportion of single parents feature in low-income statistics. By encouraging marriage, contraception and stronger restraint in sexual activity, the social problem of poverty can be challenged through moral practice and family structures. The liberalisation of society has caused much of what we refer to as poverty and the welfare system is almost encouraging this.

Structural explanations – social democratic approach

In contrast to the New Right approach, the social democratic left suggest poverty results from the capitalist system and its unfair distribution of power and wealth.

Life-chances are restricted for many to the extent that large sections of society are at greater risk of poverty due to low paid, insecure jobs. Living on low wages means you are less able to stand the financial as well as social/psychological effects of unemployment and are more likely to suffer if made redundant. As a result, poverty is not so much caused by the welfare state or any change in society's values or individual's behaviour patterns but by economic insecurity.

The growth in poverty over the last five years is caused by increasing levels of insecurity in employment. Many from this perspective argue that welfare benefits should be much higher in order to avoid a poverty trap where low income breeds low income, a cycle that is very difficult to break. For example, if you are studying towards AS and A2 level examinations, it may be necessary for you to work more hours than is academically healthy in order to support your low income family. As a result, you are more at risk of failing the exams and so having fewer life-chances at 18. This would result in less opportunity to get higher paid and more secure employment. A cycle begins that leaves you at greater risk of poverty.

A cycle of poverty/depravation illustrated

Low income = more pressure to work more hours = less time for homework = may result in lower exam grades = lower income and less secure employment = greater risk of redundancy = less chance to save and invest = less choice of place to live = having to live in a house/region that is less desirable as the more affluent move away from your region = fewer jobs and services = longer periods of unemployment = further financial pressure = more psychological pressure = perhaps more pressure on relationships = greater risk of separation = and so on goes the cycle.

The social democratic left do not fully reject the points about individual responsibility in order to avoid poverty. They argue that poverty is a cycle that is very difficult to break and is largely caused not by individuals or the welfare system but by the insecurities of the economy (largely jobs). The focus for social policy when challenging poverty is to break the cycle through increased benefit payments but also measures such as:

- the minimum wage
- training programmes
- sound careers advice
- urban renewal programmes.

According to this model, the state has a vital role to play.

?
1) **Discuss the argument that the solution to poverty lies with the individual, not the state.**
2) **Evaluate the role of the family as a sound provision for individual welfare.**

The underclass

In terms of social exclusion, the concept of underclass is explored by many theorists. The argument suggests that a section of society is emerging who are consistently isolated and ever more restricted in their life-chances. They suffer poverty and low income, long-term unemployment,

higher rates of crime, worse housing and worse health than any other group in society, creating an underclass. 'Underclass' refers to a group in society who have developed a culture distinct from mainstream society.

Some theorists and the New Right argue that the underclass are developing a distinct behaviour pattern – culture. The culture and associated behaviour involves some or all of the following:

- a disregard for authority in the normal sense, e.g. hostility towards the police force, rejection of school and the school rules
- a tendency towards criminal behaviour, in particular, street crime and robbery
- reliance on state benefit system
- greater likelihood of being a single parent household, through more separation and divorce
- low income
- low qualifications and skill levels
- greater long-term unemployment
- worse health and higher likelihood of health threatening behaviour, e.g. smoking and alcohol misuse.

The concept of an underclass is referred to by many different theorists but often they are referring to a different thing. For example, the New Right see a culture emerging on 'the council estates of Britain' of community decay, crime and welfare dependence. The culture comprises many of the components listed above.

In contrast, the social democratic left refer to a group in society who have been and continue to be marginalized in such a systematic way that they are far less able to take a full part in society than any other group. Some theorists such as Frank Field (1995) refer to groups such as lone parents, the elderly in state care, the long-term unemployed and the disabled, as groups consistently and systematically marginalized. They could be referred to as an underclass, unified by their social isolation and not necessarily because of their cultural attitudes.

Others such as Rex and Thomlinson (1979) refer to minority ethnic groups as being specifically and systematically isolated from taking a full part in society through racism and discrimination. There are consistently higher numbers of minority ethnic groups among the long-term unemployed, households on low income, and people with mental health problems associated with social problems. As a result, a group systematically marginalized by society may be developing an isolated identity – perhaps closely associated with minority ethnic groups, especially Afro-Caribbean communities.

Feminists point to the issue of women making up nearly 99% of single parents and a very high proportion of the low-income households are headed by women. The majority of pensioner poverty is experienced by women and health issues of women are not prioritised by the health service. These factors place women as a group in higher risk of poverty and the group most likely to constitute an underclass.

When many commentators refer to marginalization not all of them agree on the concept of underclass. Those who use the term are often referring to different groups. Little agreement exists over what the cultural/behavioural norms and values of this so-called underclass are. For example, not all individuals from deprived backgrounds turn to crime or reject school. Also, many mainstream behaviour patterns could be associated with the rejection of school rules or street crime and other types of crime.

?
1) Define 'underclass'.
2) Evaluate the claim that a distinct group is emerging in society where mainstream values and norms are rejected and replaced with a distinct pattern of behaviour we can associate with an 'underclass'.
3) 'When many refer to an underclass few agree on the nature and extent of it.' Discuss.
4) Identify and outline two models explaining the causes of poverty.
5) To what extent do researchers agree on the existence, definition and properties of the underclass concept? Explain your answer.

4 Literacy and education performance according to age, ethnicity and gender

This section explores the relationship between educational performance and its impact on life-chances according to age, ethnicity and gender groups. It looks at:

■ examination achievement by gender and ethnic group
■ examination achievement and subject choice by gender group
■ adult literacy
■ reasons for differences in achievement in the education system
■ education **action zones**.

Examination achievement by gender and ethnic group

Hayton (1999) offers an exceptionally thorough and readable array of aspects relating education to social exclusion.

Among educationalists the term 'social exclusion' has often been linked to other terms – disaffection and non participation … Different labels are used to describe those groups of people who are 'either impeded in gaining access to, or are unable to maintain themselves within, mainstream education and training' (Education and Employment Committee, 1998) or, more generally, who are 'detached from the organisations and communities of which the society is composed and from the rights and obligations that they embody.

Room (1995) in Hayton, A (1999) *The Future of Education from 14+: Tackling Disaffection and Social Exclusion Educational Perspectives and Policies*, **Kogan Page, pp11–12**

EXAMINATION ACHIEVEMENTS OF PUPILS IN SCHOOLS BY GENDER AND ETHNIC ORIGIN IN ENGLAND AND WALES, 1998 (%)				
	2 or more	5+ A*–C	4 A*–C	None graded
Males				
White	–	43	25	7
Black	–	23	24	7
Indian	–	52	23	2
Pakistani/ Bangladeshi		29	29	6
Others*	–	37	28	11
All males	26	42	25	7
Females				
White	–	51	25	6
Black	–	35	42	7
Indian	–	55	28	3
Pakistani/ Bangladeshi	–	32	45	6
Others	–	52	31	3
All females	33	51	26	6

*'others' includes those who did not state their ethnic origin

There has been an overall increase in the number of pupils gaining two or more GCE A levels and those achieving A*–C in five or more GCSEs. Girls have done as well or out-performed boys at GCSE level and A level since 1999. The ethnic group Indian has the highest performance at

GCSE. At A Level in 1998, 36% of Indian pupils achieved two or more A levels compared with 29% of white pupils.

Adapted from *Social Trends,* **2000**

1) What variations exist between ethnic groups and their achievement in education?
2) How do the variations in ethnic group also vary according to gender?

Examination achievement and subject choice by gender group

Although girls do out-perform boys at all levels and in all subjects (except physics), there is a noticeable gender issue for choice of subject particularly at A level. The social sciences and humanities subjects tend to be favoured by females as opposed to males preferring the natural sciences with the notable exception of biology.

AS LEVEL GRADES BY GENDER AND SUBJECT, AUGUST 2003

Subject	Gender	Number sat	% for each grade					
			A	B	C	D	E	U
Art and design	Male	18,587	16.8	16.8	20.6	19.0	14.1	12.7
	Female	36,848	24.9	21.6	21.7	16.1	9.4	6.3
	Both	55,435	22.2	20.0	21.3	17.1	10.9	8.5
Biology	Male	26,548	16.0	15.1	16.6	16.8	15.4	20.1
	Female	41,297	18.5	16.8	17.1	16.4	14.1	17.1
	Both	67,845	17.5	16.2	16.9	16.5	14.6	18.3
Business studies	Male	24,975	10.9	16.2	21.2	21.7	16.4	13.6
	Female	18,916	13.8	16.9	21.2	20.0	15.3	12.8
	Both	43,891	12.2	16.5	21.1	21.0	16.0	13.2
Chemistry	Male	23,003	21.2	17.2	17.1	15.9	12.8	15.8
	Female	23,583	23.3	18.9	17.6	15.4	11.7	13.1
	Both	46,586	22.3	18.0	17.3	15.7	12.3	14.4
Computing	Male	30,319	7.5	11.6	17.9	21.0	19.4	22.6
	Female	12,589	6.5	11.5	19.9	22.5	20.1	20.3
	Both	42,908	7.2	11.6	18.2	21.5	19.6	21.9
Economics	Male	14,274	23.4	18.5	17.9	15.1	11.8	13.3
	Female	7060	24.5	20.4	18.4	14.5	11.0	11.2
	Both	21,334	23.8	19.1	18.0	15.0	11.5	12.6
English	Male	29,053	14.9	18.1	23.8	22.7	13.9	6.6
	Female	67,375	15.7	20.2	25.4	22.1	11.8	4.8
	Both	96,428	15.5	19.6	24.9	22.2	12.5	5.3
Exp arts/drama	Male	6100	10.1	18.7	27.1	22.5	13.4	8.2
	Female	16,016	13.4	25.2	29.5	19.8	8.7	3.4
	Both	22,116	12.5	23.4	28.8	20.6	10.0	4.7
French	Male	6739	27.5	20.3	18.4	14.8	10.3	8.7
	Female	14,924	25.3	19.4	19.4	15.7	11.3	8.9
	Both	21,663	26.0	19.7	19.0	15.5	11.0	8.8
Geography	Male	21,546	17.3	18.9	20.8	18.9	13.5	10.6
	Female	18,206	25.8	21.2	19.8	15.9	9.8	7.5
	Both	39,752	21.2	19.9	20.4	17.5	11.8	9.2
History	Male	23,694	16.8	21.6	23.5	19.3	11.2	7.6
	Female	26,332	20.6	23.3	22.8	16.6	9.8	6.9
	Both	50,026	18.8	22.5	23.1	17.9	10.5	7.2

Subject	Gender	Number sat	% for each grade					
			A	B	C	D	E	U
Mathematics	Male	40,467	25.5	14.2	13.9	12.7	11.6	22.1
	Female	26,745	28.1	16.9	15.2	12.8	10.4	16.6
	Both	67,212	26.5	15.3	14.5	12.6	11.2	19.9
Physics	Male	27,958	21.3	16.5	16.5	15.0	13.0	17.7
	Female	8963	27.8	19.0	17.6	14.0	11.0	10.6
	Both	36,921	22.8	17.2	16.7	14.8	12.5	16.0
Psychology	Male	20,308	8.4	13.1	18.1	18.9	17.3	24.2
	Female	50,748	16.5	17.7	19.3	17.3	13.7	15.5
	Both	71, 056	14.2	16.4	19.0	17.6	14.8	18.0
Sociology	Male	9576	11.7	15.8	19.2	18.8	15.8	18.7
	Female	27,557	18.4	18.5	19.3	17.2	13.2	13.4
	Both	37,133	16.7	17.8	19.3	17.5	13.9	14.8
All subjects	Male	471,137	15.6	16.4	19.4	18.4	14.4	15.8
	Female	559,782	18.9	19.2	20.8	17.6	12.2	11.3
	Both	1,030,919	17.4	17.9	20.2	17.9	13.3	13.3

Adapted from *The Guardian*, **14 August 2003**

ACTIVITY

1) Refer to the data above. Which subjects are favoured by females and which by males?
2) What broad trends exist between males and females in a) exam grades, and b) subject choice? Why might this be the case?
3) Explain some of the reasons for the gender differences in education achievement.

WEB ACTION

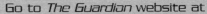

Go to *The Guardian* website at **www.guardian.co.uk** and click on 'education'. Scroll down the list and you will find AS results by gender. Click on this and the graphics give details on the results for 2003 by gender. You can do the same for A level [A2] results and GCSE. There is also an article on the gender differences in response to the results of 2003.

Adult literacy

LITERACY LEVELS OF ADULTS BY GENDER AND AGE IN GREAT BRITAIN, 1996 (%)						
	Males			Females		
	16–49	50–65	16–65	16–49	50–65	16–65
Level 1	15	31	20	22	40	27
Level 2	24	29	25	30	30	29
Level 3	33	28	31	31	24	30
Level 4–5	28	12	24	17	6	15

Level 1 is the lowest and Level 4–5 the highest ranking. Rankings based on the International Adult Literacy Survey

Adapted from *Social Trends*, **2000**

Adults with the lowest literacy or numeracy scores had long histories of it from their early schooling. This continued into employment, where they were often the most marginalized participants in the labour market. The Organisation for Economic Co-operation and Development (a group of the powerful advanced industrialised nations in the world) considers Level 3 to be the minimum level required to 'cope' with modern life and work.

ACTIVITY

1) What do you consider the likely difficulties experienced in the workplace of an individual of literacy Level 1 or 2? Consider the changing nature of necessary technical and inter-personal skills needed in modern working environments.

2) The government have set up various initiatives to tackle low levels of literacy among some adult groups. Identify and explain some of the difficulties adults might face in learning new and basic skills.

Reasons for differences in achievement in the education system

Theories offering explanations for the differences in achievement in the education system can be grouped into four broad areas. The theories can be applied in different ways to gender, ethnicity and social class.

Peer group association

Peer group is the circle of friends and people of your own age group. They apply pressure on you to conform (peer group pressure). Friends will have an impact on your learning and all students know that support from friends when studying is crucial. Support from friends to maintain focus and consistency in study is equally essential to achieving your maximum potential. Peer group pressure can have a positive and negative effect.

 Try to identify two positive and two negative effects of peer group influences on education experience/achievement.

Sub-cultures

A **sub-culture** is a group of people who break the norms of society through establishing a deviant or distinct set of values that differ from those of mainstream society (see Chapter 7).

Many anti-school sub-cultures exist in schools and communities. Associating with a negative anti-school sub-culture can be negative whether you know it or not. There are also sub-cultures where working hard is seen as 'uncool' but some are able to break the norm.

Consider the impact of friends and your peers and consider the types of groups at school and their approach to study. How did the anti-school groups perform in their GCSEs? Perhaps a reason for developing an anti-school sub-culture is a feeling that lessons are not relevant to real life. Can you think of other reasons? Consider the gender balance of anti-school sub-cultures. Was there a mix of male and female? Was there a racial or social class pattern?

Teacher attitudes

Many sociologists explore the relationship between teacher and pupil. Some argue that teachers have a general set of middle class values and backgrounds. This can lead to division between the teacher's values and those students associating with different norms and values.

It is suggested that teachers label students 'bright' or 'slow'. The labels or expectations placed upon the student by the teacher become a defining point in their relationship. Those labelled as 'bright' are likely to be understood and encouraged more by teachers, leaving those labelled otherwise outside the 'ideal pupil' image.

The middle class, largely white, teaching profession may be unintentionally marginalizing working class and minority ethnic groups and so perhaps having a negative impact on their education experience. The student may also be aware of the teacher's expectations and this may lead to them acting according to those expectations. This is referred to as a **self-fulfilling prophecy.**

In your experience, was there a language barrier between teacher and some students? The 'ideal pupil' is alleged to have a more middle class language code where words and phrases are more consistent with academic language. Any language code that is more 'streetwise' is said to be less effective in classrooms and in examinations. Working class students are suggested to use a more restricted, command like language, which is at odds with middle class elaborate codes of speech used by examiners and teachers.

Ethno-centric curriculum

Many sociologists argue that the education system tends to emphasise a white, male bias. The teachers are predominantly of this background and will find more difficulty relating to differing cultures and identities from their own. Consequently, those not of a white middle class background are considered to be at a disadvantage. The learning of history, for example, is said to be mainly about white, male, middle class activities.

ACTIVITY

In groups, explore your experiences to assess whether there is any truth in the argument that the curriculum is ethnocentric.

> 1) Do we live in a society where equal opportunity in education exists so that achievement is dependent upon ability and effort alone?
> 2) Apply each of the above four influences on learning and achievement to gender, social class and ethnic group categories. How far do they apply to each group consistently?
> 3) To what extent does ability alone determine a student's achievement in education?
> 4) Identify and explain three explanations for the variations in achievement by different social groups.

Parental/home background

The background a student belongs to influences the chances of success. Some parents are not able or willing to participate in the education of their dependents for reasons of knowledge, interest, language/culture and resources. Individuals may be disadvantaged if their parents do not get involved with their learning. For example, it is suggested that parent's evenings and school/parent associations are attended by middle class white parents more so than other groups. They are more likely to know how the system works and probably know teachers themselves. The suggestion here is that the students from middle class backgrounds are likely to have parents more able to involve themselves with the school and their dependent's learning.

Home background in terms of economic resources is vital. Learning is not cheap and many additional resources such as study guides, computers and materials all help with achievement. This costs money. Evidently, the resources of the home are significant. The home may be equipped with space and warmth to study, more so in some cases than others.

Other factors to consider

Where was your school in the league tables? Was it able to attract the 'best' teachers? Did your school have a specialist status?

All the above factors (as well as others such as ability) influence a student's chance of achievement. These factors influence some more than others in both positive and negative ways.

Education action zones

In 1998, the government introduced 25 education action zones (EAZs) in an effort to boost the achievement of pupils in disadvantaged areas in England. The number of EAZs has increased since then.

The EAZs comprise clusters of local schools in partnership with local businesses and other community groups. The idea of the zones is to give special funding and powers to boost educational achievement of the young people in the area. The EAZs have the power to:

- change the curriculum, the length and timetable of the school day
- pay for teachers and to appoint so called 'super teachers' (very experienced teachers who have moved into management but are encouraged out of promoted positions by offers of matched and higher pay for staying in the classroom).

A highly significant feature of EAZs is that one third of the money for the projects will be paid by industry and that schools are expected to team up with industry to deliver the action in the zones.

> What actions might the EAZs take to tackle truancy, low literacy and low achievement among the young people in the zone areas?

5 Health

This section explores the relationship between differences in health and social group and its impact on social exclusion/inclusion. It looks at:

- health and social class
- health and gender.

Health and social class

It is possible to identify trends linking varying levels of health to gender, ethnic and social class groups. Social inequalities in such areas will clearly have an impact upon one's ability to participate as citizens.

Baldock *et al* (1999) explores the relationships between social and economic position and ill health. They state that since the government's commissioned report *Black Report* (1980) and *The Health Divide* by Townsend, Davidson and Whitehead (1998), there has been clear evidence of a link between socio-economic circumstances and ill health. Baldock *et al* extend this evidence with more recent research.

People in unskilled occupations and their children are twice as likely to die prematurely in comparison to professionals, and that gradients in mortality by social class are apparent for nearly all causes of death to a greater or lesser extent. Men in social class 5 lost 114 years of potential life per 1000 population, against 39 years for men in social class 1, with women in unskilled occupations losing 34 years compared with 16 years for women in professional occupations … Various indicators of health such as height, body mass index, lung function, and blood pressure vary by social class … consultation rates with GPs for serious conditions are significantly higher among local authority tenants, people who were unemployed, and people both from the Caribbean or Indian subcontinent, than in the general population.

Fox and Benzeval (1995) c. Baldock *et al* (1999) *Social Policy*, **OUP, pp313–14**

ACTIVITY

Make a list of the points that link health to social class.

Health and gender

The government has a role in tackling the social problems related to health. However, there is also a role for the individual to change lifestyles and habits in order to avoid self-imposed barriers to full participation in society and maximising life-chances. The table below sets out the pattern of smoking in the UK by gender and social class.

Smoking is a singularly effective contributor to ill health both to the individual smoker and bystanders affected by passively inhaling second-hand smoke. It is also of great financial cost to the smoker and taxpayer funding the health services.

CURRENT SMOKERS (GB) BY GENDER AND SOCIO-ECONOMIC GROUP (%)	1972	1982	1996–7	1998–9
Males				
Professional	33	20	12	15
Employers and managers	44	29	20	21
Intermediate and junior non-manual	45	30	24	23
Skilled manual	57	42	32	33
Semi-skilled manual	57	47	41	38
Unskilled manual	64	49	41	45
All aged 16 and over	52	38	29	28
Females				
Professional	33	21	11	14
Employers	38	29	18	20
Intermediate and junior non-manual	38	30	28	24
Skilled manual	47	39	30	30
Semi-skilled manual	42	36	36	33
Unskilled manual	42	41	36	33
All aged 16 and over	42	33	28	26

General Household Survey, Office for National Statistics, *Social Trends,* **2000**

1) Given greater education and knowledge about dietary habits and their impact, the nation is improving its health. As well as the table above, what other areas of dietary behaviour have changed in recent years?

2) How do you account for the variation in patterns of smoking by gender and social class groups?

3) Given the points in question two, to what extent do you think individuals in the 'unskilled' social group are entirely free to choose whether or not to smoke?

6 Income, welfare and social exclusion by social groups

This section explores income and welfare in relationship to specific social groups and looks at:

- the elderly, low income and citizenship
- ethnicity, citizenship and welfare
- women, welfare and citizenship
- social exclusion and high income groups.

The elderly, low income and citizenship

Low income has particular significance to those elderly in society who are past retirement age. So called 'pensioner poverty' causes acute problems in terms of health and diet and also affects the ability of the low income elderly to engage fully in social and political structures.

As a particular illustration, living in a rural community without private transport often means reliance on public transport, which is often of a limited service. Such difficulties affect the elderly in rural communities more than other age groups on low income because the elderly are more likely to be unable to drive and less able to walk. However, it must be recognised that individuals on low income can be resourceful and able to overcome issues such as geographical isolation, not least the elderly. The crucial point is the relationship between low pay and people 'at risk' of social exclusion, in particular the elderly.

Will pension credit help the aged?

Item 1

Measures sketched out by ministers have the potential to improve living standards for many pensioners. But the package is fiendishly complex and will leave many of those it is designed to help bewildered. Much of the success of the new system will rely on pensioners' claiming what is due to them under the new system.

Last week's announcements have implications for younger people as well as today's pensioners.

The changes will ensure that the basic state pension, a non-means-tested benefit available to everyone with a relatively stable record of national insurance contributions, will play an ever-smaller role in providing retirement income in the future. Increasingly, the basic state pension will be supplemented by means-tested top-ups.

In 2003, when the new Pension Credit is introduced, the state will offer two types of top-up to the basic state pension.

The first will provide a minimum income, as is the case now, based on means testing. The aim will be to ensure that no single person has an income below £100 a week in 2003 (£5200 a year), and no couple will have less than £154 a week (£8008 a year).

The second top-up will come from the new Pension Credit, for pensioners with savings. If you have savings, the government will give 60 pence for every pound you have saved or are earning (e.g. through part-time work). But this does not apply to those with incomes on or above £135 per week (£7020 a year). For couples, the cut-off level for state assistance will be £201 a week (£10,452 a year).

Item 2

The government is now considering proposals to make second pensions (top-up state pensions) compulsory. A series of reports will be examined by the government with recommendations to review the pensions system in the UK to meet the growing demands of an ageing population (an increasing percentage of the population are over retirement age). The government is also considering proposals to increase the retirement age to 70. The 'retirement age' refers to the age at which you are eligible to claim the state pension.

Adapted from Maria Scott, *The Observer*, **12 November 2000**

1) Using Item 1, identify one criticism of this new system for pensions.

2) Explain what is meant by a) means-tested system, and b) non-means-tested system.

3) Outline and assess arguments for and against means-tested systems of state welfare.

4) Identify and explain one social problem associated with an 'ageing population' and one social benefit of an 'ageing population'.

5) Evaluate the case for and against the state making second pensions compulsory.

6) Discuss some of the reasons for and against raising the retirement age to 70 for men and women (Item 2).

Ethnicity, citizenship and welfare

In an interesting exploration of citizenship and minority ethnic groups, Patrick Roach and Marlene Morrison (1998) researched the relationship between public library use and availability and the Afro-Caribbean minority ethnic group's citizenship rights. The findings of the research suggested that availability of public libraries was a key aspect influencing citizenship in relation to public and social participation. Some minority groups have specific needs. English may be the second language and significant numbers of ethnic minority groups may live in socially deprived areas. The availability of publicly funded resources such as libraries is vital to the effective integration and access to citizenship rights of minority ethnic groups. This illustrates the important role the state plays in promoting social inclusion. In this case, local authorities continuing to adequately fund public libraries to allow effective citizenship participation among ethnic minority groups.

Race, ethnicity and welfare

Employment is a key to one's welfare standing and it is evident that welfare is a less stable aspect of life for the majority of minority ethnic groups in UK society. A number of employment, standards of living and welfare measures indicate that minority ethnic groups experience lower standards of living than the average for the population as a whole. As a result, they are more likely to rely on state welfare. Dean and Melrose (1999) identify aspects of poverty as related to ethnic minority groups.

Certain minority groups are more likely than white British people to be not only numbered among the poorest in society but to be in receipt of social security benefits.

Dean, H and Melrose, M (1999) *Poverty, Riches and Social Citizenship*, **Macmillan, p146**

The table below indicates some areas of difference in the standard of living according to ethnic group. It offers an indication of the higher likelihood of minority ethnic groups being 'at risk' from low income and poverty when compared to the majority white group.

People from minority ethnic groups who are in employment are more likely to be employed in industries renowned for low pay, such as catering, cleaning and service industries. Young Afro-Caribbean men aged between 16–24 years old were three times more likely to be unemployed than their white counterparts. Instances of social welfare inequality are more acute for women since under 50% of women from minority ethnic groups were employed in contrast to above 65% of white women.

POVERTY MEASURES BY ETHNIC GROUP IN THE UK

Indicators	White	Black (Afro-Caribbean)	Indian	Pakistani/ Bangladeshi
Average hourly pay of those in employment	£7.73	£6.88	£7.12	£6.43
Unemployment rates	8%	24%	12%	27%
Households in receipt of income support	15%	35%	20%	44%
Households in lowest quintile (after housing costs)	19%	35%	30%	63%

Adapted from Dean, H and Melrose, M (1999) *Poverty, Riches and Social Citizenship*, **Macmillan, p146**

Ethnicity, employment, income, homelessness and housing

This fact sheet from Shelter develops the issue of social exclusion among minority ethnic groups. It explores employment and housing circumstances of minority ethnic groups. Many of the problems identified below are also associated with white groups but they are experienced to a greater extent by minority ethnic groups.

ACTIVITY

1) With reference to the items, using your own words, describe the pattern of experience by minority ethnic groups in one of the three areas: employment, housing conditions or homelessness.
2) Using information from the items and elsewhere, assess the experiences which distinguish between minority ethnic groups in either employment or housing.

Item 1: Employment

The disadvantages faced by minority ethnic groups in the job market can be seen by looking at the economic activity rates and unemployment patterns for the different groups.

Minority ethnic groups are over-represented among the long-term unemployed. Youth unemployment is consistently high across all groups, but is higher for those of black origin. By 1996–7 the rate of unemployment for this group was 35% compared with 14% of white youth (ONS, 1998).

In 1991, the proportion of economically active men who were in full-time employment was highest among the white group (69%) and lowest among the Pakistani group (47%). Black African, Pakistani and Bangladeshi groups were in the worst position with male unemployment rates three times higher than their white counterparts (Housing Corporation, 1996).

Item 2: Housing conditions and overcrowding

Overcrowding is one of the key measures of housing conditions. In 1984, the Labour Force Survey found that 1% of white households lived in overcrowded conditions, compared with 28% of Pakistani or Bangladeshi households. The 1991 Census showed that this situation had not improved. If anything, overcrowding levels had risen. 30% of Pakistani and 47% of Bangladeshi families lived in overcrowded conditions, compared with 2% of white families. The Afro-Caribbeans had a lower level of overcrowding than the South Asians (5%). Overcrowding levels were lower in the younger generation (Ratcliffe, 1997). A more recent study carried out among minority ethnic groups in Bradford highlights overcrowding as a major problem. 65% of Bangladeshi and 45% of Pakistani households were living in overcrowded conditions (Ratcliffe, 1996).

Shortage of large properties

The household size of minority ethnic groups is greater than the white population. Pakistani and Bangladeshi households are on average the largest with 4.5 persons. They are nearly twice as large as the average white household (2.4 persons).

Historically, local authorities have not built many properties that have more than three bedrooms. As a result, it is difficult for local authorities to meet the needs of large households. This clearly has a disproportionate effect on minority ethnic households. For example, in Luton, not only is there a limited supply of five bedroom council houses, but they are all concentrated in one housing estate which has a poor reputation. In Glasgow, shortly after the 'right-to-buy' was introduced, 3.2% of the local authority stock was of four bedrooms and by 1993 the proportion had fallen to 2.6% (Bowes, 1998).

Item 3: Homelessness

Governments have never published figures on the extent of homelessness among the minority ethnic population. Shelter's housing advice service in London found that, in the first half of 1997–8, 82% of clients from minority ethnic groups were homeless or potentially homeless. Where research and monitoring have been carried out by local authorities, the results tend to show that minority ethnic groups, especially black people, are over-represented among homelessness acceptances. An analysis of homelessness acceptances of local authorities in the inner London area revealed that in 1996 51% of homelessness acceptances were from households of a minority ethnic group. Over a quarter (28%) of acceptances were from households from a black origin (London Research Centre, 1997).

Adapted from www.shelter.org.uk

Women, welfare and citizenship

Feminists such as Ruth Lister (1999) make the point that welfare models do not adequately consider the role of women in society. They make little effort to redress the imbalance of social inequality of women and men. The models of welfare must consider issues of gender as fundamental variables rather than assuming the differences as merely incidental. Alternative models of welfare must be developed in order to take account of gender inequality.

Single parenthood

An area of society of relevance to issues of welfare with particular emphasis on women is single parenthood. The vast majority of single parents are women. Of all families with dependent children, 22% were headed by single parents of which 95% were women. Despite efforts to extend absent parental involvement in childcare through, for example, the controversial Child Support Agency (CSA), the burden of child support in society falls largely upon women.

In terms of welfare needs, we must not assume that all single parents are in need of state support. But there are a disproportionate number of single parents existing on income below national average when compared to the population of parents as a whole. Consequently, women will be more likely to need state support, making the issue of state welfare a specific concern for women. There are also particular barriers to securing and advancing one's job or position in the workplace that are experienced by single parents. For example, not all employers provide adequate and affordable childcare and child friendly employment policies, such as crèche facilities and flexible working hours. The state may need to intervene in order to ensure employers do promote child friendly practice at work. Aspects of state intervention are of specific focus for women. Many feminists argue that any model of state welfare must incorporate the specific concerns experienced by women in society.

It is important to recognise the points made by Sue Innes (1995) on single parents. Innes argues that we must be careful when referring to the social problems faced by single parents to avoid portraying single parenthood itself as a social problem.

There is a crucial line to be drawn between recognising that many single parents have a hard life and presenting them as a social problem because they are on their own. Most public dis- *cussion manages to ignore the happy and successful single parent families – after all, they're not supposed to exist.*

Innes, S (1995) *Making It Work: Women, Change and Challenge in the 90s*, **Chatto & Windus, p191**

Innes also argues that women are exposed to greater social hardship as a result of male exploitation and control of wealth and power in society. Welfare dependence in greater numbers by women reflects the male domination and continuing control of wealth in society.

The poverty of most single mothers is a consequence of women's economic dependence, particularly when we have children, and of our failure as a society to value the work of bringing up children.

Innes, *Making It Work: Women, Change and Challenge in the 90s,* **p191**

Aside from the convincing argument made by feminists about the specific welfare challenges faced by women, the question as to what specific role the individual, the state, the family and employer should have in terms of the welfare needs to be addressed.

Feminists argue that women have specific challenges to their social welfare in contrast to men. There are aspects of identity involving race and ethnicity that further complicate these barriers to full citizen inclusion.

?

1) To what extent is it the state's responsibility, the employers' or the single parents' themselves to provide childcare services and appropriate employment conditions?
2) At what point does an individual actually cease to be a dependent child? For example, is a full-time student aged 20 years with part-time work and living at home still a dependent?
3) One of the few remaining universal benefits is child allowance. Many feminist policy makers such as Harriet Harman are strongly protective of this universal principal for child benefit. Why do you think this benefit in particular remains universal?
4) With reference to the elderly, ethnic minority groups and women, explain how social inequality affects each group.

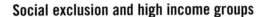

Social exclusion and high income groups

Though the major area of concern regarding social exclusion are low-income groups and the socially disadvantaged, consideration must be given to the growing social divide of an increasingly detached richer group in society. When living in isolation, it would be better to be rich rather than poor. The point is that social cohesion benefits all and social isolation damages society.

This social fragmentation is not a source of individual happiness for either rich or the poor. The rich get locked in a lonely world of competitive consumption in which material objects gradually replace human associations. Nobody enjoys living in a city or urban space in which there are increasingly no go areas.

Hutton in Carpenter, *What If. . .? Fifteen Visions for Change for Britain's Inner Cities,* **p20**

Hutton (2000) refers to a 'drawbridge' community of super-rich in the USA, a circumstance that may not yet be far off in the UK. Giddens (1998) raises the issue of an emerging 10% ghetto. Here, a rich 'super class' detach themselves from the public community, from public services, e.g. schools and health services, and social life, preferring private clubs and societies to public meeting places such as the 'pub'. Through such detachment, communities fracture and divide which undermines social activity and a collective belonging. Social inclusion and exclusion affects all sections of society directly and indirectly, even including the super-rich.

7 Challenging social inequality and social exclusion

This section explores the policies and laws designed to tackle social exclusion and assesses their impact. It looks at:

■ the Disability Discrimination Act 1995
■ the Equal Pay Act 1970 and the Sex Discrimination Act 1975
■ the Race Relations Act 1976 and 2000
■ recent policies tackling discrimination and social exclusion.

There are a number of ways that social exclusion can be challenged. Legislation and government policy are key areas.

The Disability Discrimination Act (DDA) 1995

The Act has two major parts. The first relates to employment law and outlaws discrimination on grounds of disability. Equal opportunity to compete for jobs based on fair assessment and on merit is the intended outcome of the Act. However, there are some roles/jobs that require specific tasks, which a person with a severe physical disability could not possibly do without serious threat to health and safety of themselves and fellow workers, e.g. a steeplejack or scaffolding construction worker. For these reasons certain jobs can be exempted by special permission.

The second area that the legislation covers relates to access. All public buildings and services (e.g. buses and trains) must have adequate access for hearing and visually impaired people as well as wheelchair users. There is an acknowledgement that in order to pay for and carry out the necessary changes it will take time. For example, the train service operators have to complete and be passed by DDA inspection by the year 2020. Public buildings and employers with five or more employees should have completed their access adaptations by 2002.

The Act is changing the physical environment in which we operate. The perceptions of disability issues among the whole population are being changed. The public and employers are recognising the difficulties of exclusion and discrimination faced by people with disabilities. Perceptions of the word 'able' are changing as resources and public buildings are designed with all people's needs considered. Although critics argue it does not go far enough, the Disability Discrimination Act is clear evidence of the way legislation may work to positively address social exclusion and extend citizenship rights.

The Equal Pay Act 1970 and the Sex Discrimination Act 1975

The Equal Pay Act was introduced in 1970 and stated that equal pay for the same job must be applied to men and women. However, if employers wanted to continue paying different wages to men and women, all they had to do was slightly change the job specification. Consequently, the European Community (now the European Union) in 1975, after a case in the European Court, imposed legislation on the British government stating that equal pay was to be awarded for work of equal value. It also allowed female and male employees to take employers to an industrial tribunal if they felt discrimination was occurring over rates of pay.

This shows that legislation is sometimes not particularly effective, demonstrated by the ease with which employers could ignore the rulings of the Equal Pay Act.

The Race Relations Act 1976 and 2000

This legislation made it illegal to discriminate on racial grounds in a range of areas including pay, job applications, housing (many landlords openly refused to rent to black and 'non-whites') and membership of organisations. The Act also set up the Commission for Racial Equality with powers to examine cases of unfair dismissal and allegations of racial discrimination.

The MacPherson Report on the Stephen Lawrence case has led to new legislation (the Race Relations Amendment Act 2000) and more concerted attempts to deal with racism in British society.

Legislation can challenge racist and discriminatory behaviour, but the extent to which it changes attitudes (the basis for prejudices) is limited.

> With reference to the Disability Discrimination Act, the Sex Discrimination Act or the Race Relations Act, a) explain its intentions, and b) discuss the extent to which you consider the intentions of the legislation to be successful.

Recent policies tackling discrimination and social exclusion

There are social changes required which comprise but extend beyond legislation to tackle social exclusion. In this section some recent policy initiatives directed at reducing social exclusion and enhancing citizenship rights are explored.

The government's Social Exclusion Unit summarises the problem as follows:

1 *Over the past 20 years, poverty has become more concentrated in individual neighbourhoods and states than before, and the social exclusion of these neighbourhoods has become more marked.*

2 *But this (neighbourhood renewal) is about more than*

poverty. It is about the fact that compared with the rest of the country many deprived areas have 30% higher mortality rates; 25% more people with low skills and literacy; unemployment rates six times as high; and three times as much burglary.

National Strategy for Neighbourhood Renewal: A Framework for Consultation, (September 1998) Social Exclusion Unit

Action zones

The government recognises the significance of pockets of social exclusion and has adopted a policy of action zones for education, employment and health. The specific areas considered socially deprived in one or more of the three areas are identified as qualifying for increased funding (**regeneration** grants) and resources to improve facilities. The government have recognised that social exclusion is a complex problem to resolve, requiring a range of initiatives from a number of social welfare areas. They refer to a 'joined-up government for joined-up solutions to joined-up problems'. For example, how does an individual become homeless? Are there problems in the home from which individuals are running away, e.g. domestic abuse, financial pressure? Are there mental health problems? Are individuals running from local authority care or private households? Whatever the cause, there are many economic, health and social problems that emerge as a result of homelessness. They can span a range of government and social services departments from education and employment to health and social services.

The Social Exclusion Unit

As a response to the complexity of the causes of social exclusion, the government has set up a Social Exclusion Unit whose purpose is to advise on social exclusion of all kinds and to propose policy initiatives aimed at resolving the problems.

A report from the Social Exclusion Unit, *Rough Sleeping* (July 1998), explores issues leading to rough sleeping, numbers and demographic data on rough sleeping, sources of support and policy suggestions.

Another report from the Social Exclusion Unit entitled *National Strategy for Neighbourhood Renewal: A Framework for Consultation* (September 1998), charts the problems of concentrations of poverty in specific geographical areas of Britain. The report exposes the failures of past policies. It also identifies a range of initiatives that communities can promote to restore local economies, faith in local political structures and social services. In commenting on the suggested strategy to be adopted, the NSNR states a combined effort is required in addition to existing public services:

A coalition of policies, resources and people needs to be marshalled behind a single strategy, involving action on four fronts: reviving local economies, reviving communities, ensuring decent services, and leadership and joint working.

National Strategy for Neighbourhood Renewal: A Framework for Consultation, **Social Exclusion Unit**

New Deal

Other policy areas include the New Deal for unemployed youth, long-term unemployed and lone parents. It is designed to encourage unemployed people from various backgrounds to seek work or training and to offer employers financial incentives for recruiting long-term unemployed. The policies involve inter-agency work, e.g. the Department of Social Security and the Department for Education and Employment work together with employers.

Child benefit increase

Increases in child benefit (20% since 1997) have been introduced in order to pay parents/carers directly cash benefits for each child under the age of 18. This benefit is significant for debates about universal benefit payments (universal means everyone qualifies as opposed to means tested when recipients qualify usually based on an income assessment). The principal of universality is held by those who argue that many will receive government money that they do not need. The only way to ensure that the benefit reaches everyone, is to simply pay it to everyone (i.e. the children themselves via parents/carers).

Minimum wage

There are two minimum wages:

- £3.70 for those 21 years old and over
- £3.20 for those workers aged 18–21.

The idea of a minimum wage is to avoid the growing concern of increasing numbers of people being paid very low wages. Although many advanced industrial societies including the USA have a minimum wage, there was some resistance in this country to the minimum wage from some employers. They claimed that they would not be able to afford the rate. Controversy came also from trade unions who claimed the rate was set to low. The Low Pay Commission, which is independent from government, agreed and set increases in the rate each year in line with cost of living (**inflation**) increases.

Minimum income guarantee (MIG) and stakeholder pensions

The government has set up a guarantee that pensioners will not fall below a specific income level. In return, individuals take responsibility for saving for their future retirement through private pension schemes, hence the term 'stakeholder pensions'. The idea is that with an ageing population it will be increasingly expensive for the government to maintain a universal state pension for all. Encouraging individuals to insure their own futures in return for a state minimum guarantee, eases the growing cost of state paid pensions and ensures that low-income families are the beneficiaries of state spending on pensions. A recent development has attempted to encourage individuals to get second pensions (stakeholder pensions).

1) What is the Social Exclusion Unit? What does it attempt to achieve?
2) Identify some 'action zones' and explain what they do.
3) Outline the arguments for increasing the minimum wage and extending it to cover all workers.
4) Identify and describe three recent initiatives which attempt to tackle social exclusion.
5) How might very high income groups be described as socially excluded?
6) Evaluate the likely effectiveness of two of these recent policies.

Exam questions

You must answer Question 1 and either Question 2 or 3.

1) Read **Sources A**, **B** and **C** and answer the questions which follow.

Source A

> The MacPherson Report investigated the circumstances surrounding the murder of black teenager Stephen Lawrence. In its review of the way law agencies handled the case, the MacPherson Report stated that there was strong evidence of institutional racism in the Metropolitan Police.

Source B

Last night's events in Oldchester

A violent confrontation between police and groups of Asian and white youths was narrowly averted last night. Community leaders and councillors persuaded separate groups of white and Asian young men to leave the streets in a peaceful manner. The confrontation began following the spread of rumours about a planned march by extremist white racist organisations in the Oldchester area. As these rumours spread, groups of Asian and white youths began to gather in the Middletown area of Oldchester. As police blocked off access points to Middletown, community leaders talked the groups into dispersing.

This morning, there were few signs of any trouble, other than a couple of broken shop windows and some damaged cars and vans. Police, however, warned of the potential for trouble during the long summer months ahead and called for restraint by all sections of the community.

Oldchester Herald, **11 June 2001**

Source C

Middletown Resident's Action Group formed

Over 200 residents from the Middletown area of Oldchester gathered last night in Middletown Community Centre to form a resident's group. In the wake of the disturbances of yesterday, local community leaders moved quickly to try to prevent trouble in the future.

Chaired by two local councillors, the meeting discussed the events of the previous night and their causes. One resident who asked not to be named, said that the events were the result of outside influences stirring up racial tension in what had previously been a co-operative community. Another local shopkeeper said that the problems in Middletown had been building up for years, with high unemployment, poor schools and old housing particularly affecting the Asian community.

One white resident said that Middletown was still a 'nice area to live in with friendly people'. Another, though, said that he felt intimidated at times by different groups of youths, especially at night.

The meeting agreed to establish a Middletown Resident's Action Group which would have the aim of bringing all sections of the community together. A small committee was established to bring forward ideas about how the communities could be brought more closely together and to look at other ways of maintaining peace on Middletown's streets.

Oldchester Herald, **12 June 2001**

(a) Briefly explain the term 'institutional racism'. (4 marks)

(b) Examine some of the ways in which groups like the residents of inner-city Middletown are often disadvantaged. (10 marks)

(c) Identify some of the ways in which the Middletown Resident's Action Group could attempt to improve community relations **and** assess how likely these ways are to be successful.

(16 marks)

AQA, 11 June 2002

2) (a) Examine some of the social consequences of the existence of poverty in the UK. (10 marks)

(b) 'Equal opportunities laws in the UK have failed in their aim of reducing discrimination.' Assess this claim. (20 marks)

AQA, 11 June 2002

3) (a) People are often discriminated against on the basis of their sexuality, social class, **nationality**, gender, ethnicity, disability or age. Taking any **two** of the characteristics, explain how they may be used to discriminate against groups of citizens. (10 marks)

(b) Assess explanations of the continuing existence of poverty in an apparently wealthy society such as Britain. (20 marks)

AQA, 18 June 2001

9

The Citizen and Community Participation

In this chapter you will explore citizen action in the community including:

- forms of individual participation via political parties and **pressure groups**, including the electoral process, **parliamentary action**, **direct action** and lobbying
- campaigning for change – methods individuals and groups use to bring about change, e.g. the **mass media**
- examples of actions supporting community interests, such as forms of self-help, which may enhance social inclusion
- decision-making, strategies for resolving conflict and achieving collaboration, both formal (e.g. voting) and informal (e.g. persuasion and negotiation)
- concepts, processes and strategies of a campaign and community action, e.g. motivation, group dynamics in meetings.

The chapter is broken into five sections

1 Community action and social capital (pp 198–201)
2 Techniques and organisations promoting citizen participation (pp 201–204)
3 Campaigning and communities (pp 204–211)
4 Community structures and running campaigns (pp 211–215)
5 Information and communication technology networking and citizen participation (pp 215–219)

Key terms

Community – the locality and groups existing and surrounding individuals where they live or are socially active. It can be in a virtual environment, e.g. Internet chat rooms

Democratic renewal – improving the processes of decision-making and participation within them by community members

Legitimacy – quality of being popularly accepted as rightful and just

Social capital – sum total of social networks, social awareness and participation of individuals and communities that strengthens the chances and impact of citizen participation

1 Community action and social capital

This section explores citizen participation and community involvement. It looks at:

- active participation
- active communities: Citizenship Survey 2001
- building social networks
- sectionalism
- democratic renewal.

CASE STUDY: Royds Community Association, Bradford

Royds is a self-sustaining community where local residents are actively involved in identifying their needs and implementing the means to achieve their goals.

In the recent past, Royds has experienced high unemployment, with levels of male unemployment sometimes as high as 47%, low average incomes and **demographic change**. The main cause has been the disappearance of major traditional employers from the area, with few new small businesses springing up to fill the gaps or provide work.

From the outset, the aim of the Royds Economic Regeneration Programme has been to:

- encourage new employment opportunities
- improve people's access to training
- stimulate and encourage local business.

Royds contains around 3300 dwellings spread across its three estates – Buttershaw, Woodside and Delph Hill. Many dwellings were built over 50 years ago and are highly energy inefficient by today's standards. The general appearance of the area was unfavourable, with outdated access and vast open spaces, many unkempt and unused. The aim of the Royds Physical Regeneration Strategy has been to transform the landscape making it a more enjoyable, safe, attractive environmentally improved place to live.

Since the Regeneration Programme began, the Community Association has introduced a wide range of initiatives and services to improve the quality of life. More than 1200 homes have had new kitchens, bathrooms, central heating and home security and safety devices fitted. The Association has helped residents face up to environmental issues initiating food growing, gardening projects and various recycling initiatives.

Many local residents have been involved in planning these developments. Carol Dickinson, a resident director and chair of the Physical Working Party, said, 'We were doing planning for real before planning for real was a name.'

The Royds Community Association is managed by a board of directors. 12 of the 22 directors represent the residents who live on the three estates and are elected by the residents. They serve for a period of four years. Turnout for these elections are higher than those for local council elections.

The services the Community Association organises include:

- Groundforce, its own ground and garden maintenance business. Staffed by local residents, the Groundforce team is now responsible for the upkeep of the grounds of many properties in the area as well as local schools pitches and the Millennium Green.
- Royds Consultancy, a business offering clients a full range of services including face-to-face and telephone surveys, focus groups, feasibility studies, specialising in community participation and communication.

The Association has backed the building of two community centres, a Healthy Living Centre and play areas. They also support:

- parent–toddler groups
- play groups
- youth clubs

- local schools
- breakfast clubs
- keep-fit classes
- better facilities for older people
- advice facilities for those who need help in claiming benefits and disability allowances, or in coping with debt.

New services are being developed continuously. Funding has recently been secured for CCTV. If the Association becomes a registered social landlord, then Royds will become a model for neighbourhood governance. However, the problem remains of more fully engaging younger residents, single parents, etc., in the activities of the Association. As Carol says, 'It's not that they don't want to, it's that they have so many other things on.'

For more information contact:

Royds Community Association, Sunnybank House, 506 Huddersfield Road, Wyke, Bradford, BD12 8AD.
Telephone: (01274) 414111
Facsimile: (01274) 414840
Email: andyg@royds.org.uk

ACTIVITY

In what ways is Royds an example of active citizenship?

Active participation

Citizenship is keenly debated largely because our democratic political system has been losing the support, commitment and enthusiasm of many people. Both Conservative and Labour governments have acknowledged that our democracy is in urgent need of reform and losing its legitimacy. Fewer people vote at national elections and voter turnout at European and local elections is frequently 20% or less. Many people seem to be uninterested in public affairs. There does seem to be an increase in campaigning and protests about particular issues that effect individual and local communities directly. The fuel protest in 2000, campaigns against genetically modified food, protests against new roads or airport extensions that damage the environment, are some examples. However, the massive public demonstrations in March 2003 against the American and British war against Iraq showed that vast numbers of young (and older) people felt very strongly about international issues of peace and justice.

Governments, businesses, and other bodies have come up with many ideas, policies and actions that aim to encourage interest in domestic public affairs and develop a commitment to democracy. In some areas, environmentally rooted Local Agenda 21 initiatives have helped build sustainable communities and a local participatory democracy. In discussing, choosing and working to establish meaningful indicators that show that sustainability is actually being achieved directly involves members of local communities in a form of civic engagement. The Institute of Public Policy Research has suggested a number of devices whereby democracy could be renewed and strengthened. For example:

- citizen juries
- deliberative opinion polling
- community issue groups.

Local authorities in Birmingham, Bradford, Manchester, Coventry and Cambridge have established elected youth councils or parliaments directly involving young people in civic debate, political action and decision-making. Countries like Britain and America have the formal institutions of democracy. Critics argue that our democracies do not connect with the everyday experiences of most people who perceive and experience them as either irrelevant or even a barrier to individual and social well-being.

Active communities: Citizenship Survey 2001

In 1999, the Home Office published a report called *Giving Time, Getting Involved*. It stated that:

volunteering and community activities are central to the concept of citizenship and are the key to restoring our communities. They can help with social inclusion, life-long learning, healthy living and active ageing. A strong and vibrant democracy requires active citizens participating in their communities.

It also noted the number of adults volunteering across the UK fell from 51% to 48% between 1991–7. The biggest fall occurred among those people aged between 18–24 years. This means that unless people get more active there may be no voluntary reading schemes in schools, no victim support schemes and no mentors by 2010.

In 2001, the government surveyed a nationally representative sample of people in England and Wales to find out what type of citizenship activities people got involved in. It was found that over two thirds of people were involved in social groups, hobby or sports clubs and religious or community organisations. About the same percentage of people volunteer informally to help others in some way. This may include giving advice to someone, looking after their house when they are away, or doing someone's shopping when they are ill. 39% of people undertake formal volunteering activities such as fundraising, organising an event, or providing transport. The most significant barrier to formal and informal volunteering seems to be lack of time and busy lifestyles. Only 38% of people participated in civic activities like signing petitions, contacting MPs or councillors, going to a public meeting, or taking part in a rally or protest demonstration.

- White men are most active when it comes to civic participation and Asian women least active.
- People aged 35–49 were the most likely to participate in civic affairs (44%) and those aged 16–24 the least likely (28%).
- Black men are most likely to be active as informal volunteers and black women most likely to be formal volunteers.
- Black women and white men are the most likely to be involved socially in groups and clubs.
- Generally, people in the most deprived areas are less likely to be active citizens than those in the least deprived areas.

The reasons for these differences are not yet clear. The lower levels of participation in the most deprived areas may be due to socio-demographic factors (for example, the greater prevalence of people with lower educational attainments and lower income levels in the most deprived areas).

In May 2002, the Home Office re-launched its Active Community Unit with four major aims:

1 to build the capacity of local people to lead community development
2 to promote community involvement and citizenship
3 to develop productive partnerships between government and the community
4 to develop a modern framework of laws and regulations that would facilitate good **practice**.

1) Why is volunteering good for democracy?
2) Why are young people the least interested in civic affairs? Should they be?
3) What might the government do to improve things?

Building social networks

Contemporary failures to engage people in civic affairs is seen by the American political scientist Robert Putnam as due to a decline in membership of voluntary associations that produce the **social capital** upon which real participation relies. Relationships and networks of give-and-take, trustworthiness, obligation and perceived mutual benefit are key to the generation and maintenance of this social capital. There is perhaps an important causal link between social capital and citizenship participation, political literacy and government efficiency and effectiveness. This is because the link between social or leisure clubs and civic participation is a strong one. The more you are with others the more you get to know them, talk to them and do things with them. People may find out they share the same interests or concerns and decide to do something together.

Sectionalism

Some social initiatives or campaigns may have only a short self-interested lifespan. This is affected by people's willingness to get involved. Many organised pressure groups are dominated by the educated middle classes who know what they want and how to get it. These people often risk being accused of **NIMBYism** (Not In My Back Yard).

Community action is often seen as one section or group doing something for themselves regardless of the consequences on others. This **sectionalism** is made worse by the charter approach to servicing public needs. This approach treats the individual as a customer rather than a socially responsible citizen who is concerned about himself *and* also the common good. For example, seeking compensation or writing a letter of protest for the late running of a train or a leaking roof does not necessarily accommodate the consideration of wider issues (which by their very nature encompass many people's interests). This has been one of the reasons why the values of **communitarianism** have been so attractive. Responsibilities *from all* require that a good person contributes to the common good. If you are going to be an active and responsible citizen making a valuable contribution to the community, you must also know and understand what your community stands for.

Democratic renewal

Democratic renewal must be rooted in the experience of face-to-face communities that give us our social identity, culture and shared purpose, that motivate people to look out for each other and to work together towards goals of mutual benefit. Community is something that is achieved and constructed through social interaction, dialogue and communication, and by people getting on with each other. The cure for the ailments of democracy is more democracy. The experience of community planning activities such as Planning for Real show that strong democratic practices can successfully be rooted in the life worlds, needs, feelings and expectations of local communities. People start talking and listening to each other seriously, sympathetically and maybe empathising with each other's concerns and problems. Through this they can develop those 'democratic skills' such as:

- holding coherent meetings
- making decisions
- allowing everyone the chance to speak
- learning how to debate and vote on complex issues
- learning that selfishness often backfires
- recognising that other people's concerns do not necessarily diminish one's own.

2 Techniques and organisations promoting citizen participation

This section explores ways through which citizens have and can affect influence and looks at:

- participation techniques
- pressure groups and political parties
- volunteering
- trade unions and professional associations
- campaigning and the mass media.

Participation techniques

Service satisfaction surveys

These may be one-off regular initiatives, focusing either on specific services or on the local authority's general performance. Surveys may be carried out in a variety of ways (e.g. postal or door-to-door) and may cover the entire local authority population or a particular group of service users or citizens.

Opinion polls

These may be used to find out citizens' views on on-service specific issues (e.g. community safety or the town in 2000). Opinion polls are generally used to obtain citizens' immediate reactions. 'Deliberative' opinion polls are used to compare a group of citizens' reactions before and after they have had an opportunity to discuss the issue at hand.

Interactive website

This may be used on the Internet or on a local authority-specific Internet, inviting email messages from citizens on particular local issues or service matters. We are only interested in interactive initiatives and not in the use of computer technologies simply to provide information on services or facilities.

Referendum

These allow citizens to vote on policy-specific options, as in the Strathclyde vote on the reorganisation of water services.

Community plans/needs analysis

The purpose of these is to set out priorities for local service provision and local authority policy, often on a community-by-community (or neighbourhood) basis. In general, councillors take primary decisions about the budget while citizens review (and may reorder) specific priorities.

Citizens panels

These are ongoing panels which function as a 'sounding board' for the local authority. Panels focus on specific service or policy issues, or on wider strategy. The panel is made up of a statistically representative sample of citizens whose views are sought several times a year.

Public meetings

These are a traditional method of informing the public usually with a platform of councillors and/or officers. They are based on an open invitation to members of the public to attend.

Citizen juries

A citizen jury is a group of citizens (chosen to be a fair representation of the local population) brought together to consider a particular issue set by the local authority. Citizen juries receive evidence from expert witnesses and cross-questioning can occur. The process may last up to four days, at the end of which a report is drawn up setting out the views of the jury, including any differences in opinion. Juries' views are intended to inform councillor's decision-making.

Focus groups

One-off focus groups are similar to citizen juries in that they bring together citizens to discuss a specific issue. Focus groups need not be representative of the general population and may involve a particular citizen group only. Discussions may focus on the specific needs of that group, on the quality of a particular service, or on ideas for broader policy or strategy. Focus groups do not generally call expert witnesses and typically last between one and two hours only, usually involving around 12 people.

Visioning exercises

A range of methods (including focus groups) may be used within a visioning exercise, the purpose of which is to establish the 'vision' participants have of the future and the kind of future they would like to create. Visioning may be used to inform broad strategy for a locality, or may have a more specific focus (as in environmental consultations for Local Agenda 21).

Issue forums

These are also ongoing bodies with regular meetings, but focusing on a particular issue (e.g. community safety or health promotion). They may have a set membership or operate on an open basis. They are often able to make recommendations to relevant council committees or to share in decision-making processes.

Shared interest forums

These are similar to issue forums but concentrate upon the needs of a particular citizen group (e.g. young people or minority ethnic groups). They may have a set membership or operate on an open basis and are often able to make recommendations to relevant council committees or to share in decision-making.

Area/neighbourhood forums

Such forums are concerned with the needs of a particular geographically-defined area or neighbourhood. Meeting regularly, they may deal with a specific service area (e.g. planning or housing) or with a full range of local services and concerns. They may have a close link with relevant ward councillors or with councillors responsible for the service areas under discussion. Membership may be set or open. Where there is a formally established membership (e.g. of representatives for tenants or community association in the area), members of the public may be free to participate in an open discussion session at meetings.

Enhancing Public Participation in Local Government, **DETR (1988), London**

1) What is the difference between being taught about citizenship and practising it?
2) How else might young people learn to be active citizens?
3) Is voting at local and parliamentary elections enough?
4) How might a local participatory democracy work in your area?

Pressure groups and political parties

As an individual, you might sign a petition, write a letter to a local paper, or send a donation to a campaigning organisation such as Compassion in World Farming (CWF). You might express your concern more strongly by finding out what organised groups exist that campaign actively and consistently on animal rights issues, for example. Having done that, you might then send in your membership fee, join a local group, go to a public meeting or two and maybe even demonstrate publicly with others to prevent the lorries boarding the ferries. If you feel very strongly, you may even join the Animal Liberation Front and take action that breaks the law. Some people feel that in certain circumstances breaking the law is morally justified. The suffragette leader Emmeline Pankhurst once said, 'The argument of a broken window pane is the most valuable argument in modern politics.' In other words, sometimes governments will only take notice of campaigners when they resort to direct action and possibly breaking the law.

Examples of protests

Historically, in hard times, tenants in rented accommodation have refused to pay rents if they felt the rents were too high or if the landlords failed to repair their properties. Homeless people have been known to squat in empty buildings to protest against housing shortages. Environmentalists have been known to destroy GM crops to raise public awareness about the dangers of genetic engineering. Sometimes direct action affects the privacy and human rights of the individual. Some gay activists like Peter Tatchell try to 'out' public figures who they believe to be homosexual but who conceal and sometimes speak publicly against the extension of key rights to gay people. A sit-down protest was a key technique used by civil rights protestors in the 1960s and has became prominent in many environmental campaigns in the 1990s. It was most notable during the long and ultimately unsuccessful battle to prevent the extension of the M3 motorway through Twyford Down in Hampshire. Environmental protesters have also burrowed under the proposed sites of new airport runways to prevent or delay construction work.

Although direct action rarely leads to permanent change, sometimes it does, as with the '**poll tax**' riots in 1990, which saw the government of the day withdraw an almost universally hated local tax.

To join an organised campaign or pressure group shows a greater degree of interest than simply expressing disapproval to friends and family or moaning when watching a television news bulletin. To send money indicates concern and allows professional campaigners to continue their work. Sending money, however, can be a way of soothing one's conscience – a substitute or excuse for not getting engaged. Giving time, for some people, is simply impossible because of family or work commitments. Time is sometimes more valuable than money because time means giving up the opportunity to do something else – work, decorate, walk the dog, watch television, study, etc.

Volunteering

Most members of organised pressure groups campaigning for animal rights, or environmental protection or any other issue do so voluntarily. Friends of the Earth could not survive without a huge input of time, money and commitment from local volunteers. Political parties have paid officials and may be financially well off, but without people giving up their time because they believe in the values or policies, most political parties would probably not even exist. Ordinary party members can involve themselves in party political and civic affairs in a number of ways:

- paying the subscription
- helping to raise funds from jumble sales and raffles to more sophisticated requests for donations and gifts
- attending local party meetings
- organising public meetings
- canvassing at local elections
- delivering leaflets between elections
- standing for the local council
- helping out with office and other administrative duties
- taking on a local voluntary role, e.g. producing a newsletter
- writing letters to the press or doing interviews on local radio
- voting
- going to party conferences
- attending rallies.

However, citizenship is not the same as campaigning or being a member of a **political party**. It is essentially about being active. Voluntary activity can take a number of forms. Letter writing is for most people an important voluntary activity. Although this requires a belief that it is worth doing, will make a difference, etc., it also requires a certain degree of literacy and a mastery of technique. The point of writing a letter, from a campaigning perspective, is to make a point, to have an effect, to get noticed. Often campaigning organisations like **Amnesty International**, will offer some guidance, even training, to members on how to write effective letters.

Pressure groups like Age Concern or Help the Aged campaign to improve the situation of older people. They invite people of all ages to get involved to break down social barriers leading to discrimination against the elderly. They campaign actively for such things as better pensions and healthcare. Age Concern lists the ways an individual may volunteer time to include being:

- a visitor
- an advice worker
- an administrator
- a be-friender
- a driver
- a campaigner
- an insurance clerk
- a handyperson
- a trustee
- a sales assistant
- an accountant
- a day-care helper

- a fundraiser
- a gardener
- a cook
- a writer or publicist
- a secretary.

Volunteering for Age Concern doesn't only involve caring for people who are frail

Without the help of people like you, vast numbers of older people would be alone and struggling. But volunteering for Age Concern doesn't only involve caring for people who are frail. Behind the scenes there are all kinds of opportunities for you to gain skills or use your experience.

We'll give you all the practical support you need to get the job done, and you'll be covered by indemnity insurance.

You may even gain a certificate that helps you to get a job.

You'll have a great time, you won't be out of pocket and there's even a perk! After only six months with us, our volunteers can take out Age Concern insurance, whatever their age.

I want to do something medical when I leave school. This is a really good chance for me to gain experience and understanding of older people. And it's really enjoyable because they so enjoy our company as young people.

www.ageconcern.org.uk

Trade unions and professional associations

People can become active citizens by getting involved in their professional associations or trade unions. These are organisations that are financed largely by subscriptions to promote and defend the interests of their members. The Law Society is the professional association of solicitors and barristers; the British Medical Association is the professional association of doctors, and the Transport and General Workers Union is the organisation for many non-professional working people. The membership of these bodies will elect local and national officials to do a range of things. For example, negotiate terms and conditions of service, negotiate pay scales, pension or sickness benefits, length of holidays, redundancy terms and many other things. Employment conditions have to conform to legislative standards regarding pay and health and safety. Trade unions and professional associations will seek the best deal for their members just as private companies will seek the best deal for their shareholders.

Most of the work of these organisations goes unseen and unnoticed by the general public or even the members themselves. Occasionally issues like the extremely long working hours of junior doctors or the low pay of public sector workers hit the headlines. Sometimes trade unions will campaign publicly to shame employers or governments so their case is taken more seriously. Sometimes the media story focuses exclusively on the conflict or the failed negotiations. The media tends to see conflict stories as newsworthy and the press has been criticised by academic researchers and the trade unions themselves as generally biased in favour of employers, particularly if they are private businesses. Occasionally when negotiations break down or if conciliation or arbitration fails then public demonstrations and even industrial action may take place. The Criminal Justice and Public Order Act 1994, employment legislation and the Human Rights Act 1998 provide the legal framework within which such actions take place.

Strike action

Although strike action is not illegal, there is no legal right to strike as such. Trade unions are not held responsible for any losses the employer suffers as a result of industrial action so long as the proper procedures have been taken before the action started. The membership must have balloted in favour of strike action. They must make sure that no attempt is made to intimidate people who refuse to take part in the action, etc.

3 Campaigning and communities

This section explores campaigning in local communities and looks at:

- organising a local campaign
- individual campaigns
- community action
- citizenship, **empowerment** and community action.

Organising a local campaign

Campaigning often and necessarily involves securing publicity for an event or an issue. Being able to deal with the media beyond writing a letter is often called for. Many campaigning organisations offer media training in how to cultivate local journalists, write press releases, give radio or television interviews, or organise a media event of some description. Local environmental campaigners learn to do most of these things. At first it requires considerable courage, a little self-confidence and skill, but with experience and practice it becomes much easier.

Some time ago, a local environmental group wanted to secure the support of its MP for a bill going through Parliament designed to promote **organic** farming. The local MP had already signalled his support by signing a motion in the House of Commons. The group felt it could build on this to raise the issue more broadly in the town by getting some local press and radio coverage. Campaigning is often about winning hearts and minds, arguing and justifying a case or a course of action and attempting to persuade others to agree with a particular point of view. If this can be achieved then other people might also write letters or get involved to promote the issue further.

Plan of action

The first stage involved contacting the journalist on the local paper who dealt with environmental issues to see if his editor would be interested in the issue. Organic agriculture is very worthy but not particularly exciting. If it can be dressed up in the form of an attractive media event, sometimes referred to as stunts, then other possibilities present themselves. A press release was written and sent to the paper providing the journalist with ready copy. It was also sent to the local radio station's newsroom followed up with a friendly phone call. The MP was asked, via his constituency secretary, if he would like to have his picture taken being presented with a free box of organic vegetables outside a local wholefood store. MPs need press coverage between elections in order to maintain their profile in their constituency and newspapers always need pictures and stories of local celebrities, of which an active constituency MP is invariably one, to sell copy. The event was staged one Saturday lunchtime, the

photograph taken and the week after an article on organic food and the parliamentary bill together with a picture appeared in the paper.

One of the campaigners gave a short interview at the local radio station going equipped with a series of sound bites that could easily be edited into a brief news report. A final letter calling for supermarkets to stock more organic produce at reasonable prices was sent to the local paper. The event also involved the whole local group and many ordinary people who, when passing by, noticed the MP holding a box of vegetables in front of a photographer and wanted to show their support. They stood by the MP and had their picture taken too. This was a classic win-win situation in which many people enjoyed participating actively in a public event. Citizenship and campaigning can and should be fun.

Journalists want news stories. It is not easy to describe what makes a good news story, but a key ingredient is something involving local people or local personalities. Other elements include controversy; previously unpublished facts (hence the number of items which include lines such as, 'A leaked Council report shows . . .' or 'Shock new research reveals . . .') as well as visual appeal. What you find interesting, or important, is not necessarily news. Opinions are not usually news either. You can (and of course should) express an opinion, but only if you are presenting news. External events often make a good story. Disapproving of plans to build a new road past your home may only become news if campaigners organise a demonstration of outraged homeowners, some dressed in costumes, at the meeting councillors are expected to vote for the plan.

Gilligan, E & Watson, A (2000) *How to Win: A guide to successful campaigning*, **London, Friends of the Earth, pp58–9**

The key to securing the interest of the media is to know what they want. Modest events, which strike a chord with journalists and their readers, can be very effective and success gives the local group a boost and a sense of achievement. Citizenship is participation with a human as well as a political purpose. It is also a way of directly influencing the democratic process by directly influencing the views of a Member of Parliament who in the future may ask questions, make speeches, as well as vote on issues that further the cause or defend the interests a local campaigning group supports.

Individual campaigns

Sometimes individuals and their families have to fight long and hard to get things done or to win justice for their families.

Community action

Reaching compromise and resolving disputes often requires making decisions that do not suit all people. Below are three case studies of issues where more than one side to the issue emerges. Study the cases and consider them from both sides of the argument and explore ways through which compromise could be reached.

CASE STUDY: Bristol Heart Children's Action Group

'I have a caption on my mobile phone that says Justice for the Children. That's the only thing that motivates me. These children can't speak for themselves – all you can do is try and extract as much justice for them as you can,' says Steve Parker, chairman of the Bristol Heart Children's Action Group (BHCAG).

The story of the 'Bristol Heart Babies' is a familiar one. The deaths of many children who underwent heart surgery at the Bristol Royal Infirmary between 1984–95 and the subsequent investigation into why has been in the headlines for the last five years.

But headlines don't always tell the full story. The story, that is, of the campaigners' long struggle to get justice – the endless meetings with government officials, the legal wrangles and their sheer determination to succeed.

Parker's wife Diana lost her daughter Jessica, before they met, after she underwent heart surgery at the Infirmary in 1989. Parker is one of those at the centre of the battle.

How it started

The campaign only began in 1995, when Stephen Bolsin, the anaesthetist present during many of the operations, spoke openly on TV about his concerns over the number of babies who had died. Before that, many parents hadn't realised the extent of the problem at the hospital. 'When your child goes into hospital, you know there's a risk. If they die, you tend to think, "I'm just one of the unlucky ones",' says Parker.

'And you're so traumatised, you tend not to be in a state to question it.' After Bolsin spoke out, several families got together and formed the Bristol Heart Children's Action Group. But Parker was reluctant to get involved. 'At first, I thought that my wife, having lost her child, was just searching around for reasons why,' he explains. 'You never believe that there's something seriously wrong at a hospital.'

But before he knew it, he became deeply involved in the campaign for the public inquiry during the General Medical Council's inquiry into the hospital's practices.

Under the media spotlight

The GMC inquiry was the turning point for the campaign. Carrying little black shoeboxes with crosses on the front for each child who died, the families made their way to the inquiry in London. Media attention was huge. 'The families were thrust right onto the front page,' says Parker. 'The fact that it was babies who had died made it a big story for the press. I don't think they would have been as interested if it was geriatric patients.'

'But the intense media spotlight was a hindrance as well as a help,' says Parker. 'The difficulty is that the press likes to focus on the bad things. They ask questions like, just how upset are you? And they keep going until the person cries. It's cruel. They should be asking how we can make sure it doesn't happen again.'

Nevertheless, Parker acknowledges that the media helped to bring about a public inquiry.

The public inquiry

Once in place, the public inquiry, which lasted two years, was hard going. As well as the trauma of reliving their nightmares, the group had to read through mountains of evidence, compile arguments and give daily comments to the press. The report that followed the public inquiry found that around one third of all the children who underwent open-heart surgery at the Infirmary between 1984–95 received 'less than adequate care'.

More importantly, it found that 'in the period between 1991–5, between 30–5 more children under one died after open-heart surgery in the Bristol Unit than might be expected.'

Sheer determination

Parker believes the families' refusal to give up has been crucial to the group's success. 'The dedication and sheer perseverance of the families who, considering how traumatised they were, still kept on pushing, has been astounding.' But he admits it hasn't been easy for the families to keep the group together. 'When dealing with emotions, people want to do their own thing. For some, the need to tell their child's story to the media became an end in itself. And that annoyed others who felt it was the same people, time and time again, in the press.

'The fact that we still exist is amazing. Lots of groups disintegrate after a period of time.'

The future

'The public inquiry report was just that – a report. We now need implementation of the changes – a proper system for investigating doctors' mistakes, audit mechanisms, cultural changes. The families also want a memorial for their children.'

And is Parker still keen to lead the fight? 'I don't know. You go through phases of being enthusiastic, then apathetic. Having to work two or three hours extra a night after work, trips at weekends, saving your holiday up to work on the campaign – it's hard to keep your energy levels up.' But he adds: 'The negatives are far outweighed by the positives. At the end of the day, even if it only saves one child's life, it's worth it. It's the only way to honour these children.'

This article appears on www.JustDoSomething.net, a website published by international educational organisation Common Purpose

ACTIVITY

1) How effective was the campaign?
2) What could have been done differently?
3) Was Steve Parker's motivation purely personal?
4) What does this case study tell us about the nature of citizen action?

CASE STUDY: Campaign to halt the closure of care homes in Burnley

Join march to stop closures

The Lancashire Evening Telegraph is today urging YOU to join a protest march to stop the closure of 35 old folks' homes.

We want readers to take part in the event next Saturday to show county hall bosses the anger over plans to close the care homes.

The march will take place in Burnley town centre and is being backed by our MPs and politicians.

Kevin Young, editor of The Lancashire Evening Telegraph, said: 'This march is a great opportunity for the people of Lancashire to demonstrate their opposition to the ill-conceived plans to shut down these homes.

'It's a unique chance to show solidarity with hundreds of senior citizens who have given so much to this country and who now face a dreadful uncertainty over their futures. Let's hope it sends a clear message to the County Council that what they are doing is quite simply wrong.'

A Lancashire Evening Telegraph campaign to stop the closure of 35 of the council's 48 care homes – 19 of which are in East Lancashire – has already got the backing of 2000 of our readers.

Lancashire County Council leader and Rossendale county councillor Hazel Harding or councillor Chris Cheetham, head of Social Services, are expected to be at the bandstand to receive a petition signed by protesters.

The council is in the middle of a four-month consultation on whether to shut the care homes to save spending £14.5 million on repairing them and bringing them up to new national standards.

Some of the residents living in homes in Burnley have already been moved once, when Lancashire County Council closed a home in the town in 1998.

Councillor Birtwistle said: 'We are just putting the final preparations in place. We hope it will be as big as the protests in Preston when they closed the last lot of homes in 1998. There was a massive turnout to that.

'People in the homes will be joining us if possible. We are hoping to get wheelchairs and sticks so people can join us, but we need friends, relatives and supporters to come along as well.

'We have to halt these closures.'

He has also set up an anti-home closure group of relatives who have people living in the affected homes that meets regularly to plan action to try to ensure the proposal does not become a reality.

The Lancashire Evening Telegraph, **15 April 2002**

1) To what extent do you think a march is appropriate for elderly people who may have mobility problems?
2) A celebrity, Claire Raynor the agony aunt, was expected to attend the march and rally. How do you think this could be exploited to secure further media coverage for the campaign?
3) Discuss the role of the local newspaper in organising and promoting the march. How important to the success of the campaign is this media involvement?
4) The review of council spending of £14.5 million may lead to alternative provision at less cost. Write a short report to the leader of the campaign supporting the use of the funds for alternative provision.

CASE STUDY: Unhappy landing: ancient heronry threatened by airport plans

They appear as fantastic shapes – angular, elongated, with almost a touch of the prehistoric about them, as if pterodactyls were swooping through the skies.

But these are herons, scores of them, floating from the marshes where they have spent the day hunting, to their roosting place in an ancient wood. The flap of their great wings is languid and deliberate, the bringing forward of their gangly legs seems clumsy in the extreme, but unfailingly they come to rest in the top branches of the oak trees uttering hoarse squawks – an unearthly sound in the still evening air.

The spectacle is astonishing. This is Northward Hill Wood in Kent, the largest heronry in Britain, where more than 160 pairs of the great fisher birds breed every year. And if government proposals, reissued yesterday, for a new airport at Cliffe on the Kent marshes go ahead, it will be bulldozed.

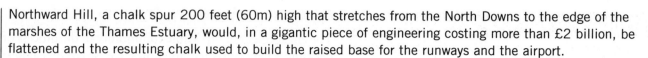

Northward Hill, a chalk spur 200 feet (60m) high that stretches from the North Downs to the edge of the marshes of the Thames Estuary, would, in a gigantic piece of engineering costing more than £2 billion, be flattened and the resulting chalk used to build the raised base for the runways and the airport.

The heronry, with its 320+ inhabitants, contains virtually all the herons of the lower Thames. And for several years it has held a growing population of little egrets, the smaller, white relatives of the heron, which began breeding in Britain in 1996.

The proposed new airport is in the middle of one of the most protected areas, in conservation terms, in all of Britain. The lower Thames Estuary is blanketed with protected sites under the Ramsar Convention, the international treaty covering wetlands, and the European Union Birds Directive; and the airport would directly affect five nature reserves run by the Royal Society for the Protection of Birds (RSPB), including Northward Hill. The area contains up to 200,000 wintering wildfowl; in summer, it hosts more than 100 breeding pairs of avocets, the bird that is the RSPB's symbol.

Michael McCarthy, *The Independent,* **28 February 2003**

ACTIVITY

1) Make a case for and against the decision to build the new airport. Consider the local economy, the wider need to build more airports as the public demand to fly increases, and the natural environment and tourism.
2) Suggest campaigning strategies that the RSPB could adopt to stop the plans.

ACTIVITY

1) How might the Youth Unity Project involve PC Fisher in its efforts to promote unity between the racial groups?
2) Suggest other activities the group could organise to appeal to young people and suggest how these might be publicised.

Not all community action for change has to involve campaigns and petitions. The case study below illustrates effective citizenship through taking initiative to promote community participation.

CASE STUDY: Youth Unity Project

The Youth Unity Project is run by a group of Asian youngsters aged between 18–25, aimed at improving social integration in all sections of the community. The project sprung out of the Burnley task force report following last year's riots, which called for more integration between racial groups in the town. The initiative will be launched with a fun day at the youth centre. Longer-term projects include anti-vandalism schemes and awareness days. PC Nick Fisher said, 'I have worked with young people for more than 13 years and this project is the most dynamic I have ever come across.'

Adapted from *The Lancashire Evening Telegraph,* **13 April 2002**

Citizenship, empowerment and community action

If citizenship is about doing things then, apart from having the skills, knowledge and perhaps connections to make oneself heard, what is also important is the existence of structures that make this possible. A free press can only exist without oppressive or restrictive censorship. People can only participate in the affairs of local government if there are ways for this participation to take place. You can only write so many letters and receive only so many non-committal or bureaucratic replies before one feels the whole 'system' is a conspiracy against you or the values of a participatory democracy are purely idealistic. If one has the means and access to the appropriate channels then citizens are able to act effectively. However, **empowerment** involves both feelings and beliefs in one's political effectiveness and hard evidence that actions really do have an effect on the way decisions are made and the way policies are formulated and carried out. Empowerment and capacity building are valued highly but they need to be realised in the real world of social and political action.

It may be asking too much to expect local government to get people shouting from the rooftops. But it is not too much to expect most people to care enough to vote or to know who to praise or blame for what is going on in their locality. [...]

But it is not just **representative democracy** *that needs to be strengthened. We all need to look at other democratic initiatives that will strengthen community leadership. Councils need to avoid getting trapped in the secret world of the caucus and the party group. They should let local people have their say. Some authorities are doing this. Citizen juries are helping to build consensus for tackling difficult issues. Local surveys are being used more and more to identify local concerns. And the local referendum could become part and parcel of a council's toolkit to help it exercise its leadership function.*

Tony Blair, Prime Minister, IPPR (1998) *Leading the Way: A new vision for local government,* **London, pp14–15**

Participation and citizenship can be rather disturbing even annoying for those who believe that democracy is too important to be left to the people. It makes the whole process of decision-making more cumbersome, messy and perhaps even more costly. Some politicians feel the public is an interfering nuisance and would prefer to channel or control their participation in public affairs. They are sometimes right, but citizens need to reflect very critically on the types of participatory procedures local government or other bodies are offering.

One way of forming this is to relate what type of citizen participation or empowerment is being experienced with a hierarchical measure. Is this consultation real or just for show – purely cosmetic? Am I being heard and if so, are these people actually listening to me? Am I making a difference?

Prior to the 1998 DETR document *Modern Local Government,* many local councils would hardly have gone beyond the citizen non-participation zone. With focus groups, citizen juries, visioning exercises and the setting up of area committees, many are now moving into the citizen participation bracket, though not many are in the citizen control zone where neighbourhood committees are given direct control over budgets or services. This is part fear of the democratic process being hijacked by un- or anti-democratic bodies made real by the British National Party's local election victory in Tower Hamlets, Oldham and Burnley, or the destructive disagreements evident in Walsall between national and local politicians.

Engagement of communities

The engagement of the whole community in the process of deciding where and what amenities, e.g. shops or schools, are most appropriately located is becoming a means whereby people can actively apply their citizenship skills. This is community planning and requires decision-making to be located at the lowest effective level, e.g. the neighbourhood community. If community planning works then it will not be 'them' doing things to 'us' but us deciding for ourselves what should be done or where things should go and monitoring effective implementation of those decisions.

Planning for Real

There are many techniques which facilitate community participation and so help to empower individuals. One example is Planning for Real, in which a large 3-D model of the local neighbourhood is made and used by local people to show their needs in a non-confrontational way. Local schools and local groups help to make the model, which is then taken around to different venues to raise awareness. Interest can also be generated through surveys designed by residents to identify local resources, skills and experience. The model is used at open meetings, which are held at places and times suited to the community. Women only consultations may be organised in Muslim communities or special events may be staged to attract young people. The suggestion cards and the publicity materials are often translated into local languages. At the Planning for Real exercise lots of illustrated suggestion cards are available covering issues such as:

- community facilities
- crime and safety
- the local environment
- health
- housing
- leisure
- traffic and transport
- work
- training
- the local economy.

Blank cards are also available for people to make their own suggestions. The use of the model, on which participants place their suggestion cards, ensures that full participation is achieved. A model is much more easily understood than a map. Using suggestion cards means that ideas can be put forward without participants feeling the need to be verbally articulate or self-confident. The pictures on the suggestion cards assist those with poor literacy skills and those whose first language is not English. As Wares (2000) notes, these directly accessible methods appeal to people of all ages. Planning for Real events have happened all over the country, from densely populated urban areas in London and Leeds to small rural communities like Satterthwaite in the Colne Valley. Further information can be obtained from the Neighbourhood Initiatives Foundation.

4 Community structures and running campaigns

This section extends the exploration of community action and examines the structures and systems that exist in local communities through which individual and group action can be undertaken. It looks at:

- community planning
- effective meetings
- building communities through citizen participation.

Community planning

The [Planning for Real] concept is already used by local authorities and community groups in over 100 localities: in England, Scotland and Wales; and in Tanzania, Zambia, India, Cambodia, Germany, Australia and the USA. The Planning for Real process usually involves resident-led surveys, which are conducted face-to-face at each house. These seek to identify hidden practical talents of residents who would not always be adept at communicating in the more traditional form of consultation – the public meeting. Following the surveys, an action plan is drawn up where everyone agrees what should be done immediately, soon and later. This also determines what can realistically be done by residents unaided, with a little money and advice, or jointly with an outside body.

Adapted from Neighbourhood Initiatives Foundation promotional material

Community planning is not particularly new and may be traced back to initiatives in community architecture and co-operative building in the early 1970s. The Jagonari Centre for Asian Women in Whitechapel, East London, was developed with the full and direct involvement of its future users, a feminist designed co-operative and the Greater London Council. The main ideas developed from the Jagonari women's images of buildings and the scheme

that emerged reflected the group's functional requirements and concerns – a courtyard that imitated traditional Asian design and security from possible racist attacks. The main hall and seminar rooms were located on the first and second floors giving users privacy and safety from the public domain. The building was completed in 1987. Community planning requires a developmental approach to community learning and decision-making. Creative Spaces integrates issues of the built environment with social issues such as:

- unemployment
- crime
- health
- education
- housing.

It creatively involves local people in designing sustainable solutions to urban problems. Outcomes cannot or should not be pre-set or prejudged.

John Thompson, a veteran of over 50 community planning exercises, writes:

People deserve the opportunity of being able to find out what they really need. They may not know at first. Initial responses usually reflect negative perceptions – 'We don't want any more people round here – there are too many cars on the road already and the schools are all full.'

At Lea View House [in Hackney], the shopping list of improvements that the tenants had already demanded would have done little to alleviate their real problems. Nobody had asked them if they needed a new way of living, merely what was wrong with their flats. The solutions that eventually emerged were new, radical and only became obvious when discovered.

Active and genuine participation on housing estates can ensure **regeneration** and renewal, as the experience of the Hulme and Royds inner city estates testifies. Significant government funds are regularly directed towards improving depressed areas where there exists low levels of economic activity, often high levels of crime, drug abuse and social and personal alienation. Strategies to involve the local community in regeneration processes provide a schooling in citizenship, which perhaps even prefigures a form of community self-governance itself. It is through experience of taking part, of analysing issues, listening to others, making decisions and seeing them carried out that citizens feel and become empowered.

Participation schemes

Participation schemes have usually focused on groups experiencing specific and serious disadvantage and marginalization. The government's National Strategy for Neighbourhood Renewal, Lifelong Learning: The Active Community Initiative and the New Deal for Communities projects are designed to address issues of unemployment, deprivation, crime, poverty and social exclusion. Critics of earlier participatory initiatives have noted that they tend to mirror areas where the state can most easily intervene to shape the form participation takes. They suggest that non-involvement or exclusion is in some way a consequence of the particular social characteristics and educational deficits of the excluded themselves. The policy emphasis focuses on life skills and if this is all that is required then any reform of the formal political structures, institutions and processes need only be modest and limited in scope. The problem remains, however, that if democracy is to be genuinely deepened then structures and institutions will require radical reform and new values and new social relationships will need to develop.

In a study of mass housing in Northern Europe, Anne Power notes that the key to reinvigorating democracy and encouraging participation is to concentrate on areas small enough for residents to identify with. Commitment to a place is significant but so is the capacity to pool resources, to meet and work together in a context the citizens have some influence on.

> 1) **How might community planning activities empower citizens?**
> 2) **Why should people get involved?**

Find out if any community planning or similar activities have taken place in your area.
■ What did people do and what did they think of it?
■ Were they empowered?

Effective meetings

Community participation often means meetings. Each meeting will have a number of people who, although sharing the same or similar concerns or values, will bring with them something distinct derived from their individual knowledge or experience. It is important to recognise that groups are more than the sum of their parts. They take on a life and personality of their own. Some are chatty and co-operative. Others are sullen and quarrelsome. Certain members may take a different view on the gravity of the issue than others and differences, even conflicts, may result. However, the object of holding meetings is to reach some type of conclusion or agreement.

Conflict in meetings

Conflict may be valuable if it means people being able to express their viewpoints, but this needs to be done sensibly, recognising that others, too, have a view worthy of respect and attention. Sometimes it is difficult to accept some views and occasionally ideas expressed may seem so bizarre or perhaps even offensive that they should not be tolerated. If this situation occurs, then problems could arise. Ground rules need to be set from the beginning. There should be no badmouthing other people's contributions, no racist or sexist language, no swearing or blasphemy, etc. If members find it difficult to understand or appreciate where someone is coming from, then a useful exercise is to attempt to see the problem as the other sees it, to empathise with his or her feelings or experiences. This may not lead to agreement but it may at least help communication and mutual understanding. Free expression enables issues to be examined from a variety of perspectives but even this may not lead to consensus among the group. What is more likely and probably more pragmatic is to reach a shared understanding of the main points, accepting that differences may remain. Democracy, citizenship and neighbourhood or campaign group meetings should deliberate rationally, allowing members the space to persuade or the opportunity to negotiate an outcome. Groups may sometimes come to a decision by **voting**, but sometimes voting simply shows up divisions and does not help to bring people together.

Participation experiences

The experience of participation and of deliberative democracy often has a transforming effect on the participatory process itself and on the people involved in it. A learning process emerges whereby getting involved enhances the experience of everyday life. This can then have a mobilising and motivating effect in the wider community. Selfishness or NIMBYism no longer seems as significant as it initially did, as collective achievement demonstrates that concern for others' needs do not necessarily diminish one's own benefits. The experience of community participation, of being a part of a group and contributing to meetings, enables people to develop democratic citizenship skills:

- holding coherent meetings
- allowing all to speak
- learning how to debate and vote on complex issues where choices are multiple.

There are numerous guides to conducting good meetings and many accessible textbooks on group dynamics discussing at length how to deal with common problems groups experience. What follows are simply a few tips and pointers which might help with some of the problems of managing something like a community council or voluntary group meeting.

- Participants should have clear roles and responsibilities.
- Objectives should be set which are SMART – Specific, Measurable, Achievable, Realistic and Time limited.
- Action plans could be developed.
- Activities could be organised to break the ice or facilitate networking.
- Fun should be on the agenda.

Being SMART

Specific, Measurable, Achievable, Realistic and Time limited objectives are important because they keep people focused. If an objective is specific, then what is to be done is easily understood, e.g. getting new computers for a local youth and community centre. If the objective is measurable, say two computers, then getting one is obviously not enough. If a community group is able to raise money for four or five, then setting a higher target would not be realistic or achievable. Putting a time limit on an objective keeps people on track. Not specifying a time or specifying too short or long a time would be unhelpful. Being SMART is something like a group saying 'we intend and are able to raise money to buy two new computers for our youth and community centre by Christmas'.

Dealing with group problems

If the group is not working well together for whatever reason, ensure the ground rules are adhered to. It may be that no one should speak twice until everyone has had the opportunity to say something. Sometimes groups become affected by a dominant personality who may be loud, negative, cynical or just domineering. His or her views should be acknowledged, perhaps with a joke, but the meeting should be moved on to allow others to contribute. It might be useful to break the group up into smaller units to affect this. Sometimes people start muttering privately about lack of progress or direction and although this is not recom-

mended, a dedicated period for review and appraisal could counteract the drift towards disillusion and resignation. There is no magic formula for conducting meetings.

It doesn't take much to know when things work well and when things are badly wrong. Often it is just a case of good habits being swamped by bad ones. Groups get stuck in bad meeting habits for a variety of reasons. They may be reluctant even to acknowledge they have a problem. Change can only happen with the consent of the group or at least its key people. Unfortunately, these can be the very people whose behaviour creates the problem! Ideas about change will then have to be introduced subtly, in such a way that no one feels undermined by them.

Friends of the Earth briefing

Citizenship is a continuous learning experience acquired through processes of participation and empowerment.

? The playwright George Bernard Shaw once remarked that the problem with socialism was that it took up too many evenings. What do you think he meant?

Building communities through citizen participation

In Britain, the New Economics Foundation, the Worldwide Fund for Nature, Friends of the Earth and the Community Development Foundation have published material to help individuals and community groups get involved and make a difference. People need to examine their communities to see what is good, what is bad, what can be done to improve them, and to encourage people to be more active. This leads to developing techniques that facilitate community participation and the identification of **indicators**, which show what progress, if any, is being made towards developing more sustainable communities.

Many communities in Britain are developing sets of indicators to measure the local trends that directly matter to them. Many activities are co-ordinated by the local authority and some are organised by community activists or environmentalist groups. People are measuring trends in large inner city districts and small rural villages. The problems of inner city decay and rural isolation, poverty and social exclusion, and depressed local economies means that **sustainable development** and regeneration are frequently one and the same.

How to protect and enhance the environment	Examples of popular community indicators
Use energy, water and other natural resources efficiently and with care	Number of buildings measured for energy efficiency Water leakage (in litres/property/day)
Value and protect the diversity of nature	Wildlife in rivers and streams Wildlife diversity
Protect human health and amenity through safe, clean, pleasant environments	Number of asthma cases Skin cancer incidences Number of asthma treatments prescribed
Meet needs locally wherever possible	Percentage of shops selling locally produced or processed foods Basic services within walking distance Alternative means of transport: kilometres of dedicated cycle routes
Ensure access to good food, water, housing and fuel at reasonable costs	Homelessness: number of households applying to local authorities Average house prices Availability of a healthy food basket

McGillivray, A, Weston, C, and Unsworth, C (1998) *Communities Count!* London, New Economics Foundation. Adapted from pp152–5

In all these projects it is local people deciding together what is important to them and agreeing how best to measure whether things are getting better or worse. This results in increased social awareness and feelings of empowerment that helps build agreement about what should or could be done. As the New Economic Foundation states, when communities start to look at things and are empowered to make decisions about their way of living, Local Agenda 21 becomes real. When armed with facts people are able to:

- participate in their communities. People have a great deal to offer to their communities but are all too easily excluded. Increasingly, central government, local authorities and other bodies are appreciating the value of the participation of as many people as possible in the running of their communities.
- strengthen their arguments, raising awareness about the need for action, demonstrating the benefits of what local groups are doing, and building the case for outside support and funding.
- build capacity, learning new skills and developing community relationships. Working with indicators helps people to decide on priorities, decide what action to take, monitor progress and celebrate achievements. It can even be fun!

Sustainable development

Sustainable development also means community based economic enterprises, e.g. farmers' markets, credit unions, time banks, retail and producer co-operatives, Local Exchange and Trading Schemes (LETS), which may contribute to the regeneration of local economies and communities of mutuality that sustain them. LETS are an innovative approach to resource and equipment sharing involving trading networks in which people use a local currency – the bobbin in Manchester, the nidd in Nidderdale – to pay for goods and services offered by other members. There are around 450 LETS in the UK and about 50 across mainland Europe concentrating on the provision of services to meet needs rather than consumption of material goods.

In the process, social relationships within communities are nurtured and strengthened, individual skills are developed, and for those on low incomes, self-esteem may be regained because the financial costs of participating in community life are removed. People offer to baby sit, loan their tools or knit a jumper, teach a skill in return for having their kitchen painted, their hair cut or getting use of a computer. LETS has the potential to address issues relating to:

- poverty
- unemployment
- social and financial exclusion.

Women seem to be more active in LETS than men and the large pay differences that exist in the formal economy are not replicated in LETS trading. In many schemes, work that has traditionally been low paid, such as childcare, are rewarded more generously.

Local actions can have wide social implications and impacts on policies supporting sustainable urban development.

Local people's participation in the planning of their own community developments, participating in the design of their own community's architecture, enhances interest in a political process that becomes directly relevant to the improvement of people's quality of lives and even livelihoods. It is a way of building citizenship, eco-conscious neighbourhoods, democratically designed public space and inclusive communities, as the experience of redeveloping and regenerating on the Hulme housing estate in inner city Manchester testifies.

?
1) What are community indicators?
2) How might LETS make a difference to people's lives?
3) What are the lessons from Hulme?

5 Information and communication technology networking and citizen participation

This section explores the impact on campaigning using information and communication technology. It looks at:

- Internet campaigning
- ICT enhancing democratic debate
- online campaigning and e-democracy.

Internet campaigning

US activist and community networker Ed Schwartz wrote a book on the use of the Internet for campaigning called *NetActivism: How Citizens Use the Internet*. He comments:

The heart of political organizing and advocacy is communication. At any given moment, we need to be able to reach one another and to speak out to the people in power. Up to now, we have to rely on snail mail, telephones, and fax machines. All are expensive and limited in their outreach. Only large organisations or movements with sizeable budgets could make full use of them.

Email now adds a powerful new resource to the list. It is not simply a 'me-to-you' broadcasting system. It is a powerful 'we-to-us' communications system. It is this system that permits people from all parts of the world to connect simultaneously

CASE STUDY: Hulme

The lessons from the redevelopment of Hulme in Manchester show clearly that communities that have taken generations to create can be destroyed virtually overnight. Only by ensuring that a firm and trusting relationship is created and maintained between tenants and local authorities can the necessary affordable housing be built which meets all the social, cultural and community needs of local people. Tenant involvement with housing professionals actually makes things happen faster: much to the surprise of sceptics who may feel local people only get in the way of redevelopment.

As the Joseph Rowntree Foundation report, *Lessons from Hulme*, states: 'The houses and flats that are currently being redeveloped incorporate many of the layouts and practical ideas suggested by residents. For example, plans for a network of cul-de-sacs were rejected in favour of the tenants' proposals for a traditional street grid with a more "urban" mixture of houses and flats … Tenant involvement on the Hulme model is a principle that could be extended from social housing to other decision-making about shops, schools and wider planning issues.'

Joseph Rowntree Foundation, www.jrf.org.uk

with one another quickly, easily, and at minimal cost. This is the system that holds the greatest for the Internet in politics.

Schwartz, E *NetActivsim: How Citizens Use the Internet* **(1996), O'Reilly**

Information and communication technologies (ICTs) have the potential to offset certain disadvantages derived from social deprivation and physical disability. People may be able to overcome problems with the use of standard computers with additional software. Multiple sclerosis sufferers may continue to work at home by having their keyboards retuned to different reaction speeds or new software installed so the same things may be accomplished by different means. Cost, access and awareness will always be a problem until resources are made broadly available by government and other agencies. The 1998 Social Exclusion Unit report, *Bringing Britain Together: A National Strategy for Neighbourhood Renewal,* noted that the lack of access to ICTs may lead to or reinforce disadvantage and prevent active citizenship in a number of ways.

- For children, not having access to computers and the Internet at home or in the community may make it hard to keep up in school.
- For adults, computer literacy can be important for re-entering the labour market.
- For the community as a whole, access to communication networks can improve the quality of services, make it easier to realise opportunities in other areas, and possibly enhance social capital.

Advantages of ICTs

New technologies have the potential to develop social, community and employment related skills. In the Westvale Resource Centre in Knowsley, Merseyside, adults with learning difficulties are using ICTs to produce their own community newspaper and in the process are developing basic literacy and numeracy skills and personal self-confidence. ICTs may operate in a similar way in deprived neighbourhoods to support community development projects and enable communities to regain self-respect and some social solidarity. The Artmedia project in Batley, West Yorkshire, uses multimedia technologies and digital arts to enable Afro-Caribbean women to record their own experiences of immigration and settlement in the UK. Others used ICTs to develop a digital community archive. Local artists and photographers used ICTs to produce a digital gallery. New technologies can also help communities function on a more practical level if local authorities are able to establish 'one stop shop' approaches to information and services through things such as information kiosks, council websites, the Internet, call centres and video conferencing.

In Lewisham, South London, residents can log their housing problems on the Internet without having to visit council offices. In the Harrogate district, covering over 500 square miles of North Yorkshire, people are able to find their nearest recycling centre by using an interactive page on the council's website. ICTs can be both a positive and negative force. Online shopping, for example, may benefit the elderly in one way but may reinforce isolation in another. The technologies are not ends in themselves but a means to an end. Social, community or more broadly, citizenship activities should not be focused on technology but supported by it. This is the case with the successful development of certain IT based community resource centres, e.g. the Grimethorpe Electronic Village Hall.

The government report, *Closing the Digital Divide: Information and Communication Technology in Deprived Areas* (2000), states:

Healthy, sustainable communities depend on levels of formal and informal community activity. Where people are organised and support one another informally in neighbourhood life, they are likely also to be in a position to articulate their needs effectively and work with authorities to address those needs. Access to common resources, which includes ICTs, can stimulate community involvement in a range of activities leading to greater social cohesion, reduced welfare dependency, education opportunities and economic development.

However, many of the hopes for a cyber-based participatory democracy expressed by activists can probably be realised only with the help of long-term public funding, community development work, appropriate learning support, and significant changes in political culture. There is the additional problem of the rich excluding themselves from mainstream society and living within privately walled communities, buying private healthcare, CCTV protection, education and pensions, perceiving their obligations to be primarily, maybe exclusively, to themselves. Others are to be feared or hired rather than helped.

ICT enhancing democratic debate

Miranda Mowbray researches social and practical issues in running online communities at Hewlett Packard Laboratories.

'The Internet is not just a library. Although it's a good idea to put useful civic information online, it's a pity not to take advantage of the possibilities for two-way (and multi-way) communication. Similarly, although it's good to put educational material on the Internet, e-learning works best when there is also an opportunity to contact other human beings for discussion and teaching.

'The Internet has a role in enhancing democracy, but not through simplistic enthusiasm for e-voting.

'To increase voter turnout, allow postal voting. It does increase turnout, it's accessible, and we know how to make it reasonably secure and private. E-voting is riskier.

'As for e-plebiscites, I agree with the e-envoy, Andrew Pinder; that they lead to "hastily-formed and ill-informed judgements". Giving citizens the ability to make instant votes, and the ability to email their representatives rather than just writing a letter, won't do much for democracy. To enhance democracy, you need to enhance the quality of democratic debate, and the Internet can help with this.

'Online is not a substitute for offline. For best results in the civic use of the Internet, have offline meetings as well, and work with offline organisations.'

Wilcox, D and Pearl, M, *Civic and Community Technology*, http://www.makingthenetwork.org/docs/journal2.htm

Online campaigning and e-democracy

Tearfund, an organisation campaigning for Third World debt reduction, arranged an Internet link-up between the Chancellor of the Exchequer Gordon Brown and Elinata Kasanga, a poor woman with seven children living in Balakasau, Zambia. The Internet made information readily available to all debt campaigners and in the summer of 2000, cyber campaigning reached a peak when the Italian government closed its email account after receiving 65,000 emails calling for debt cancellation in a single day. Cyber-campaigners, such as the Electrohippies Collective, are now establishing their own virtual organisations to defend the Internet from what they see as dangerous attempts by various states and corporations to establish censorship and control. The potential for an IT influenced democracy is quite real if its interactive and dynamic dimensions are properly exploited.

In December 2000, the government launched the UK Online Citizen Portal, (www.ukonline.gov.uk) as part of its wider initiative to ensure universal access to the Internet and having all government information and services online by 2005. Cabinet Office Minister Ian McCartney said that:

In time, the portal will help revolutionise the relationship between government and citizens by turning public services inside out. Instead of being organised around government bureaucracy, they'll be organised for the citizen's convenience.

There are also significant concerns relating to human and civil rights abuses. On one hand, ICT allows for the creation of a surveillance culture, on the other, a couch potato subjectivity. Although largely silent on the effects of computer technologies, Putnam (2000) identifies television viewing, an essentially passive and private experience already associated with low social capital and the corrosion of character, as the prime suspect in explaining the decline of civic participation in the USA. Active citizenship involves changes to what we value, what we do, and how we live our everyday lives.

1) Why is the government developing its online portal?
2) Give examples of how ICT could promote active citizenship.
3) How can ICT help communities develop?

Conclusion

Material poverty and a lack of education and skills need to be addressed if we are to feel able to participate effectively. People should not be excluded or forced to conform. Conflict will need to be channelled in productive ways so that trust and community are reinforced. Some sociologists argue that people are bound together more by verbal conflict than by (immediate) verbal agreement. In an attempt to resolve conflict situations, people work hard at communicating and learning how to listen and respond to one another even when differences are felt keenly.

- Social conflicts may actually be good for democracy.
- Freedom is found in the way people resist domination through the creation of new social identities or by organising protests and campaigns.
- Strong civil societies will allow conflict to take place and be resolved. Existing structures, relations and processes of power, systems of administration and government will need to be challenged as well as reformed.

- New habits, perspectives and values need to be nurtured and developed along sustainable lines.

Recent evidence from the urban regeneration projects set up under the New Deal for Communities scheme show an increased interest and participation in local issues, partly as a result of having the opportunity to cast votes by post and partly because people are seeing themselves as having real influence. Elections to New Deal partnerships have attracted turnouts of over 50%, something virtually unheard of in local government elections. Global protests too have resulted in positive outcomes, e.g. some debt relief for the developing countries. Many people see the emergence of a **global civil society** with citizen action based in local community activities or with individuals sitting at home writing a letter on behalf of Amnesty International.

1) How might discussion and argument bring people together?

2) What are the most important factors in helping people get active and be empowered?

ACTIVITY

Investigate how a local group organises itself or campaigns on an issue in your local community. Address the points in the list below.

- How is it organised?
- How many members are there?
- Is everyone involved?
- What knowledge and skills do people have or need?
- How are meetings conducted?
- What are the group's objectives?
- What relationship does the group have with the local media?
- How successful is the group?

Exam questions

You must answer Question 1 and either Question 2 or 3.

1) Read **Sources A** and **B** and answer parts (a)–(c) which follow.

Source A

> From the top of Plynlimon Mountain in the heart of mid-Wales, the view is staggering. The grandeur is undeniable, but for some the view is ruined by the sight of more than 250 wind turbines dotted around the landscape in every direction. Energy companies have been attracted to the area because mid-Wales is ideal wind power territory – economically depressed, under-populated and near to the National Electricity Grid.
>
> The government supports the development of more renewable energy sources. Its plans to build another 34 huge wind turbines in the area have horrified the Cefn Croes campaign, a group of people opposed to further wind farm developments in mid-Wales. Their spokesman said, 'This land is under threat. 44% of all the wind turbines in Britain are situated in mid-Wales and the planned site for the next 34 is in a designated environmentally sensitive area and next to one of the largest sites of special scientific interest in Wales. Furthermore, the wind turbines will bring virtually no benefits to the local economy.' Almost all local community groups have made their opposition to the new site very clear to government ministers. However, the local County Council overwhelmingly passed the scheme after a series of consultation meetings.
>
> **Adapted from** *The Guardian*, **20 February 2002**

Source B

> Some groups have disagreed with objections to the plan for more wind turbines. The British Wind Association's spokesman in Wales said, 'The Cefn Croes group claim to represent local communities, but they don't. Any opposition could affect the long-term development of the Welsh countryside. They seem to want a landscape with no one living in it. The key point is "whose landscape is it?" Is it the property of a few unelected groups of preservationists or does it belong to local communities? Rural communities keep saying: "Give us jobs, bring us economic development". Wind farms bring work and rental money which feeds into the local economy.'
>
> **Adapted from** *The Guardian*, **20 February 2002**

Your answers should refer to the sources as appropriate but you should also include other relevant information.

(a) Explain **two** reasons why the Cefn Croes group is opposed to further wind turbine developments in their area. (**Source A**)

(4 marks)

(b) Briefly examine some of the tactics which the Cefn Croes group could use to gain media coverage in support of their campaign.

(10 marks)

(c) Assess how far it might be possible to reach a solution that satisfies both the Cefn Croes group and the British Wind Association.

(16 marks)

2) (a) Briefly examine some of the ways in which the content of the mass media may be biased.

(10 marks)

(b) Assess the extent to which members of different social groups may experience unequal life-chances. (20 marks)

3) (a) Briefly examine some of the effects of poverty on individuals and families. (10 marks)

(b) Assess the ways in which governments can attempt to reduce discrimination against particular social groups. (20 marks)

AQA, 3 June 2003

The specification, the exam and revision

Introduction to the AQA AS Social Science: Citizenship specification

The guidelines on what to study in this subject are written by the exam board (AQA) and are referred to as a specification. Below are the main components of the AQA specification for Social Science: Citizenship. The full specification can be obtained from the AQA. See www.aqa.org.uk

Some background to the specification

The specification Social Science: Citizenship was first developed as a pilot in 1998–9 by the then NEAB examination body. The first examinations were sat in June 1999. Since then the specification has been taken over by the new AQA examination body.

Some detail on the modules in the specification

All three modules are broken into three areas, with each having two sub-sections.

The first module has a legal, state and welfare theme. The second has a politics and political participation theme, and the third section has a social identity and community participation theme with a case study based approach.

All three modules have three sections and each has two sub-sections as set out below.

Module 1 The Citizen and the State

- Area 1: Characteristics of Citizenship in the Modern State
  Sub-section (a) The nature of citizenship
  Sub-section (b) Citizens' rights and duties
- Area 2: The Citizen and the Law
  Sub-section (a) The legal system
  Sub-section (b) The criminal justice system
- Area 3: The Welfare of the Citizen
  Sub-section (a) Welfare
  Sub-section (b) Citizen's charter

Module 2 The Citizen and the Political Process

- Area 1: Representative Democracy
  Sub-section (a) The functions and levels of government
  Sub-section (b) Elected representatives
- Area 2: Political Participation
  Sub-section (a) Forms of political participation
  Sub-section (b) Influencing political decision-making
- Area 3: Political Ideology and Political Action
  Sub-section (a) Political ideologies
  Sub-section (b) Knowledge of a particular campaign

Module 3 The Citizen, Society and the Community

- Area 1: Socialisation
  Sub-section (a) The impact of socialisation
  Sub-section (b) The role of the media in the creation and maintenance of social identities

- Area 2: Life-chances and Inequality
  Sub-section (a) Differences in life-chances based on class, ethnicity and gender
  Sub-section (b) Poverty and inequality
- Area 3: The Citizen and the Community
  Sub-section (a) Group dynamics and conflict resolution
  Sub-section (b) Community based forms of action

Key themes and concepts

The specification lists a number of key concepts that students will be expected to understand and use. Ensure you understand and can use these terms and concepts in an exam situation as some (not necessarily all) will be in your examination paper and should therefore be in your answers.

Authority, co-operation, conflict, democracy, equality, fairness, freedom, justice, order, power, rights and responsibilities. We can add more relevant concepts than these but be sure these terms are clear to you.

Some detail on the assessment/examinations

The three module components are assessed by three unit module examinations, each of one hour. Each module unit has exactly the same weighting towards the final grade (33.3%).

The module unit examinations are available for entry in January and June. You will need to speak with your teacher, or examinations officer, or training provider to find out how to enter for the examination. In the case of independent candidates, you should contact the exam board directly. Back copies of exam papers and mark schemes are available from the AQA for a fee.

The examination papers are closed, meaning no books are allowed into the exam room. Each module is assessed by what are called assessment objectives (A01, A02, A03, see below). The examination papers are marked by exam board appointed and approved markers who are all experienced teachers and trained in the marking process.

The assessment objectives

What skills and knowledge do you need to show on your exam papers?

A01 Recall, select and deploy knowledge and understanding of citizenship concepts and theory accurately and with examples where necessary or appropriate.

A02 Apply skills of analysis, interpretation and evaluation by forming written arguments and explanations.

A03 Communicate arguments and explanations in a clear and structured manner, making use of a range of relevant evidence and vocabulary appropriate to the study of citizenship.

The exam and how the marks are awarded

The exam paper lasts one hour. There is one paper for each module, meaning you need to sit three exams to get the AS qualification.

The exam paper is broken into two sections. There is one question in section 1 and two questions in section 2. You **have** to answer the question in section 1 and one question from section 2. The first question is compulsory but there is a choice from two in the second section. In section 1 there will be some stimulus material to help you. The questions will ask you to refer to this material.

Question 1 has three sub-parts. The maximum mark for question (a) is 4 marks, question (b) is 10, and question (c) is 16 marks. You **must** answer every question. In section 2 the two questions have two parts and the maximum mark for (a) is 10 and (b) is 20.

Do not be rigid about the length of answer but as a guide, the 4 mark question should require at most a short paragraph. You are usually asked to identify something and explain it. The 10 mark questions should require about a side of A4 paper, the 16 mark questions a side and a half. The 20 mark questions should require about two sides of A4 paper.

How do the questions relate to the assessment objectives?

Question 1(a)	A01 – 4 marks
	Maximum mark 4
Question 1(b)	A01 – 3 marks
	A02 – 5 marks
	A03 – 2 marks
	Maximum mark 10

Question 1(c)   A01 – 5 marks
                 A02 – 7 marks
                 A03 – 4 marks
                 Maximum mark 16

Question 2(a)   A01 – 4 marks
                 A02 – 4 marks
                 A03 – 2 marks
                 Maximum mark 10

Question 2(b)   A01 – 8 marks
                 A02 – 8 marks
                 A03 – 4 marks
                 Maximum mark 20

Question 3(a)   A01 – 4 marks
                 A02 – 4 marks
                 A03 – 2 marks
                 Maximum mark 10

Question 3(b)   A01 – 8 marks
                 A02 – 8 marks
                 A03 – 4 marks
                 Maximum mark 20

Look very closely at the assessment objectives above and how the three areas are shared out for each question. You will notice that question 1 is knowledge A01 alone, yet questions 1(b), 1(c), and questions 2 and 3 have A02 marks. The examiner marking your scripts will give a mark for each of the three assessment objectives. You must be aware of the different skills domains of knowledge and understanding A01, analysis and evaluation A02, and use of language A03.

In terms of marks for each paper and pass rates/grades, as a rough measure, you need about 28 out of 60 for a grade E, and to be safe, 45 out of 60 for a grade A.

Summer 2002 results (%)

A – 14   B 28   C – 47.7   D – 69.2   E – 84.8

Nearly 85% of candidates passed the examination.

- 14%   gained grade A
- 14%   gained grade B
- 19.7% gained grade C
- 21.5% gained grade D
- 15.6% gained grade E
- 15.2% failed.

Revision guidance

Remember it is you and you alone, who has to answer the exam questions.

We all have our own style of revision but some methods of revision are helpful to most if not all students. A good starting point is to reflect on the key concepts of the specification (listed above) and see if you can explain each and illustrate with an example.

- Plan before you start revision but be aware that revision starts after the first lesson and not when the course ends. Efforts in revision during the early and mid stages of a course will pay great rewards at the end. Ensure to review all your notes and findings as you progress. Draw up a revision timetable. You will have heard this said countless times but it is good advice.
- Be sure to plan your study with all your subjects in mind. Balance is essential to success. Set out a revision timetable that is realistic. If you have a work or social commitment on one or two nights every week, e.g. going out on Saturday night, do not allocate this for revision and study, but you will need to find time elsewhere in the week. It is advised by many that you should spend 4–5 hours each week studying for each of your subjects. If you are consistent throughout the year, this time frame is realistic even when the exam is very close.
- Ensure you know whether you are taking a module in January and if so which module it is.
- Devise a checklist with page numbers from this book that relate to the learning checkpoints. Ensure you have a response to all the learning checks. These will not be enough on their own but they are a good basis to work from.
- Do the same for the questions/activities, for the web action points and for the exam questions. If there are gaps, fill them quickly. This checklist is something you can draw up in the early stage of the course because it will help you monitor your progress as you advance through the course.

Revision sessions should not be ordeals but more a time of proud reflection of your achievement. Be proud of your file and the work in it, you have worked hard and the later stages are when you can look back on the work produced not just as a pile of work but as a personal achievement.

Exam tips

- Look back at the beginning of this chapter and remind yourself of the assessment objectives and how they spread across the different questions in terms of marks. Be aware of this and think about the significance of it for your answers.

- Plan your answers! Many candidates run out of time in exams. Be prepared by having a set plan on how you will answer the questions and in what order. Never start writing straight away. Allow yourself five minutes to plan a strategy and to fully reflect on what you are going to write. Set out plans for the longer questions before answering them. Do not forget the shorter questions are also vital to a good grade despite their being for fewer marks.

- Personal experience of citizenship activity and specific examples known to you will be rewarded by the examiner. Set out a few ideas of what examples/ illustrations you may use for the longer mark questions in your plans for answers.

- Some questions refer you to the items. In this case, you must refer to the item. If the questions do not refer you to the item, you can still use it, if it is relevant. In using the item you will be showing the examiner application and interpretation skills. Be very sure to use the item when asked to.

- Arrive early for the exam. When you take your seat sit in it quietly and look forward. Breath slowly and deeply for a few minutes. This will relax you. Organise your pens and pencils on the desk and read the instructions on the exam paper to get your mind thinking, but also to remind yourself of the exam paper format.

- Go to bed early before an exam. Staying up worrying does not help. You may as well be lying down if you are going to worry. Do not go out with friends before an exam.

- Talk through your understanding of the key themes with a friend, this will help you remember and explore the themes better. Compare your answers and their marks with others to seek further ideas on how best to approach a question.

- Read the question. Then read it again. Then read the items. Break the question down into sections and identify the verb in the question. Read the items again and begin planning. Sometimes the answer for the first question comes to you easily, other times it can be confusing. Leave the question if you are unsure and move on to the next but be sure you remember to return to it later.

- Leave time to read through your answers at the end. Do not simply scan across the words you have written. Re-read the question and pretend you are an examiner marking your answers. It is never too late to seek advice.

- Good luck in your exam results.

Useful addresses and websites

Alphabetical list of some useful web addresses

www.aqa.org.uk   Assessment and Qualifications Alliance

The exam board! Follow the links to social science citizenship to find data on exam results. The site also covers general themes on exam board issues and some past papers, mark schemes, etc.

www.atss.org.uk   The association for teachers of social sciences

Very helpful for all areas of social science, with an extensive list of useful web addresses.

www.bbc.co.uk   The BBC broadcasting, news and current affairs site

www.channel4.com   Channel 4 broadcasting and current affairs site

Both are very useful for campaigning themes, current issues and good links.

www.byc.org.uk   British Youth Council

Organised by young people for young people. Operates as a voice to parliament for young people and contains a wealth of advice on active participation.

www.charter88.org.uk   Campaigning for modern and fair democracy

Covers a range of citizenship themes: democracy, rights, issues of current relevance, campaigning themes, etc.

www.chrisgardner.clara.net   A social science (mainly sociology) site

Some helpful tests to check your knowledge online. You will have to sift through for the relevant areas.

www.citizen.org.uk   The Institute for citizenship

Contains a vast array of relevant materials.

www.citizen21.org.uk   Citizenship education and the national curriculum site

Good for detail on bill of rights, freedom of information, parliament and voting. The key stage 4 material is aimed at GCSE level but is still very useful as background.

www.citizensconnection.net   'Common purpose' activist site

The 'Just Do something' initiative designed to encourage participation on all levels. Very useful for practical advice on how to take action at whatever level you want. There are stories relating personal experiences, factual information about a range of issues and organisations as well as links to other sites.

Offers a campaigning advice toolkit.

www.citfou.org.uk   Citizenship Foundation site

Covers a wide range of themes, such as education for citizenship, democracy, European issues, legal issues, etc.

www.courtservice.gov.uk   The courts service site

Explains how the legal system works and how to use the courts. Has a 'what's new' section raising issues of current legal significance.

www.cre.gov.uk   The commission for racial equality

Promotes awareness of and challenge prejudice towards aspects of ethnic and racial identity and history in multicultural Britain.

www.csv.org.uk   Community Service volunteers site

Good advice on participation and support for Community Service Volunteering. It also offers case studies of action and a directory of local community organisations.

www.explore.parliament.uk   The UK Parliament site

Useful resources and worksheets, and includes some of the historical background to the Houses of Parliament.

www.europarl.eu.int   The European parliament site

(the UK section is found at www.europarl.org.uk)

Explains the role and functioning of European parliament. Follow links to the detail on economic, civil, political and social rights of EU citizens (www.europarl.eu.int/charter).

www.feminist.com   Feminist issues site

Site promoting feminist beliefs and action to challenge sexism in society. Useful for exploring citizenship issues from a feminist perspective. Has a useful 'activism' section.

www.hansardsociety.org.uk   The Hansard society

Publishes government documents and transcripts of the various bodies of national government. Seeks to promote effective parliamentary democracy. Has a section encouraging participation by young people (www.cypu.gov.uk).

www.jrf.org.uk   The Joseph Rowntree foundation site

A social policy research organisation, publishes readable social exclusion research. Government policies are evaluated and there are all sorts of publications.

www.legalservices.gov.uk   The community legal service site

Advise on how to use the law, what to do if accused of crime. It replaced the legal aid board in 1999.

www.lga.gov.uk   The Local government association

Explains the local government system and issues involving local government funding, council tax and spending. Easy to find links to local councils.

www.nya.org.uk   The National Youth Agency

Explains rights of young people and explores PSE issues.

Also click on their sister site at www.youthinformation.com which gives information on issues of employment, equality, health, housing, justice, money as they apply to young people.

www.obv.org.uk   Operation black vote

Encourages voting among ethnic minorities especially 'black' groups. Raises issues and awareness in government and democracy and explores 'your role in democracy'.

www.ukonline.gov.uk   The UK Government online

Plenty of detail on current government activity with useful and easy to use search facilities.

www.socialexclusionunit.gov.uk   The government's social exclusion unit site

The social exclusion unit has all sorts of data, publications and policy statements on social exclusion as well as some useful research material.

www.politicalcompass.org   political ideology and awareness

Good on ideology, helping to make sense of the main political ideologies. Take the test. It is challenging and insightful of your own ideas and their connection to other ideologies and leaders. Where do you fit on the graph?

www.schoolcouncils.org   The schools council site

School councils support pupils to be partners in their own education. As well as information about what they have done and could do, the site offers advice on setting up your own council.

www.sociology.org.uk   Sociology academic site

Very useful for social science themes, from family and education, to crime and mass media.

www.statistics.gov.uk   Government online statistics site

Official statistics on a whole range of areas. Plenty of data material that may enable you to add specifics to an issue.

www.ukelect.co.uk   UK election forecasting

Useful for data on past general election in colour map form. Also has prediction for the future in map form based on opinion poll evidence.

www.ukyp.org.uk   The UK youth parliament site

Aims to give young people a voice. Explains how the youth parliament is structured, elected, run and what it does and has done. Also tells you how you can get involved.

General

Campaign for Freedom of Information
Suite 192
16 Baldwins Garden
London EC1N 7RJ
Tel 020 7831 7477
www.cfoi.org.uk

Commission for Racial Equality
Elliot House
10-12 Arlington House
London SW1E 5EH
Tel 020 7828 7022
www.cre.gov.uk

Friends of the Earth
26-28 Underwood Street
London N1 7JQ
Tel 020 7490 1555
www.foe.co.uk

Law Centres Federation
Duchess House
18-19 Warren Street
London W1T 5LR
Tel 020 7387 8570
www.lawcentres.org.uk

National Council for Voluntary Organisations
Regent's Wharf
8 All Saints Street
London N1 9RL
Tel 020 7713 6161
www.ncvo-vol.org.uk

National Association of Citizens Advice Bureaux
Myddelton House
115 Pentonville Road
London N1 9L7
Tel 020 7833 2181
www.nacab.org.uk

Neighbourhood Initiatives Foundation
The Poplars
Lightmoor
Telford
TF4 3QN
Tel 01952 590777
www.nif.co.uk

New Economics Foundation
Cinnamon House
6-8 Cole Street
London SE1 4YH
Tel 020 7407 7447
www.neweconomics.org

Glossary

Action Zones: particular areas usually of a geographical nature that have been identified by government for special action e.g. raising educational standards or participation as in Education Action Zones

Adversarial: a political and legal system which pitches one party against another

Advocate: a member of the legal profession employed to make a case on behalf of a client. A term common in the Scottish legal system

Ahistorical: a social perspective that takes no account of historical development or context

Amnesty International: a pressure group campaigning on Human Rights issues

Anti-social behaviour: acting in a way that caused or is likely to cause alarm, distress or harassment to another

Autonomy: a term signifying a freedom to act independently or without undue constraint of social and political authorities

Balance of probabilities: when one course of action seems more likely to occur than another

Ballot: a measure of feeling among a group often carried out by a vote, perhaps by show of hands but usually on paper, hence the term ballot paper. Trade unions ballot their members on whether or not to carry out strike action

Best value: a term applied to local government aiming to ensure the most efficient and effective working of local services, not necessarily the cheapest

By-elections: a constituency election that occurs outside the time frame of major or General Elections, usually as the result of a councillor or MP standing down or perhaps dying

Charities: a legally constituted non-profit organisation, usually with a social or educational purpose

Circuit judge: a judge presiding over proceedings in a county or Crown Court

Committal proceedings: process whereby a case is transferred from a magistrates court for trial in a Crown Court

Committee: group of people established to consider specific issues requested of them by a person or group in power e.g. a school student committee to explore issues of concern to students set up by the governing body. This is where the term 'standing orders' comes from. A committee is given a number of issues or a single issue to explore and this is the purpose or reason for the committee standing (standing orders). Some committees are very powerful and have the power (right) written in their standing orders to demand an individual or group make a submission e.g. the Committee for MPs' standards

Communitarianism: the philosophy that the community rather than the individual or state is and should be at the centre of our value system

Community Involvement Teams: groups of local councillors, religious leaders and other people in prominent public positions aiming to identify best use of council funds for local communities

Community Service: a form of punishment, in place of imprisonment, requiring the offender to work for the good of the community

Conservatism: a set of ideas or a theory suggesting we should be cautious about change and consider events today in the light of past experience and established traditions. It is associated with the Conservative political party

Constituency: a geographic and electoral boundary returning representatives to either local government (councillors) or Parliament (MPs)

Democracy: a process of government where ultimate political authority lies with the people

Democratic Socialism: a socialist political system operating according to democratic principles and procedures

Demographic change: widespread changes to populations that take place over time

Direct Action: political action, perhaps violent and illegal, aiming to achieve a particular goal or influence governmental decision making

Ecoism: an approach or social perspective that places great value on the environment and preserving eco(logical) systems

Empowerment: the practical enabling of groups and individuals to participate effectively in civic society by increasing knowledge, skills and capacity to act

Environmental Rights: rights of individuals, groups and societies that refer to the maintenance of environmental well-being

Equality: the idea that every person has an equal right to have his or her material, spiritual and other interests respected by other people

Ethics: commonly used as referring to a set of standards by which a particular group or community decides what is legitimate or acceptable in the pursuit of their aims

Ethnicity: refers to cultural practices and outlooks that distinguish a particular community of people

Extra Parliamentary Action: political action that takes place outside legal and constitutional procedures

Feminism: a political and social movement that emphasises the rights and significance of women

Gender: socially defined and approved behaviour associated with one's biological sex. Femininity and masculinity are examples. Society expects us to behave in certain ways dependant upon whether we are male or female. Be aware, however, that males can behave in feminine ways and females in masculine ways, but consider the social responses to this deviance

Global Citizenship: the notion that our rights and duties extend to all peoples and perhaps life forms that exist on our planet

Global Civil Society: institutions and organisations operating beyond the confines and rationale of nation states and national governments

Green paper: a consultation, the first draft (reading) of a proposed law

Indicators: identifiable signs showing that a particular policy is achieving its objectives

Indictment: a formal document accusing someone of committing an indictable offence read to the accused at the trial

Inflation: an economic term referring to a rise in prices

Information and Communication Technology: computers, videos and other forms of electronic communication and data gathering

Injunction: a legal remedy in the form of a court order preventing or requiring someone to do something

Liberal democracy: a democratic political system emphasising the liberal freedoms of the individual, of speech, of assembly, of free elections, of conscience etc

Liberalism: a political philosophy emphasising the rights, obligations and cultural importance of the *individual* in society

Litigation: the process of one party taking legal action against another

Maastrict Treaty: the 1992 treaty of the European Union member states marking the deepening and widening of the organisation

Magna Carta: a written agreement signed by King John in 1215 limiting the arbitrary power of the monarch

Mandate: the political authority usually gained by individuals and political parties through electoral victory to carry out the terms of a manifesto

Manifesto: a political and policy programme put to the voting public at election times that will form the basis of political action if the party achieves governmental power

Marxist: a political perspective derived from the revolutionary philosophy of Karl Marx

Mass media: various forms of communication including television, radio, newspapers, aiming to reach a mass audience

Monoculture: a single culture sometimes used in Environmentalism to designate the cultivation of a single commercial crop

Nationality: a social and cultural articulation of certain traits and symbols that pertain to the membership of a national community or nation-state

New Right: a strand of political conservatism emphasising free market economic policies and the rights and responsibilities of individuals

NIMBYism: a tendency on the part of individuals and groups to react negatively to new developments, meaning 'Not In My Back Yard'

Ombudsman: an official with the powers to investigate the proper workings of an organisation e.g. compliance to financial regulations

Organic: the process whereby plants and vegetables are grown without the use of artificial or chemical fertilizers, pesticides, etc.

Overtime bans: action taken by trade unions whereby members refuse to work hours longer than they have been contracted for

Parliamentary Action: constitutional and legal action following Parliamentary and constitutional procedures

Patriarchy: male dominance in society and culture

Political party: an organisation designed to achieve power in local and national government usually by electoral means in order to pursue a political programme

Poll tax: a tax levied on everyone by virtue of their existence irrespective of their ability to pay

Polygamy: the cultural right and practice of having more than one wife

Practice: an intelligible and meaningful course of action undertaken individually or collectively

Pressure group: an organisation that seeks to advance the interests of a particular group or promote a particular issue

Primary socialisation: the process of childhood socialisation mainly taking place within the family

Probation: a period of time following an offender's release from prison in which s/he is under strict supervision by a probation officer to prevent re-offending

Pro-choice: the position taken in the abortion debate stating that women have the right to choose whether to have an abortion or not

Pro-life: the position taken in the abortion debate stating that the unborn child's right to live usually supersedes all other considerations

Prosecute: the pursuit of legal proceedings against someone accused of committing a criminal offence

Racial mixing: the social or institutional mixing of racial and ethnic groups

Referendum: a political process where the entire eligible voting population is called to vote on a particular political issue e.g. devolution of political powers to Scotland and Wales

Regeneration: the redevelopment of a given community or area socially, economically and culturally

Relativism: a social and philosophical perspective that recognises the equal worth of different values, attitudes, cultures, behaviours

Representative democracy: a political system whereby constituency councillors and MPs are elected by people to represent their views and pursue approved manifesto commitments in legislative bodies e.g. Parliament

Secondary socialisation: the process of socialisation experienced by young people and adults involving such agencies as the mass media, peer groups, work organisations, schools, etc

Sectionalism: a process of breaking away from political mainstream to represent specific sections of a community e.g. Catholics or Protestants in Northern Ireland

Secularisation: a process involving the decline in the importance of religion in society

Self-fulfilling prophecy: a tendency to persuade oneself that a certain viewpoint or course of action is inevitable

SMART: criteria for project evaluation referring to objectives that are Specific, Measurable, Achievable, Realistic and Time-limited

Social capital: the network of social relationships of trust and reciprocity that enables individuals and communities to operate effectively and harmoniously – often linked to citizenship

Socialisation: a social process whereby children learn the key values and norms of the wider society and in so doing develop a sense of self

Socialism: a political system in which the means of production, distribution and exchange are under social ownership

State: governing body responsible for making and enforcing the law and the protection of the citizens belonging to it

Sub-culture: a segment of society distinguishable from the rest of society by its cultural habits, behaviour, values, ways of dress, etc

Substantive citizenship rights: rights pertaining to the citizen that exist and are enforced

Substantive moral rights: rights of an ethical nature that are embedded in social and legal practices

Sue: to claim legal remedy in a civil court for wrongful action e.g. libel, breach of contract

Sustainable development: a process enabling all people to realise their potential and to improve their quality of life in ways that protect and enhance the Earth's life support systems

Tax: money gathered from citizens and businesses by government for its spending purposes. Avoiding paying tax is illegal. Taxes can be direct from income or profits and indirect, added to prices of goods in shops (VAT) Others include airport tax, tax on some roads e.g. in inner London, inheritance tax

Universal Declaration of Human Rights: a publication of a series of rights by the General Assembly of the United Nations in 1948 outlining the 'inherent dignity and the equal and inalienable rights of all members of the human family is the foundation of freedom, justice and peace in the world'

Universal institutions: otherwise called 'universal values' which are common to all individuals (in general) rather like an institution surrounding an individual. Examples may include respect for the law, the value of formal education – going to school, fashion or the importance of working. Some refer to the universal values of fairness, respect, hierarchy, freedom, justice

Warrant: a legal document authorising action e.g. a police search or arrest

Welfare state: a social and political system providing a wide range of social benefits to its citizens

White paper: The final stage (reading) of a proposed law voted on by MPs in the House of Commons and, if passed, sent to the House of Lords for their approval. After which it becomes written into law (statute book)

Working to rule: action by a trade union whereby members will only carry out functions that are strictly expressed in rule books or by contract

Youth courts: courts of law where criminal proceedings may be brought against children (10–14) and young people (14–17)

Index